GRAHAM THORPE

GRAHAM THORPE

the autobiography

RISING FROM THE ASHES

CollinsWillow
An Imprint of HarperCollins*Publishers*

First published in UK in 2005 by
CollinsWillow
an imprint of HarperCollins*Publishers*
77–85 Fulham Palace Road
Hammersmith, London, W6 8JB

1

A catalogue record for this book
is available from the British Library

ISBN 0 00 720596 1

Set in PostScript Linotype Sabon by
Rowland Phototypesetting Ltd, Bury St Edmunds, Suffolk

Printed and bound in Great Britain by
Clays Ltd, St Ives plc

To my children Henry, Amelia, Kitty and Emma

Photographic Acknowledgements

The Publishers would like to thank the following sources for supplying photographs for this book: **Acton Images** 9br; **Empics** 2br, 3b, 4b, 5t, 8rcr, 8rcl, 9tl, 91ct, 9bl; **Getty Images** 2t, 2c, 2bl, 4tc, 4cr, 4bc; **Graham Morris** 2b, 5(all), 6, 8tl, 8tcl, 8bcl, 8br, 8bl, 9tr; **Philip Brown** 8tr, 9tm, 91cb; **Reuters** 4t, 4m, 5b; **Sunday Mirror** 7tr.

All other photographs provided courtesy of Graham Thorpe.

Every effort has been made to contact the copyright holders of the photographs included in this book. Where there have been omissions, the publishers will endeavour to rectify any outstanding permissions on publication.

Contents

ONE

Incredible Journey

I DON'T THINK I'm a typical professional sportsman. I wear my heart on my sleeve more than most. I'm emotional and sensitive, though sport has taught me when to be tough, but my life has not been all about cricket. In my heart I often put family first, and I am not sure that's usual in sport.

Being harsh on myself, I'd say I was selfish in my early career. There were times when I got wrapped up in my own game. In fact I saw a certain amount of that selfishness in some of the early teams I played in at Surrey in the 1990s and, when I started with England against Australia in 1993, the need to make sure you were a success was intensified because many of us lived under the cloud of 'two bad Tests and you're out'. That also created an unhealthy environment, and not everyone wanted to play for England then. It could be an unpleasant, intimidating experience. And not everyone in the team was always happy for you when you did well.

The whole ethos of the junior cricket and football I played, and the one taught me by my father, was that the beer tasted sour in the evening if you'd lost, however well you'd done yourself. But I stuck to the belief that if I was going to go down, it would be on *my* terms. I wasn't going to be fearful of failure, or be seduced into trying to be stylish for the sake of it, or intimidated into playing a cautious game. I never thought of myself as having a lot of talent. I learned how to survive at the crease, then to score runs.

I was very lucky in my cricket. With both county and country I survived to enjoy happier times when there was a lot of collective success, and the winning became more important than personal achievement. That is a rare state to achieve. In my final 18 months with the England team, it was a privilege to be part of such a successful, stable and selfless side. The cynicism had gone. Now everyone shared in everybody else's success. It was a much happier dressing-room.

WHEN I WAS YOUNGER, I was proud of playing cricket for England but found myself operating like a bank, churning out money for my family against the day I finished. I was desperate to do well, but didn't enjoy it as much as I should have done. I didn't give very much as a person in those days. I was shy and uncommunicative. Ultimately it didn't create happiness, and there came a time when I would have given back all my Test runs and Test caps to be happy again.

I don't think I'm a difficult person but I'll stand up and say what I think. Some people mistook my inability to wear the right kit as subversion, whereas it was mere disorganization, but I really was quite anti-establishment in my younger days. I was a kid, and kids inevitably mess up, and to make matters worse I didn't always see managers actually doing what they were supposed to do – manage. You'd be amazed how many people in authority didn't really understand those under them. For my part, as I grew up, I learned it was better to face up to things than grumble about them.

Naturally, I'd dreamed of finishing my England career with an Ashes Test on my home ground of the Oval – who wouldn't? – but, as I well know, life doesn't always work out the way you'd like. I had no hard feelings about being dropped for the start of the 2005 series. The better England had got, the harder selection had become, and I appreciated that they were striving to improve in any way they could.

Having sunk to a place from which I thought I would never pick myself up – after my depression and traumatic divorce and the drinking – I'm more careful now. When you've been hit by a juggernaut, you tend to look left and right. But I'm still basically a trusting person.

If you can't come to terms with what's happened to you, you can never be happy.

When I look back to how things were a few years ago – after I'd tried to retire from the game and was cracking up, refusing to go out, getting paranoiac, desperately missing my children, battered by journalists and bills from the divorce lawyers, shocked by my wife's lies in the Sunday papers – it seems incredible that things turned round the way they did, both in my personal life and in cricket, in such a short space of time. I expected nothing, but found redemption twice over. I've made mistakes in my life, but came to realize that that doesn't necessarily make you a bad person. What has happened to me in the last few years has changed me. I'm more appreciative of life now and try to enjoy every day. I guess I've mellowed a bit. Having gone through some very bad times, I feel I've come through a better person.

TWO

Sleepwalking

I FIRST gave up cricket three years ago. I remember it was July 2002 after the Lord's Test against India, but that's practically where my sure grasp of the facts stops. I was in a zombie state at the time, and my mind is blank about many things in that terrible period. Perhaps I couldn't fully acknowledge it then, but I was going through a mental breakdown.

England played very well in that match, but when I think about that Test it feels as though we lost. The only fragments of memory I can dredge up about the rest of the guys are that it was Simon Jones' first Test, Nasser Hussain got a hundred, and we won quite comfortably on the last day after India were left chasing a big score. When I think of what I did, I see myself as another person, someone I am watching on TV – not me, Graham Thorpe. It wasn't me playing in that match, it was someone else. I was in another place altogether and it wasn't nice, believe me. My state of mind all through that game was just down, down, down. I had become so depressed I was incapable of making a decision about anything. I was walking around in a heavy black fog. I think I'd reached rock bottom.

To say I was going through a messy divorce is an understatement. I had separated from my wife Nicky the previous year, but for months had kidded myself that we would eventually get back together. I suppose I had been in denial about the possibility that it might be permanent. It had been easy to persuade myself that things were not really as bad as they were because I'd carried on playing cricket. I'd spent much of the previous winter of 2001–02 touring Zimbabwe, India and New Zealand, so in that sense life had been pretty normal. I had told myself I was just spending time apart from Nicky and our two children, Henry and Amelia (who were then five and three), whom she'd taken with her, because that's what I spent a lot of my life – too much of my life – doing. Being apart from them, playing cricket.

When I had been prepared to really think about the situation I was in, I often ended up convinced that Nicky would take me back, and that we'd end up together. Quite what evidence there was for such optimism I'm not sure because divorce proceedings were underway. But I clung to the hope like a life raft, which in a way it was.

During that harrowing week at Lord's, supposedly

the best place in the world to play cricket, the reality of my shattered world was finally sinking in. In the four months since I'd come back from New Zealand I had been living alone in the family home, without Nicky and without the children, and I could not delude myself any longer.

For a long time I had viewed my life as virtually perfect: a wife and young family I loved, a comfortable five-bedroom home near Epsom in Surrey, and a successful career. Top England players had started to be paid well. Then, the regulars could earn over £200,000 a year, and nowadays that figure has risen to more than £400,000. I was admired as one of England's best batsmen of recent years, someone who, ironically now, was considered cool in a crisis. What more could I have wanted? But I began to fear that everything – my house, my family, my career – was collapsing all around me. Everything was out of control and there was no way back. I was staring into an abyss, scared. I couldn't see a way out, ever. I couldn't even see beyond the next few hours or minutes. Throughout that week, I was seized by one long series of panic attacks.

As it happened, I'd not played for about a fortnight before that Test against India and had spent a lot of time at home in the lead-up to the game. I might have played in Surrey's championship match at Canterbury but they'd not needed me. They had a strong squad – they were leading the table and had been for most of the season – and trying to fit in the contracted England players on the few occasions we were available wasn't easy. I had come to dread the time at home because it meant time alone and time on my hands; time to think about all that had gone wrong. I'd pretty much abandoned training by this stage. I was drinking and smoking every day and had been for several months; that was far more my idea of the way to get through a day. Not the ideal preparation for a Test match.

I found it hard to cope, and about a week before the match finally got up the courage to visit my doctor and ask for help. It wasn't an easy thing to do but I was getting desperate. I'd actually been thinking about it for months. My parents, who knew I was in a pretty bad state, had suggested I go for counselling but I didn't see the point. My attitude was that there was only one person who could help sort out my situation, and that was Nicky.

I'd never met the doctor before but I think he knew who I was, which only added to my embarrassment. My problems had been splashed all over the newspapers during the last few months, and made my situation even harder to bear. I explained everything and every symptom, that I was waking at 3am most mornings, my mind buzzing. I was unable to get back to sleep. I was down about everything. Depressed.

He listened to what I had to say and said, 'Look, I think you're clinically depressed. Maybe it wouldn't be a bad idea to try to stabilize.' So he put me on anti-depressants. My parents were against them and warned me not to get hooked. I'd tried other things to get me through the solitary nights, and thought anti-depressants couldn't make me feel any worse. But they didn't make me feel better straightaway. I know I probably should have continued to take them for a bit longer, that they might have helped, but I was scared off them by what happened next. When you start taking them you hallucinate. And I was taking them during the Lord's Test against India.

I wasn't thinking rationally. I was trying to get through each day as best I could. I was gambling with my future – though, frankly, the future was the last thing on my mind.

Sportsmen, especially, need to respect their bodies, and unsurprisingly I eventually felt the toll of filling my system with alcohol. Had anyone been able to observe me at really close quarters during this period, they would not have been impressed with me. I wasn't impressed with myself. What I did was not good for me, except that it helped me escape my situation. I was depressed and desperate.

I kept playing cricket because I felt it would help me keep a grip on things. What else was I supposed to do? But I could feel this grip on things becoming more tenuous by the day. I didn't know how long I could keep going, pretending I was okay. And at Lord's, it all started to unravel.

All of a sudden, I felt extremely vulnerable. I became acutely aware that I was on a big stage and, for the first time in my life, I didn't want to be there. I wasn't just terrified that my marriage might be over, but that I was the last person to have worked this out. I was overwhelmed by public humiliation. I looked round the dressing-room and saw other people who were really quite enjoying themselves. I tried hard to enjoy it for them, almost forcing myself to be up for the game, but it was hopeless. '*Could someone please, please, help me. I can't do it any more. I just want to go away and hide forever.*'

THAT GAME was the slowest torture. I reckon barely a minute went by without me thinking about my children. I tried to fight against it, but even catching a glimpse of children in the crowd was enough to trigger me off. I should never have played. I went through those five days with tears near to the surface with almost everything I did. I was constantly seconds away from breaking down. You can't just walk off the field when you're playing for your club or county, let alone England, but that's what I wanted to do. Hide. But I knew I had to carry on. I knew how vulnerable I was but I also knew that tens of thousands of people, at the ground and on TV, were watching me. Sometimes you just have to put on a face, even though you're feeling awful and your self-esteem is on the floor. Inside I was looking at my life and thinking, *'I can't go on any more.'*

I remember a night or so before the game going with Dominic Cork and John Crawley to a pub around the corner from where we were staying in Swiss Cottage. Corky had been through divorce himself, and told me it was a process you eventually came out of. When you're the one forced out, you fight against it. What I mainly remember about that evening is me yakking on, going on and on about my divorce. The children, the emotional cost and the friction, the money . . . you start to hate yourself, going on like a broken record, constantly explaining why, why, why.

On top of that I was nearly late for the start of the match. On the first morning, I had to deal with a phone call from my solicitor. He was trying to get a financial settlement with Nicky, as well as trying to work out contact arrangements for the children. The solicitors on both sides were in full flow – the parasites! I was getting letters from them every week and the bill was getting out of control. All of a sudden I was looking at my watch and thinking, *'Shit. It's 9.30am. I'm supposed to be out on the ground and here I am, in the car park, on the phone.'* I was still in occasional contact with Nicky and found myself ringing her. 'Can't we try and work this out between us? Have you seen the size of the bills?'

I dashed through the Long Room – late, late! – and sprinted onto the ground. All the boys were looking at me. They were already involved in their warm-ups. I was like, 'Sorry, sorry, sorry . . . Sorry!' I got on with my warm-up, finished, batted for five minutes in the nets. I went into the dressing-room thinking, *'Yeah, we're batting. I'm into this . . . I've got to be.'* I tried to settle myself down and focus but I was struggling. Really struggling.

As I prepared for my innings that day – if 'prepared' is the right word – my attitude was pretty much, 'Get out there and try your best. Things haven't been great this morning but maybe you can drag it back. You might get a few quick runs and all of a sudden start enjoying it and carry on from there.' It was how my mind worked at that time. There was no proper plan, no preparation. It was all a wing and a prayer.

One of the special things about Lord's Tests, of course, is the social side. Spectators take picnic hampers, and you always know when the lunch interval is approaching because the stands start emptying as people slip off for lunch. And many aren't in too much of a rush to get back promptly for the re-start.

Well, there must have been a few who missed my innings. I was down to bat at No 4 and not 5, where I'd been batting the previous few months, because Marcus Trescothick had been ruled out with an injury and we'd rejigged the batting order. As it happened, the second wicket fell only minutes before lunch, leaving me to negotiate a tricky little period. No time to get myself in, but plenty of time to get out. Fortunately, Anil Kumble served up a full toss first ball which even I couldn't fail to put away to the boundary. But he beat me the following ball and, in the next over, the last before the interval, Zaheer Khan went past my bat too.

Zaheer is a lively and intelligent left-arm swing bowler, and I wasn't surprised to see him preparing to continue when Nasser and I walked out for the afternoon session. Nasser played out the first over to put me back on strike at the Nursery End against Zaheer. Because of the slope running across the square, batting at Lord's is all about getting used to two totally different ends. As a left-hander, I don't mind the Pavilion End and can get into better positions there, but I have to fight not to fall over and lose my sideways position at the Nursery End, where the movement of the ball angled across you is accentuated by the drop.

Zaheer was right on target, bowling me a really good sequence of balls. He probably should have saved it for someone else, but then he didn't know he wasn't bowling to Graham Thorpe but his shadow. He beat me once, angled a couple into me that I had to play, before giving me one that pitched middle and leg and left me. I didn't spot the movement, didn't move my feet, and played down the wrong line. Then came the clatter of stumps.

I walked back to the dressing-room, unstrapped my pads and slumped into the big chair on the left of the window, opposite Freddie Flintoff, and threw down my kit. I had chosen that chair in the hope that it would bring me a change of luck. This was my tenth Test match at Lord's, but I'd never scored a century, never got my name up on the honours board, and I'd been in the habit of moving seats in the hope it would alter my fortune. Maybe the missing hundred had something to do with the slope, but I think it was just one of those things. In the past, I'd revelled in the atmosphere and crowds at Lord's, and certainly not everything there was against batting. The outfield was usually fast, so the ball raced away, and though I'd once been whacked over the temple by a ball from Courtney Walsh that I'd lost in the trees above the sightscreen at the Nursery End, having to spend a night in hospital, I'd returned to score 40. The last time I'd played India there, in 1996, I was confident of making a century until I got an inside edge off Javagal Srinath on 89. And now, surprise, surprise, despite the switching of chairs, my luck was still out.

I'd been smoking pretty steadily for some months by then, so I took my packet of cigarettes out of my bag and smoked two or three straight off. Mark Butcher said later that he remembered me for much of that match just sitting there in that chair, every lunch break, every tea break. All I remember thinking was, *'Do I have to get back out there?'* Those sessions seemed like the longest and slowest I'd known.

The end of each day's play came as huge relief, except that the relief quickly gave way to anxiety. In the back of my mind I'd be calculating that I'd got five or six hours of being awake – awake and totally miserable, before, if lucky, getting off to sleep. And sleep was hard to get. The anti-depressants hadn't improved things, and I reckon I probably got only three or four hours of sleep a night during that match. I'd get up at 3am, feeling down, and light another cigarette. And I kept thinking, '*I don't want to be doing this. I can't keep fucking doing this. This is killing me.*'

I just couldn't find any strength. I wished there was a magic switch I could flick to wipe away my entire memory-bank so I could just get back to living a normal life. But there wasn't. If I was lucky I might drift off to sleep again for 30 minutes or an hour. Then I'd be up again thinking, '*Now I've got to go out and play again.*'

If batting was bad, fielding was worse, and there was a good reason for that. Not only had my wife left me, she'd left me for someone who was also in the public eye. He was Kieron Vorster, who was Tim Henman's fitness trainer at the time. Naturally this made the whole affair that much juicier to the papers, and there'd be no shortage of wags in the crowd with a few beers inside them ready to crack tennis jokes when I retrieved the ball from the boundary. Sure enough, the wisecracks started when we fielded, but I wasn't strong enough to take them. '*Bitch . . .*' [that was often my first reaction] '*. . . for doing this to me.*'

There were many times when I just wanted to walk off. I'd go onto the field, look up at the clock and think, 'A two-hour session. *Two hours*.' Then I'd look again. One hour, 50 minutes. I just wanted the next break now, to get off. I think I stood at first slip next to Alec Stewart quite a lot of the time and prattled on about things off the field, as you do. I'd played more cricket with Stewie than perhaps anybody. He'd been on the Surrey staff when I'd joined 14 years earlier, and we'd changed next to each other in the dressing-room for most of that time. We were chalk and cheese in some respects. He was good at concealing his emotions and if something had been going wrong for him off the field, as with me now, you'd probably not have noticed. He would have been his usual professional self.

I remember finding it really difficult to encourage the bowlers; I probably did it occasionally because I felt I had to. In fact I hardly touched the ball, but I did have a chance early on to catch Sachin Tendulkar which I put down. Brilliant. '*I've only gone and put down the world's leading batsman. I don't think I can do this again. I can't play for England again.*' Some of the lads knew something was badly wrong, but no-one said anything.

On the second night of the game I reckon I got off to sleep about midnight, maybe 1am, and was up again by about 3 or 4am, having woken sweating like a proverbial pig. I often did around then. The drinking was making me a bag of nerves. Maybe three or four beers or a bottle of wine and I'd wake up in the night, sober, in a cold sweat, my mind jumping. And I wasn't looking forward to the cricket at all. I told myself to try and find something positive to latch onto but there was nothing, just that clock ticking round, the lunch and tea breaks and the moment I could get off the pitch. I must have been tired by then. Really, really tired.

On the third day, the Saturday, a solicitor and barrister came to see me. It was a completely surreal experience. Here I was playing a Test match for England at the greatest venue in the world, being interrogated in a lunch break about my finances. It was perhaps an indication of my state of mind at the time. I should never have let it happen, and it showed how easily manipulated I was at that time. I was so racked with guilt over my marriage break-up that I was always trying to accommodate people, and show what a decent bloke I could be.

We went through my whole financial situation, how much a settlement was likely to cost, how much Nicky was likely to get, and in the back of my mind I'm thinking, '*You're discussing my future earnings, discussing my next year's salary and what maintenance I'm going to pay, and I'm not even sure I'll be earning a penny then.*' I had an England contract but they were renewed – or not – each September, and I wasn't certain I was going to be in England's thinking in one week's time, let alone two months.

After tea, I batted again. We were already well ahead and preparing to set India a big target. We were 60-odd for two when I joined Michael Vaughan, who was already playing well and on course for a century – he was then in the early stages of a golden run that lasted for the next 12 months. It was after tea, and there was still a while to go until stumps. Even if I'd been in a great state of mind it was the kind of situation I'd have found awkward. I was rarely great when the match didn't demand much of me. I preferred it when we had our backs to the wall – but now that only applied to my private life.

I remember walking out to bat and looking around the field, supposedly to take in where the fielders were positioned, but knowing full well that I wasn't going to do a thing. I had absolutely zero game-plan. A couple of balls came down from Kumble and I just swung my arms, feet planted at the crease. Somehow, in the next over from Ajit Agarkar, I squirted one out on the leg side for a single. That got me back down to Kumble's end. I remember registering that he'd decided to go round the wicket to bowl into the rough, but I thought, '*I don't really care.*' I blocked one, then left one, before having another wild swing. The ball leapt out of the rough, hit high on the bat and my drive went uppish to a fielder in the covers.

My over-riding feeling as I trudged off was huge sadness that I could have played in such a state of mind, but there was anger too, anger that Nicky, I suspected, would have been happy to see me go through this torment. She had spoken of getting her revenge – and if that's what she wanted it must have been sweet. I kind of made up my mind there and then to pack it in, walking off the field and trudging through the Long Room to an embarrassed silence.

It would have been almost completely silent in the dressing-room, too. It's usual for someone to say, 'Bad luck, mate', but that was one thing I always hated because often it wasn't bad luck and, even if it was, I didn't want to hear it. So I'm pretty sure it was quiet. I felt a sense of relief as I sank back into my chair thinking, '*This is definitely the last time. I can't go through that again.*'

WE WON the Test with quite a bit to spare, late on the final day. I remember taking the winning catch: I have this picture in my head of holding the catch off Simon Jones low down at gully, throwing it up and seeing the boys running together. I simply turned and walked off.

Nasser knew one of his players hadn't really been at the races. I'd spoken to him during the game, out the back of the dressing-room where there's a TV, and told him I didn't think I could do this much longer. That was shortly after I'd had that session with the barrister. Like Duncan Fletcher, the coach, Nasser knew very well I'd been having severe marital problems for several months.

I told him I couldn't get my mind into any decent place to play cricket. Playing for England, you're meant to have your whole heart and mind in it. I said that I didn't feel I was giving him anything, wasn't giving the team anything and that, to be honest, he'd have to get rid of me in a game or so anyway if I carried on the way I was. It really was best if I went away and tried to sort myself out. He reminded me that two games ago I'd got a hundred. 'Yeah, and do you know how I managed it? Because I'm not sure I do.'

Alec Stewart and Mark Butcher, my Surrey muckers, were very good at the end of the game. They stayed around. Butch had gone through a separation of his own a couple of years earlier and said I reminded him of himself then, playing cricket but not really wanting to be there. Butch said he admired me and that I would eventually come through, stronger. I felt on a good level with Butch. We both understood that although there was a game going on out in the middle, occasionally things off the field had to take priority. They were kind words of encouragement, even if I found them hard to believe at the time.

I hadn't really said anything to Duncan during the game, but could tell the wily old fox had been keeping an eye on me. Duncan had been England coach for three years, and I had learned that I could speak honestly with him. His public image was dour but there was a lot more to him than the public saw. He was always sensitive to how his players were getting along as people. I knew he cared about us and I trusted him. He'd had his own difficulties in life, growing up in Zimbabwe and taking the big step of leaving for South Africa in his mid-thirties with little money in his pocket and few firm plans in his head.

Soon after the finish, I called him onto the balcony. 'Are you all right?' he said. 'No. I don't think I can do this any more,' I replied. 'I don't want to carry on the way I've been during this game. I really need to get away from cricket and have a break. I'm not giving you anything. To be honest, I'm totally fucked up at the moment.'

'I can tell your mind's not on the job . . .' He was trying to cajole me. 'But what are you going to do? I'm concerned about you as a human being. All right, there's the cricket side, but I'm more concerned about you. You come away from the cricket now and what are you going to do? Sit at home and your problems are going to multiply by 10.'

'I just can't go on the way my mind is,' I explained. 'I'm not freezing out there, but I am becoming a wreck. I think I'm losing control of my mind.'

'All right,' he said. 'But, you know, you've got to do something.'

A few minutes later, I spoke to Keith Medlycott, the coach at Surrey, and Richard Thompson, the club chairman, and asked them to support me because I had to withdraw from all cricket.

And so there I was, left to pack my bags.

As I walked through the Long Room, I looked around for one last time. '*This is it*,' I thought. '*I'm never going to play at Lord's again*.' If you'd told me that I would not only play more Test matches at Lord's, but the next time I'd help Nasser knock off the runs for victory, I simply wouldn't have believed you.

Honestly, my over-riding feeling then was of utter relief. I didn't know what I was going to do, but I knew I couldn't go through another match like that again.

THREE

Clinging to the Cliff-Face

I HAD BEEN battling to keep a grip on my mind ever since Nicky had dropped the bombshell the previous summer, in late August 2001, that she wanted to separate. The traumatic weeks that followed were the start of my spiral into the depression that gripped me during that awful match the following summer at Lord's.

A few days after she'd announced this, I was due to have a meeting with Steve Bull, the England team's psychologist, ahead of England's one-day series in Zimbabwe in September 2001. It was a routine meeting: recently, before every season and tour we had individual meetings with Steve to discuss our goals, personally and for the team. The Test matches that followed in India and New Zealand were the serious part of the schedule, and the original plan was for me to rest from what was a low-key tour of Zimbabwe (the controversies surrounding tours of that country came later), but I'd been called up when Craig White reported unfit. Steve had been with the team a few years and I'd used him a lot in 1999 when I'd had difficulties with the management (I was unhappy at their refusal to allow me paternity leave, among other things, and they thought I was sometimes a bad influence) and he'd helped me try to channel my anger in the right direction. I was meeting Steve at the David Lloyd Centre in Wimbledon, and must have been pretty keen because I sat in the car park for about an hour waiting for him to arrive.

When we sat down, Steve started pulling some sheets out of his case. I got a glimpse of one headed, 'England's Mentally Strongest Cricketers', and saw that somehow I'd sneaked into the Top 10. I thought, *'Really? I feel as weak as shit at the moment.'* Then he asked me to do some tests but I just butted in and said, 'Steve. I think it's best if I stopped you right there . . .' And I explained to him what'd happened. We ended up spending about an hour together talking it over.

I told him I was ready to go to Zimbabwe and to try and get on with things, but he warned me I'd have to train my mind to be active and to stop dwelling on my problems with Nicky. But that was far easier said than done. You can train your body but it's very hard to train your mind, and there were times after that when I would just say to him, 'Steve, I don't know how I'm going to cope with this. I'm trying to train my mind, but I can't.'

I left for that tour in a state of shock. I hadn't really

comprehended what was going on with Nicky. I suspected the worst but clung to the hope that things were not as bad as they seemed, and that though she'd spoken about a trial separation she would quickly lose interest in the whole thing and we'd get back together. Maybe it was just a phase she needed to go through.

I'd no idea that there might be someone else involved, but my phone-calls home from Zimbabwe only confirmed the impression that she wanted to go off and do something else with her life. Rather than face up to the fact, I increasingly sought comfort in a haze of drinking and smoking as I tried to dull the pain. So much for training my mind.

I wondered how long I'd be able to hide things from my team-mates, and the unsurprising answer was not long. It's hard to be up when you're down, and it didn't help that every morning on the team bus we'd listen to that wrist-slitting REM song 'Every Day Hurts'. I managed for three or four days before Nasser got to me one morning and said, 'What the hell's up with you? You've hardly said a word all tour.'

'No, nothing,' I lied. 'I'm all right.' But I told him soon enough about how Nicky had asked for a separation a few weeks previously. Nasser and I had known each other a long time. We had first come across each other in county schools matches, and since then had played a lot of cricket together for England for almost 10 years. Our views on a lot of things were similar. We'd spoken about the strain professional cricket puts on relationships, and agreed we didn't want to play just for our marriages to go down the drain, so I knew he was someone who'd understand better than most. When he asked me what I thought about the whole thing, I told him I honestly didn't know. I admitted I was wondering whether I should go back home or not. In the end I stayed but sat out a couple of matches, and in the ones I did play in I was terrible.

Once my situation became general knowledge among the squad, Ben Hollioake, one of my closest friends in the Surrey team, was a big help. He regularly came knocking on my door to check I was all right in the evenings, and would persuade me to go out and eat with him. He was always trying to distract me and was so understanding, amazing for someone who was only 21. I think he was pretty shocked. He'd viewed Nicky and I as a stable couple.

In normal circumstances, given that I'd got a young family, I would probably have been one of the guys who'd have questioned whether I should have gone on the Test tour of India about a month later, because there were security fears following the September 11 terrorist attacks. If we'd been happy together I'm sure Nicky would have told me I shouldn't go, but not now. It was, 'Go on, you've got to get on that plane.'

THE WARM-UP GAMES in India were a real struggle. I played in the first one in Hyderabad but scored few runs and sat out the second in Jaipur, even though I could have done with the practice. The original plan was for me to play but I pulled out. I was so depressed that I struggled to get out of bed and phoned Dean Conway, our physiotherapist, to tell him I wasn't sleeping and couldn't play. This was one of the hardest periods I went through. I wanted to go onto anti-depressants but Dean wouldn't let me, and told me to cheer myself up by getting into the gym. I managed it once but came away utterly exhausted and defeated.

The time difference was awful, my sleep pattern was awful and my fitness was awful, and all that in a country where the heat was stifling. I was on Sudafed to keep me awake during the day, and on sleeping tablets to drive away the demons at night. Two sleeping tablets occasionally got me through from midnight to 6am, but often I woke much earlier. Nicky wouldn't speak to me until the children were in bed, and that was 3am in India. Sometimes that'd be when I was waking. I often spoke to her for about an hour. I was still trying to get her back. She just wouldn't give ground but I thought I could persuade her. I would often end up in tears, begging, pleading.

My routine, such as it was, was to try and practice – and stay awake – during the day, and in the evening spend a couple of hours with Ashley Giles and Michael

Vaughan on the PlayStation. For me, this was the best part of the day, a couple of mates around me with whom I could try to have a laugh. The worst part was being alone in my room at night, and I began to have a bottle of Scotch to hand. Normally, I wouldn't have dreamed of doing such a thing, especially in such a humid country. I might have had one or two glasses of wine during the evening but this was madness, drinking and smoking – I'd taken up smoking as well – and generally making myself unhealthy.

By the time of the first Test in Mohali, I was incapable of concentrating properly. We batted first and I found myself facing a swing bowler called Iqbal Siddiqui playing his first Test. He kept drifting the ball away from me. I hadn't prepared for this type of bowling and, after driving him through the covers a couple of times, was caught off a lazy front-foot drive. Later, as India amassed a big lead, I remember standing in the field, fortunately with sunglasses on, tears in my eyes, wondering what was happening to my life. I also dropped an absolute sitter off Richard Dawson, our spinner. The batter literally lobbed it up to me. Everyone just stood there, looking at me. '*Shit, shit, shit, shit, SHIT!*'

Somehow I batted for about three hours in our second innings, ninth out for a top score of 62, but it was a surreal experience. For the first time I could remember, I was batting for my country and didn't really care what happened. I knew we were almost certainly going to lose because we'd conceded a huge first innings deficit and India's spinners, Anil Kumble and Harbhajan Singh, were in their element. As they ran in to bowl to me, I kept thinking about my private life, Nicky and the children, and how long I could cope. I thought '*Whoops, there's a Kumble googly. Whoa! . . . Harbhajan's other one.*' Sometimes I'd put a straight bat on one and think, '*How the hell did I do that?*' I wasn't thinking about footmarks or how much the ball was turning, I was thinking '*My life's a mess.*' I was playing from memory.

I had the wicket-keeper chuntering away, and at one stage turned round to him and said, 'Why don't you cut it out? I don't give a shit. I'm probably going to get out any moment. What you say isn't going to make any difference.'

If anyone had known what was going through my brain they would have packed me off to The Priory, no questions asked. In the end, I chipped a return catch to Kumble and we lost with a day to spare.

TWO NIGHTS before the second Test in Ahmedabad, during another seriously bad phone call to Nicky, I finally realized that she might be in a relationship with Kieron. Perhaps somewhere at the back of my mind I had suspected as much, but if I ever thought about it at all I probably dismissed the idea as ridiculous. A couple of mates of mine had suggested she must be involved with someone else – you don't just suddenly want to separate for no reason – but I'd just waved it away. The realization that she might be seeing someone, and someone I had once called a friend – because Nicky and I used to socialize with Kieron and his former girlfriend, Laura – sent me into a hurt rage. How could Nicky behave like this in the house we'd bought together only a few months earlier, while I was halfway round the world trying to support her and the children?

I decided I had to go home and try, however hopeless it seemed, to sort things out. I spoke to Nasser and Duncan the night before the game, and neither tried to dissuade me. I think they knew my mind was made up, and that I wasn't in the habit of being talked out of things.

My decision to abandon the tour failed to achieve anything, and merely succeeded in splashing my problems all over the newspapers. I was met by a television journalist at the airport asking me whether my marriage was on the rocks, and when I got back to my house there were half a dozen reporters camped on the doorstep. The tabloids felt sure there was substance to the rumours now circulating about my marriage because I was returning home early. That morning *The Sun* had printed a photograph of another man – unnamed in the newspaper but it was Kieron – going into my house with Nicky. How juicy.

I didn't believe Nicky's and Kieron's claims that nothing was going on between them, but told the reporters that Kieron was a family friend to get the reporters off my case. Nicky and I 'gutsed' it out living in the same house, arguing in front of the children, Nicky saying she wanted to separate but unsure if she wanted a divorce, me wanting . . . what did I want? Just to wake up from all this.

Things got worse. About a week after I got back, a girl from Cheshire called Lizette Roberts, who was trying to launch her pop career, claimed in the *News of the World* that she'd met me after a one-day international in Manchester five years earlier and had had sex with me six times in a night. Of course it wasn't true, but it made things between Nicky and me all the harder, especially as I'd previously admitted to Nicky my one infidelity in New Zealand back in 1997. I did take advice about suing this woman but was warned against it – something about it being my word against hers.

Everything was out of control. I was someone who'd always wanted my private life to be private; now I was probably the most public cricketer in the land. I was in territory I knew nothing about. I didn't even want a divorce, let alone to answer nasty questions – and they were pretty nasty – from reporters. It would've been hard enough to cope with all this in private, as any break-up is, but the constant sniping questions from reporters made it awful.

In the end, I moved out of the house and went to stay with Alistair Brown, who lived nearby. I'd known Ally since we were 13. He was then a confident lad who bowled big leg-breaks and had a talent for hitting the ball out of the park, testimony to some of the quickest hands and eyes in the game. Although slightly suspect against the fastest bowling, I think he might have sorted this out had he been exposed to Test cricket, and he was without doubt one of the best batsmen I ever played with at Surrey. We'd joined the county staff at the same time.

I stayed with him for about three weeks before I went back to staggering on with my cricket. To be honest I didn't really know what else to do and, as my dad said, I needed to keep working because someone was going to have to pay the legal bills if Nicky and I did divorce. Little did I know how many bills, but it was good advice. I decided to go back out to India for the remainder of the tour. I gave a press conference when I got there because it seemed like the best way to deal with the loads of questions the reporters wanted to ask. Hopefully I'd get all that straight out the way. I recall someone asking me whether I accepted that my marriage was over. I said 'Yes', but don't think I really meant it.

I made a conscious effort to appear happier, but behind the scenes was not making the necessary sacrifices to get my game back to where it should have been. I was still drinking and smoking and not training. I'd missed the last two Tests by returning home and we were now involved in a series of six one-day internationals, which was even more physically demanding. I remember a game in Kanpur in which I held the innings together with an unbeaten 36, and felt good that I'd contributed something.

We tied an exciting series 3–3 but, despite my efforts, my heart wasn't in it which was disappointing because India's like no other place to play cricket. You're on a level with movie stars, mobbed by thousands of fans, and that's just going to a net session. But there had been too many sad moments earlier in the tour for me to enjoy it.

When we moved on to New Zealand I tried even harder to pick myself up by socializing more. What I was actually doing, though, was running away from my situation. I got it into my head that I had to enjoy myself, and I was determined to make the most of every day. It turned into quite a boozy trip. For me there was certainly more drinking on that tour than on any other I'd been on, but I did briefly train hard.

I HAD A BAD EXPERIENCE during the one-day series at the beginning of that 2002 tour, and it brought me face to face with the pain of my position and reminded me that escape was not that easy. A group of New Zealand supporters had formed themselves along the lines of England's 'Barmy Army', called 'Beige Thirteen', and they could be relied on to give the opposition plenty of stick. In the second match in Wellington, they singled me out for treatment, sledging me mercilessly while I was fielding on the boundary. This was where the tennis jokes started. They shouted out stuff like, '15-love!', or 'Vorster's shagging your wife!', or 'Who's feeding your kids?'

I remember coming off the pitch and Nasser saying to me, 'What was that all about? What was that bloke with the megaphone shouting?'

'Mate, did you not hear them?' I said, incredulous. 'They were going on about my wife, yelling, "15-love!". You must have heard them.'

'Oh mate, sorry. You should have told me. I'd have moved you.'

'Well, it's too bloody late now.'

It was an appalling experience and cut me up badly.

Once the first-class programme began, I got off to a terrible start in the first warm-up, a horribly windy match in Queenstown, but was happy to miss the next game and just practice in the nets the day before the first Test. For some reason, maybe because I wasn't having so much contact with Nicky now, I was more focused than I'd been since my life started going out of control.

One of the problems I'd had in India was that I'd started to question my ability as a cricketer. Could I, this bloke whose wife had left him, still perform on the big stage? I struggled to picture myself scoring another century for England but, somehow, in the first Test in

Christchurch, miraculously it happened. Everything just went for me. The wicket, earlier in the game a green seamer on which both sides were bowled out cheaply, had calmed down by the time we batted again, and Chris Cairns had injured his knee and could not bowl.

I went out to bat early on the third day with the bowlers fresh, and was dropped in the slips second ball by Nathan Astle. My second bit of good luck was batting with Freddie Flintoff, a good distraction. Fred was then the side's promising young all-rounder but he was without a score for a long time, and was getting a lot of stick. I thought he just needed to understand what was required to achieve at the top level.

I liked him and wanted him to do well because he was a big spirit in the dressing-room. I'd played alongside him for England on and off for three years, and had tried to give him advice a few times, but maybe he just hadn't been ready to listen. Now, I just kept telling him to play his natural game but keep a tight defence to the good balls. Meanwhile, I played quite aggressively at the other end. That we'd gone out the night before, playing pool and drinking Guinness – five or six pints in my case – in the Irish bar across the road from the team hotel, boosted our comradeship. It was an incredible partnership to be involved in, and I was thrilled when Fred got his maiden Test hundred.

In the state of mind I was then in, I didn't give a great deal of thought to what I was doing. I just went for everything pitched outside off stump. One of the square boundaries was quite short – I used my nous as much as I could and took it on. Fred and I dealt in boundaries, basically. I hit 18 fours in my hundred and Fred had 21 in his. Later on, I hit five sixes – not something that often happened! I gave a bloke called Chris Drum a fearful beating and Fred got stuck into Ian Butler, who was making his Test debut. There was a period when we were charging along at more than ten an over!

A cold shiver went through me when I reached my hundred. I felt proud that I'd managed to score a century again for England, but still didn't want to take my helmet off to acknowledge the crowd. It was strange, but I didn't want people to see my face. I felt as though I'd shown people I was trying to climb back up again, but I knew I still didn't have a grip on things. That innings was pure escapism, and one of the reasons things went so well was that I didn't want it to end. Being out in the middle, batting was so much better than sitting in the dressing-room thinking about my problems. We declared when I got to 200. It felt like a big achievement – I didn't find out until later that it was the second-fastest double-century ever scored for England – but even as I was walking off I was thinking what I was going to say to the press. I wanted to dedicate those two hundreds to my children, Henry and Amelia, which is what I did. Despite an even faster double-century from Astle himself, we won the game on St Patrick's Day and some of us – especially me, Fred and Butch – took it as a cue to celebrate for two or three days.

To the outsider, it certainly gave the impression that I was okay; perhaps it even convinced me for a time. But had Astle clung onto that chance, my contribution to the winter tours would have been nothing special. Not that I gloated at his dropping me. In the 1996 World Cup, I cost us our opening fixture against New Zealand in Ahmedabad (as you can imagine, not my favourite city in the world) by putting him down early on in his century. I'd also once dropped Matthew Elliott in an Ashes Test at Leeds before he reached 30, and he went on to make nearly 200, so I knew all about the humiliation of standing in the field watching a bloke who should be back in the pavilion enjoying himself at your expense.

The euphoria was short-lived. The next day, Nicky dropped another bombshell and did something she'd always said she'd never do. She did a spread in the *Sunday Mirror* saying, 'He's no hero, he's a serial cheat.' My brother Alan read it to me over the phone. This was the first newspaper article done by either of us about our private life and it devastated me. It was something she'd said she would never do. It was clear to me that the sole intention of the piece was to portray me in a bad light and in order to do that had fabricated many incidents. It was so unfair, and I felt she had publicly betrayed me. It showed how far things had deteriorated between the two of us.

Back on the pitch, we couldn't hold onto our lead in the series, which ended 1–1, a fair reflection of how the sides had played. We were distracted, to say the least, by the news of the tragic death of Ben Hollioake (which I'll come to later) during the second game, but New Zealand wanted it more in the final match in Auckland where our attempts to slow down the over-rate, after rain had ruined the first two days, badly backfired. A new rule had come in, allowing play to continue on grounds where there were floodlights and Eden Park, a rugby venue, certainly had those. But they were far from perfect for cricket, and there was, as yet, no provision for coming off when the natural light had been over-taken by artificial light (as happened later). So, on the fourth evening, New Zealand were able to bat on until nearly 8pm, by which time the moon was shining bright and the fielders lost any balls hit high up against the black sky. Even if it was legitimate, it was an utter farce and allowed New Zealand to put enough runs on the board to give themselves a chance to bowl us out on the final day.

To make matters worse, I was given out caught behind off Daryl Tuffey by local umpire Doug Cowie, even though the only contact was bat brushing pad. It was my own fault. At one point the previous night, we'd gathered round the umpires in an attempt to persuade them that whatever the regulations stated it was simply too dark for us to field. I'd rather unwisely overstepped the mark in my arm-twisting. And earlier in the game I'd been at the non-striker's end when Cowie had given out Flintoff caught behind, even though his bat was inches away from the ball; I could see the gap from where I was standing, and was amazed Cowie hadn't seen it as well. Now, I said to him, 'Look Doug, you had problems seeing it in daylight, let alone late at night . . .' It raised a smile from Fred, but Cowie wasn't impressed. 'There's no need for that,' he said sternly.

I don't know whether it influenced his decision the next day but, on reflection, I realized I'd given him an opportunity to exercise a bit of revenge and it might have been much better if I'd kept my mouth shut. He might have given me the benefit of the doubt.

UMPIRES CAN HOLD GRUDGES. Early in my career, Surrey were not a popular side and at times we pushed things to the limit with our gamesmanship. We faced accusations of excessive appealing and, in the 1991 season, ball tampering. Some officials seemed to think of us as 'city slickers' who needed taking down a peg. In the end, we realized that the only way to change things for the better was to clean up our act, which we did. But I remember, during an early season game against Durham, showing my displeasure at Don Oslear giving me out lbw to Ian Botham, then in the twilight of his great career. I glowered at Oslear as I trudged away, so slowly that Botham shouted at me to get off the field, sharpish. In later years I became firm friends with 'Beefy', but back then to him I was just another whippersnapper.

After play, I was summoned to the umpires' room where Oslear warned me that I was heading up a few cul-de-sacs in life if I thought I was never out. I was unrepentant and pretty outspoken. I knew he didn't like Surrey because he had accused us of ball-tampering the previous season. I told him that I thought England's best all-rounder had got him under his thumb. As it happened, he didn't spend much more time on the umpiring list, but needless to say Don didn't do me too many favours thereafter. It was clearly a lesson I'd forgotten, come Auckland 2002. It pretty much summed up my life at that stage. My luck was out.

I got back to England in early April. I took a taxi from the airport to the house, opened the front door, dropped my bags on the floor and looked around at what was now a deserted home. I'd paid Nicky enough money to buy a four-bedroom house, and Kieron had moved in with her. Here, now, for the first time, I was confronted with the full awfulness of my situation. What I saw was a sight I'd been trying to avoid thinking about.

I'd come home to a silent house with no children. Nicky had left me just one bed, one TV, an old two-piece sofa and, I soon discovered, a broken central heating system. I sat at the foot of the stairs, feeling utterly devastated, and I cried. I'd finally run out of distractions.

From this point, I became increasingly incapable of compartmentalizing my life, keeping my private problems separate from my cricket. I just couldn't do it. Sometimes I'd think I could cope, but then something would drag me back down. It was like trying to climb a mountain of ice, with nothing to cling on to. Occasionally I'd get so far up and then, bam, back down again.

I tried to motivate myself in my cricket by saying, 'Come on, do it for the children', but then I'd hear or see something, maybe children walking down the road who were a similar age to Henry and Amelia, and all of a sudden tears would well up. '*Fucking hell, get me out of here.*' So I'd have another beer, another smoke. '*What's happening to me?*'

I was starting to realize that I was doing myself damage and that this wasn't a way out. I was becoming seriously unfit, short of sleep and my mind was all over the place. The way I was carrying on was just a way of escape, and even then it only lasted a few hours at a time. I had to deal with it but I didn't know how.

I did play one more big innings, though, before that India Test at Lord's, and it was another of those times during this period when finding a partner to bat with – Matthew Hoggard, our No 11, in the second Test against Sri Lanka at Edgbaston in June – took my mind off things, and briefly enabled me to function again. Once I got a feel for an innings and a situation, I could still do it, but it was very sporadic.

We were well in control by the time I went out to bat late on the second day. Inspired by some high-quality bowling from Andrew Caddick, we'd bowled out Sri Lanka for 162 and a big stand from Trescothick and Butcher had helped push us to 176 in front when I went out to bat. It was another of those times when it would have been easy to give it away, but the pitch was quiet and we wanted a big lead otherwise it was quite possible Sri Lanka would bat their way out of trouble. A steady trickle of wickets at the other end helped concentrate my mind and, when Hoggard walked out with a bat in his hand not long before lunch the next day, I was still there, on 61, having seen six partners depart.

A lot was in our favour – Muttiah Muralitharan, Sri Lanka's match-winning bowler, was not fully fit – but it was still an amazing partnership. So much went as planned. I think Hoggie and I stayed together for 30 overs, and we controlled the strike so well that in all but one over I was on strike for the first ball. It really demoralized the fielders. Not that Hoggie was a mug with the bat; as he was quick to tell everyone, a couple of years after this he almost scored a century for Yorkshire as night-watchman. His talent was just keeping things simple: blocking, leaving, trying nothing fancy. By the end, I was happy to let him face most of the over, and overall I think he took slightly more of the strike than I did during our partnership.

We had some fun setting ourselves targets, 10 runs at a time, his score, my score, our partnership. By talking us through things, I managed to keep us focused. In the end, I was out first, cutting high to third man, but by that point I'd got 123 and was pretty happy with what we'd achieved. We'd built up a lead of almost 400, and it was enough to set up a commanding win.

It was great to escape the reality of my personal situation for as many hours as I could manage on the pitch. It's funny, but I found myself relaxed and feeling more in control during that innings than I had felt for weeks off the pitch. My mind had been doing strange things to me. I was in increasingly bad shape, physically and mentally. I began to question the point of my playing cricket. When men went out to work, they did it for their families, and that became their motivation. I didn't want to play just for myself. I thought, 'Yeah, well, you may have just got a Test hundred against Sri Lanka, but did it really give you a lift?' And the answer was, 'No it didn't.' As soon as the applause stopped and I came off the field, I felt empty inside. I needed the happiness of a family to go back home to if my cricket was to have a purpose. I was desperately missing my children.

My condition wasn't helped by an incident before the next Test against Sri Lanka, at Old Trafford, when I tripped over Michael Vaughan. We were playing a warm-up game of football and I badly hurt my ankle. I still played in the Test but there was a lot of bruising, and I wasn't fit going into the triangular one-day series that preceded the Tests with India. I only played a few times, missing an epic final against India when we scored a massive 325 but still lost.

Even before the problems began with Nicky, I had talked to Nasser and Duncan about the possibility of retiring from one-day cricket, telling them that something had to give because I was on the road too much. But the truth was that by this stage I was so messed up I wasn't practising hard or training at all. Sometimes you can get away with a few things in Test cricket, but in the one-day game you can't get away with anything. You've got to be very agile in the field, and I knew how the coach viewed one-day cricket. Duncan wanted energy and athletes, not some bloke whose mind kept drifting off and who wasn't working at his game.

On the day of the final, I publicly announced I was giving up one-day cricket. The press release said something about me wanting to spend more time sorting out my private life, which was true, but whatever the outcome this was a permanent decision. The next World Cup was only a few months away but I wasn't coming back. I was done and dusted with one-day cricket.

I remember standing with Marcus Trescothick on the outfield for the presentation ceremony that evening. In his enlightened state – he'd scored a brilliant hundred that afternoon – he could see that, all right, we'd lost, but it had been a great final, in front of a full house at Lord's. 'Thorpey,' he asked in his Cornish accent, 'You're going to give all this up, are you? You don't want to do this any more? Don't you think you'll miss it?'

Maybe that showed how other people can't see what's going on inside you. But maybe it also summed up what a poor state I was in; over the years I'd had so much enjoyment out of cricket, the winning, the losing, the camaraderie, but now I just couldn't see the point. I could no longer feel a thing.

'Tres, mate,' I replied, 'I couldn't give a fuck.'

But if I thought retiring from one-day cricket would help keep me together, I didn't know how low I'd become. All I could see was pain and heartache. Sport could not provide me with an escape any longer. Walking away altogether was going to be pretty embarrassing but, by the later stages of the Lord's Test match against India, which came just two weeks after that one-day final, that was my over-riding desire. I just didn't want to be in the spotlight any more. I'd been an England cricketer for nine years and now it was enough.

All sorts of things were buzzing through my head but, increasingly, I was having these fantasies. *'I'm going to leave the country. I'll go to America and start a new life.'* I found it hard to imagine still living in England. And I think I would have left but for the fact it would obviously have made seeing Henry and Amelia all the more harder, if not impossible. And, crazy though it sounds, I hadn't given up on Nicky having me back.

FOUR

I Don't Like Cricket, I Hate It

THINGS DIDN'T get better after the Lord's Test against India in July 2002, they got worse. Much worse. In my new state of 'retirement', I found myself with even more time to spend in the family home near Epsom Town, a bloody great pile with five bedrooms and a big garden in the middle of nowhere and just me rattling around inside, me and my tortured thoughts. It might have been an expensive house in a desirable area, but it felt to me like an open prison. I started referring to the house as Colditz.

Nicky and I had bought it in the summer of 2001 intending it to be our dream home, but that idea soon became a sick joke. Many bad things happened in that house as it became the central battleground between the two of us after Nicky announced she wanted a separation. It may be an exaggeration to say that that house ruined everything for us, but it seemed that everything took a turn for the worse after we left our previous house in Ewell.

When I went to Zimbabwe in 2001, it was the first time Nicky had been alone in the new house for any length of time and she didn't like it. I can remember once speaking to her on the phone from Zimbabwe and she said something about how Kieron – who'd just split up from his girlfriend, as it happened – had come over because she was scared of being in the house on her own. Of course, at that point I'd not twigged what was going on, but that house had helped bring them together.

My god, that house. I hate to think about it. This was the house from which Nicky practically tried to exclude me after she first said she wanted to separate. She rarely wanted me in the house at the same time as her, so we alternated periods of staying there, taking it in turns to look after the children, and when I was the one meant to stay away – which was a lot of the time – I was at a loss as to what to do.

This went on for most of the month I was at home between the Zimbabwe and India tours, and I found myself virtually homeless. There were not that many people I felt I could turn to. I knew it was a situation that only myself and Nicky could really sort out. I spent some time at my parents' house and also with Alistair Brown. Basically, I was living out of my car. I carried around with me two or three bags of clothes, sometimes washing them at home, sometimes at my parents and sometimes Alistair's wife Sarah was doing a bit of washing for me. It was a pathetic existence, but I guess it's not that uncommon when you separate.

I spent god knows how many hours just driving around, without knowing where I was going. I can remember once being behind the wheel, thinking, 'Where in fuck's name are you driving? You can't go back to your house because Nicky's there. You can't go to your parents' house because they're probably not in . . . You've got nothing to fall back on. *Nothing*. What are you going to do?' Occasionally, I'd go and see a couple of mates, mates who've since said to me, 'Christ, you were a mess at that stage. Totally lost.'

Then, one night during this period, I'd been over at a friend's house, where I think I'd been drinking, and I was on my way back to Brownie's house. But between these two places was my house, and all of a sudden I was doing the thing you should never do and slowing up outside to have a look, seeing what's going on. It was around 1am and, sure enough, there was Kieron's car parked in my drive. I'm thinking to myself, 'I only bought this house two months ago and now I'm in my car outside looking in and there's this bloke inside . . .'

My first thought was to do his car over. But then I thought, 'No. Christ. Criminal damage.' So I got out of my car, walked up to the house and rang the door bell.

God knows what I was planning on doing or saying, but I was in a dream-like state, and it felt like I had no control. Eventually, Nicky opened it.

'Right,' I announced. 'I want to come in, thanks very much. This is my house. I'm coming in.' Nicky said, 'Fuck off,' as I suppose you would at that time of night. I ignored her. 'This is my house,' I said. 'I've bought it with my hard-earned money. I'm going to spend the night here, thanks very much.' Looking back, I was almost in an hysterical state.

At this point Kieron came down the stairs drawling in his South African accent, 'Nah, let 'im in.' Well, I'm thinking to myself, you're hardly going to say anything else, are you, given that you are actually in *my* house. I walked in. I was struggling to control myself, but even in my highly agitated state I was aware that the children were asleep upstairs. Probably in an attempt to calm me down, Nicky suggested we talk about things and we all trooped through to the kitchen. It was completely surreal. Unsurprisingly the discussion went nowhere and we quickly ended up just shouting at each other. Then I turned on Kieron, this bloke I'd entertained in my home with his girlfriend at various times over the previous year, and who was now carrying on as though he owned the place, and told him to get out. Nicky said he couldn't go because he had been drinking. So I started screaming: 'He's fucking getting out of here! Get him out of here! Now!' I think Nicky could see I was in a desperate state and eventually she told him to leave. Suddenly I felt completely drained, exhausted. I started to feel sick and weak and stumbled off to the spare room. I still have no idea why I went there that night, and what I hoped to achieve, but driving by and seeing Kieron's car outside just made something inside me snap.

What hurt most, I think, was that I felt totally betrayed by the people close to me. The month before we bought the new house, I had given Nicky a new car. It became pretty clear that she had worked out precisely when was financially the most advantageous time to leave. As it turned out, Nicky left me just as the last cheque from my benefit year had cleared.

My wish to escape public attention by stepping down from cricket in the summer of 2002 was not immediately granted. The newspapers wanted to know all about what was wrong with this bloke who had run away from his job. I was back on the front pages again, just as I had been when I rushed home from India. All I could say to them was that I was in a bad state, and trying to sort it out. Some of them wrote that I was having a breakdown. Probably, yes, I was; but I didn't actually want to admit to it in a newspaper. The attention only made me more reclusive and soon enough I was left alone to do what I'd said I wanted to do when I announced I was stepping down from cricket – concentrate on my family. I now had time to do that for hours on end, focussing on what had gone wrong and what I was missing.

Seeing the children were bitter-sweet times. In happier days, I could obviously take Henry and Amelia out of the house no questions asked, down to the shops, on a bike ride or to the swimming pool, but now all these things had to be painfully negotiated and without the co-operation of Nicky they were next to impossible to make happen. While I was allowed to see the children from time to time, it was not always in the way I wanted. I always felt she was in control.

What I found hardest to comprehend about her attitude was that she wanted to take away the special relationship between me and my children. Fortunately, Amelia was not yet three and perhaps too young to know what she was missing but Henry, at five, was not. I'm sure he must have been desperate for me to watch him play football more often than I could, or for more of our trips down to the driving-range.

Basically I was on my own. I had effectively cut myself off from cricket and soon found that all those people on Nicky's side, who I had thought were friends, had turned away. I was left to rely heavily on my parents, although that was not easy as there had been a time when I'd not spoken to them for two or three years at the start of my marriage because Nicky hadn't got on with them. Unbeknown to me, she had written to my parents a few weeks after our wedding saying how awful they were, that they'd spoilt the wedding day – she even called my father a philistine! – and she said she wanted nothing more to do with them. It put me in an impossible situation, and I ended up siding with Nicky which created a rift with my parents, something I really regret now. I was so grateful to find that they were there for me at this time. It was quite a humbling experience.

A few friends in cricket kept in touch, but only a few like Mark Butcher and Ray Alikhan, and I noted those who didn't. I first met Ray, who had been my best man, in my second season at Surrey. He had joined us from Sussex. He was a few years older and we couldn't have been more different. He was this elegant, princely figure while I was this terrier-like bloke with no style whatsoever, but we just gelled. He'd summoned me to bowl at him in the nets. 'Old boy, come over and throw some to me, will you? . . . Just bowl them nice and short.' And he just kept pulling me away for miles. We sometimes trained together and, when he was let go by Surrey a few years later, we carried on training and playing squash together. He said that I had helped him then, and I was grateful for his support now.

Butch and I went back a long way. I first remember him as an 18-year-old with a big hairdo, strolling out at No 9 to join me in a Sunday league match at the Oval and almost pulling off an amazing victory by smashing a quick 40-odd. He was three years younger than me and saw me, he once said, as something of a role model, but the respect was always mutual. As fellow left-handers, I suppose we had a natural affinity. Socially, we weren't that close to start with. I kept myself to myself in those days, and was notorious for being unable to remember people's names. I was pretty wrapped up in my cricket and spent an unhealthy amount of time thinking about it. Butch always had a better perspective on things and thought nothing of a night out. I came to realize that it wasn't a bad thing to chill out now and again, and by the end I reckoned I was as close to Butch as to anybody I'd known in cricket.

There were, though, times when outside circumstances put our friendship under strain. Our wives – Butch was married to Alec Stewart's sister Judy – did not hit it off (but then come to think of it, on looking back, Nicky didn't hit it off with many people). That made things difficult for a while, and we also had a period of a few months when we didn't speak after Butch was named stand-in England captain ahead of me during the home series with New Zealand in 1999.

That was a complicated situation. I was going through a bad patch with the England management, which ought to have made it no surprise that they chose someone else, but I was annoyed because in the previous game at Lord's, when Nasser had left injured, he put me in charge. When Nasser was ruled out of the next Test in Manchester, the selectors opted to give the captaincy to Butch. Given that the two ex-captains in the side,

Atherton and Stewart, were reluctant to lead again, I was the senior available pro. There was really no reason to hold anything against Butch – it wasn't his fault he was chosen – but I behaved in a pretty shitty way throughout the Test at Old Trafford. I should have accepted the situation but didn't and my attitude was poor. All in all, I behaved pretty childishly, in retrospect.

Butch was having his own problems at that time which plunged his life into the sort of crisis mine was now in. His marriage to Judy was breaking down. Like me, he started to drink more and his game began to collapse under the strain. I wasn't on the 1999–2000 tour of South Africa when his struggles really began, but well remember one day the next spring him throwing his bat down during a net session at the Oval, and slumping onto the ground in tears. We hadn't spoken for a long time but I went up to him and asked him if he was all right and he told me what had happened. The time to mend bridges was long overdue. I told him that I was sorry there had been problems between us and said that if there was anything I could do to help him I would gladly do it.

It was an important day in our relationship, and after that we grew a lot closer. He lost his England place for a year but came back strongly against Australia in 2001 and established himself as the side's No 3. So, when my problems started, Butch recognized the situation straightaway and gave me encouragement and advice. But there was only so much others could do. When I did occasionally go out socializing I wasn't really there. I was still low and lost in my thoughts.

God knows how many days I spent in that house, staring at the walls, each numbing day indistinguishable from the next. The soul-searching now began in earnest. What exactly was I going to do? As Duncan Fletcher had said, I had to do something, but I ended up doing very little except getting wasted on my own every night. Each night I might drink three or four glasses of wine, though perhaps once a week it might be a bottle of Jack Daniels instead. It was the booze that really affected me. It would make me wake up in the night with my mind buzzing.

I was trying to come to terms with what had happened. Deep down, I still wanted to get everything back – my marriage, my children – and was trying to figure out how it might happen. But Nicky, who was enjoying being in control of the situation, seemed to have no intention of taking me back. She knew I was unhappy and struggling to cope, but showed little sympathy. In fact, she gave the impression she was loving every minute of it.

As a sportsman in self-imposed exile, I felt completely lost. My career was gone, my reputation ruined. All of a sudden I was in the position where I was being labelled a loser. Along with the loss of my children,

I was mourning the loss of my place in the world, my identity. Retirement is something all sportsmen have to cope with, but that doesn't make it any easier when it happens.

And in that scary state, removed from the public spotlight, I began to think that although there were things about cricket I missed, there were also things about it I hated. I looked back on my career and thought of all the sacrifices I'd made.

There's this image some people have that playing cricket for England is one long party, interrupted by a few matches at glamorous locations. If it was like that in the old days when touring was more leisurely, it certainly isn't now. God knows how many lonely, anxious nights I spent in hotel rooms in strange cities preparing for the next day's Test match. It was often bloody hard, but I used to rationalize it by telling myself this is what I had to do. I was earning a living to support my family, and it made me proud to be able to do that. That was what got me out of bed in the morning; it motivated me.

Now things looked different. What had I gone through all that shit for? For this? Was this how it was all to end? A divorce and my life splashed over the newspapers? That was not what I thought I was buying into. Nicky had always complained about my cricket taking me away from home for such extensive periods, and, for a long time, I felt very guilty about it and my attitude almost became 'I shouldn't be doing this, it's not good.' Perhaps that's partly why I gave up.

I looked at cricket and reflected that the game had done me over. I'd dedicated so much of my life to it and it had bitten me on the arse. And the more I thought about it, the more I realized what cricket had *not* done for me. It had not, for instance, taught me many 'life skills' during 15 seasons as a professional. It had taught me about playing the game, and taken me to quite a few countries, but international sportsmen, it now dawned on me, were thoroughly pampered. Sport wrapped us in an artificial circuit of cricket grounds, hotels and airports. We had to deal with performing in public, that's true, but in return we were well paid, stayed in nice hotels and flew business class. In truth, most of these luxuries were recent introductions – for a long time England cricketers were neither well paid nor treated anything like that – but by 2002 we had little cause for complaint. Virtually all our needs were catered for. We had people to tell us when to practice, when matches started, when to attend functions and when we should speak to the press. They even did our laundry. We lived in a cosy, privileged sanctum.

The world beyond cricket, I now discovered in bachelor-hood, could not have been more different. If you didn't do it yourself, it didn't get done. I had little experience about the ordinary day-to-day activities that came naturally to most people. I'd gone virtually straight from living at home with my parents to living with Nicky, and I'd had next to no experience of time on my own.

They say sport builds character, but I'm not sure it does it enough. Being exposed to the big, wide world, as I was now, was a bit of a shock. I hadn't got the grounding to get out there and survive. Doing the washing was a conundrum. Even going out to get milk and basic food was an ordeal. I can recall going shopping to my local supermarket shortly after I began my new, bachelor life. I wasn't sure what to buy and didn't like being there, but knew I had to do it. I hated it. It took me an age to decide what I needed.

My main concern was that someone might recognize me and know I had split from my wife. I was terrified they would have read about my circumstances. So there I was, unshaven and wearing a baseball cap, hoping no one would recognize me but afraid if they did they'd be thinking, 'There's that bloke in the papers . . . His life is fucked.' I was riddled with guilt and paranoia.

I was definitely not a natural at looking after myself. When I began, there had been no book on how to cope with professional sport. There was no training in handling the media, let alone coping with the wider issue of being at college one day and two years later touring the world as an England cricketer. When it came to real life, I was an absolute novice.

When, the following year, in 2003, it became public

what Frank Bruno had gone through, it really struck a chord. Bruno's wife had left him and taken their three children and their divorce, along with the end of his career as a heavyweight boxer, had brought on severe mental illness. There were stories in the papers about how he'd been sleeping in a boxing ring in his garden and had delusions that he was not actually himself but someone else – Frankie Dettori, I think – and he'd ended up in a psychiatric hospital being treated for a breakdown. '*Christ, mate,*' I thought. '*I know exactly what sort of shitty place you're in. I was so nearly there myself.*'

If I was hoping to tidy up the mess of my life, and stabilize myself, I didn't manage it. The trouble was, I just had no idea how to make things better.

I went through some bad times. The nights were terrible and the mornings little better. I'd typically wake in damp sweat-soaked bed-sheets, with my heart racing, and stumble downstairs wondering how I was going to get through another day feeling like this. My first port of call was often the fridge. A beer. I'd get it and wander over to the sitting room to find the remnants of the previous evening . . . empty bottles, overflowing ash-trays, a PlayStation. There'd been no party, just me, an evening of torture I'd grown used to. I felt like I was going mad, talking to myself. The curtains were closed, and stayed closed all day. It was scary.

I remember one midday hearing the door-bell ring

and freezing. 'Don't move,' I thought, 'they'll never know you're here.' Who is it? Not more journalists? The gardener (who I was paying far too much to look after my garden because I'd decided to try to sell this awful house, and who would put his bill under the door if I didn't answer)?

Rather than see him, I'd write a cheque out and put it in the post. I just didn't want to be seen, so I wouldn't answer the door. I went up to the bedroom and peered past the edge of the curtain to see who it was. I think it was embarrassment that made me that way. After all, most people knew the wheels had come right off.

On this occasion, I saw it was my dad. '*Oh shit.*' I didn't want him seeing me like this, unshaven and bleary-eyed. But I knew he'd know I was inside, so I went down and opened the door. He'd been working in the area, he said, and was just popping round to see whether I was up and about. He sometimes did this. He was trying to help me get back on my feet again. I could tell he was checking me over, but he didn't say anything. In the end, he persuaded me to go and help him do some gardening.

If he was seriously worried about me, and I'm pretty sure he was, he had every reason to be. I was further away from getting better than ever. Later, when my life improved, if I ever woke up facing a tough day, I'd look back and tell myself nothing could be as hard as getting through what I did then.

FIVE

House of Cards

I WAS THE youngest in our family and often the most junior member of the teams I played in when I was growing up, so perhaps I came to accept there were always others around to take the big decisions and occupy the limelight. I was happy enough keeping quiet in the background. But in cricketing terms, I was reckoned to have a good head on my shoulders from a young age. In fact younger brothers in sporting families often grow up fast by playing alongside their elder siblings – Robin Smith and Ben Hollioake, for example – and it certainly helped me.

Being the youngest of three boys – Ian was four years older and Alan two – I had to fight for every little reward I could get. Being bigger and stronger, they dominated our games of football and cricket, and I had to learn fast and work extra hard just to keep up. I wasn't exceptionally stylish or talented but I was tenacious, determined and confident. We were always encouraged by my father, who played sport at the weekends, and my mother who, in later years, became an expert scorer at our various cricket matches.

Things weren't easy for the family. My father worked as a draughtsman and later as an engineering surveyor, but I don't think he earned a particularly big salary. I shared a room with one of my brothers until I was eight, when we had an extension built and we all got our own bedroom. With fields at the back of the garden we had lots of space to play in and, frankly, that was all we wanted.

We were lucky to live in a village that had several youth teams. Wrecclesham, a couple of miles west of Farnham in Surrey, had four sides from the under-11s to the under-17s, and every Friday night up to 40 kids would turn up for practice sessions run by a guy called Tony Hughes. I remember once playing for the under-17s at the age of eight. Someone dropped out and, as we only lived up the road from the ground, I was asked if I'd go along. I was very nervous. I didn't have to bat – they'd stuck me down at No 11 – but I took a catch, pretty straightforward, but was thrilled when these big lads patted me on the head and said, 'Great catch, youngster.' It felt like I'd done something really good. Like my father, but not my brothers, I batted left-handed, though I was pretty much right-handed at everything else.

I was 13 when I first played for Wrecclesham first XI, the village team, in the I'Anson League. The team was basically made up of adults. Late in my second season, I scored my first century at a lovely ground down at Frensham when we'd only needed around 150 to win. I think I was the youngest person ever to score a hundred in the I'Anson League, but I never played for the village again. Alan and Ian were already turning out for Farnham where there was a better standard of cricket, and I was encouraged to follow them by a chap called Jim Banks, who was involved with Farnham but also helped run Surrey's youth set-up.

The Surrey Championship, in which Farnham played, featured a lot of county second XI players, so by the age of 15 I was facing some pretty good adult players. I scored 90 in my first game for the first XI. Playing on some ordinary club wickets helped shape my technique, teaching me to play soft and late, judge a run and place my shots. One of my best knocks was a hundred against Morden Wanderers, Alec Stewart's old team, who had a lot of second XI wide boys playing for them who were quite chirpy.

Surrey had a good youth system that processed a lot of young players like Martin and Darren Bicknell, Alistair Brown, Mark Butcher, Adam Hollioake and myself. I was involved with the county from the under-11s upwards. I can remember once my granddad coming to watch me play for the under-11s at Morden, and me getting out for nought and saying I didn't want to play any more. I also recall playing in front of Micky Stewart, Alec's father, who managed Surrey and was about to go on and do the same job for England, and Geoff Arnold, the club coach, who sometimes gave me lifts home when I started going up to the Oval. In the winters, the county held youth sessions in Guildford and you'd go over there, have your nets, and get a little report at the end of it. I was also invited to have net sessions with the Surrey squad in the winter at Roehampton when I was 16. It served as a useful opportunity to have driving lessons with my dad on the way, which meant we were usually not talking by the time we got there!

It hadn't really crossed my mind that I could make a career out of cricket until Surrey offered me a two-year contract for the 1988 and 1989 seasons. I was 18 and had just finished at Farnham College, where I'd spent the previous few years re-taking some O-levels and starting, but not finishing, a couple of A-levels. My results clearly showed I devoted more time to sport than homework.

I had spent the summer happily earning a bit of money gardening and driving a van for an off-licence, while playing a few games for Surrey under-19s and in representative schools cricket. I'd first played for the county under-19s at 16 which, while probably a sign of a good player, was not unheard of. No surprise that *Wisden* described my captaincy of English Schools Under-16s against Wales and Scotland as being 'quiet and efficient'.

Surrey's offer wasn't difficult to accept. They were to pay me £3,000 for each of the two seasons, which seemed riches indeed (this rose to £12,500 after I got my first XI cap in 1991). Whereas my brothers had seemed to know what careers they wanted, I hadn't had a clue. Whenever my parents asked, I'd say something like, 'I'll be all right. Something will happen.' Well, now it had, and they seemed happy for me to give cricket a go. I think Micky Stewart, who once generously described me as the most talented young sportsman in the country, had a chat with them about the pros and cons of a sporting career.

The only complication was that I was also invited for football trials with Brentford. I loved football and was also above average at that. I'd played a lot with my brothers and the Bicknell boys, Martin and Darren, for Old Farnhamians in the Guildford and District League, and we were a pretty competitive lot. The Thorpes made an uncompromising midfield trio. I'd already been to trials with Southampton, although I'd chosen not to finish them, and even once decided not to go on a three-week cricket tour of Australia with Surrey under-17s because I didn't want to miss playing football. I was 15. For a long time, football came first.

But my football career was about to go belly-up. That winter, I spent several weekends going up to Lilleshall on the train with a mate of mine, Dean Fosberry, for trials with the England Schools under-18s and was selected as sweeper for a series of internationals. But meantime I got sent off in a local club match after some bloke crashed into me with a double-footed tackle. It was the sort of crude challenge that was pretty common in the games we played on Saturdays. The guy was still on the ground when I came down on him with a right boot, bang in front of the ref. This got back to the English Schools FA, who suspended me for the last match of the tournament against Scotland.

I was devastated that a minor incident in a minor match had reached such high quarters. The Schools FA asked me to travel to Scotland to talk about my indiscipline, but I told them I wasn't prepared to go all that way for a chat. So I was already showing signs of being headstrong back then. I continued to play with Old Farnhamians for two more seasons before giving up after an opponent head-butted me, a few weeks before I was leaving for my first England A cricket tour. Martin Bicknell and I both found that becoming professional cricketers made us marked men in football. It wasn't worth the trouble. It was ironic when 10 years later the Schools FA management guy who'd asked me up to Scotland congratulated me at an Oval Test match, and said I'd made the right decision!

BEING A SMALL-TOWN BOY whose horizons had yet to expand, I was filled with apprehension at the idea of joining Surrey. It was a big club with an imposing tradition of success, even if it then hadn't won a trophy for several years. The pavilion was full of reminders of the great side of the Fifties that had won seven championships in a row, and of the many great England cricketers like Sir Jack Hobbs, Ken Barrington, Peter May, Jim Laker and Sir Alec Bedser.

I looked around the staff and saw people like Sylvester Clarke, Tony Gray, Monte Lynch, David Smith and Jack Richards, who'd all played at international level, and Alec Stewart and Martin Bicknell who'd come up through the same system as me but already appeared destined to play for England. I'd first played district cricket with Martin at the age of nine, and teased him that I'd got into the England Under-15 team as a bowler ahead of him. We were the same age but he'd signed for the county two years earlier at 16, and had already enjoyed quite a lot of success. I certainly didn't regard myself as his equal.

I was excited and nervous; I really wanted to do it. Perhaps it helped that dad was keener on football than cricket. He just wanted me to enjoy it but my mum, on the other hand, was really enthusiastic. I remember being really embarrassed when I overheard her telling Mike Edwards, the Surrey Young Cricketers manager, that if they didn't sign me she would make sure that Sussex did!

I had embarked on a huge change. My university was second XI cricket and England A tours. I'd caught the occasional tantalizing glimpse of this life when playing for the under-19s against the Surrey second XI. During a rain break I watched their lads playing cards, with a big pot of money in the middle. Now I was one of them, playing cricket during the day and going out on the pull at night!

My first away trip was to Glastonbury. We started the first evening in the bar, as you do. We had a drink, then something to eat. Then another drink. One thing led to another and before I knew it we'd had half a dozen pints. I eventually got to bed thinking, *'Christ, I've got to get up and play cricket tomorrow.'* I clearly remember a few of the lads being sick in the dressing-room the next morning. Such was the culture I had entered. At 18, of course, you think it's all bloody marvellous.

We had a pretty strong side in 1988 and won the second XI championship without being beaten. I don't know if it was the culture shock, but I made a pretty moderate contribution with the bat before putting together a couple of hundreds towards the end of the season. One was on a quite lively wicket at Old Trafford, where Tony Murphy, who joined Surrey the following year, gave us a real going over. He was a tenacious bloke who'd have a few pints and then try and hit you on the head the next morning. My overall figures for the season weren't too bad. I played in every championship match, scored more than 700 runs and took 25 wickets with my little away-swingers.

In June, during a spate of injuries, I was given my first run in the first XI. I played three matches at the Oval, two in the championship and one against Cambridge University in which I scored an aggressive, unbeaten hundred. Looking at the scorecard in *Wisden*, I must have scored some runs against Cambridge captain Michael Atherton's filthy leg-breaks. Our bowling careers lasted about as long as each other's!

The Cambridge match wasn't as intense as the second XI championship, and certainly nothing like as competitive as my first-team debut the previous week against Leicestershire. I think I was preferred to the likes of Alistair Brown because of my bowling (!), and throughout that season Surrey struggled to field a settled attack. We had problems with our two West Indian overseas players: Sylvester Clarke was troubled by injuries and was suspended after failing to report for a match in Swansea, and Tony Gray lost form completely. They stuck me down at No 8.

It was another huge jump. The bowling seemed unbelievably quick and certainly tested your nerve. Leicestershire had Phil DeFreitas, George Ferris and Jonathan Agnew in their attack, and on the Oval wickets in those days any half-decent fast bowler could make it go through. I was hit god knows how many times. DeFreitas in particular gave me a horrible going over and dished out a few verbals to go with it. Nothing too nasty, but comments designed to intimidate a kid like me.

I didn't respond, I just kept my mouth shut and hid behind my helmet. I was dropped in the gully before I scored my first run but held up an end in both innings, scraping 15 runs in the first and 16 in the second. But I got a couple of wickets, and good ones too: David Gower, one of England's greatest left-handers who the previous week had helped England save the Trent Bridge Test against West Indies, and Peter Willey. I was lucky with Gower: he was given out lbw off a big inside edge, something both he and I remember to this day. I made the papers for the first time, my local one writing up my first appearance as a momentous occasion. It felt good.

After my century against the undergraduates, I not only kept my place in the side to play Derbyshire but was moved up to No 3. It proved an over-promotion because I didn't get many runs. Michael Holding, who was in his mid-thirties but still brisk, was Derbyshire's spearhead, but it was another West Indian who gave me most trouble. Allan Warner, who had a dangerously quick bouncer, hit me on the helmet twice. Facing Holding was a huge thrill. If anything had got me interested in cricket it was watching the West Indians tour during that long, hot summer of 1976 when I was seven. The sight of Viv Richards with the bat and Holding and Andy Roberts bowling was awesome.

With Alec Stewart fit again for the first team after

breaking a thumb, I spent the rest of that 1988 season – one unsuccessful Sunday league appearance aside – back in the second XI. But those two championship games told me I could expect a lot more quick bowling around my head in first-team cricket, and that this was something I'd have to work on. In truth, I was then a limited, orthodox player. I was too static in my stance, really just bouncing up and down on my feet without taking my hands back, but I did present the full face of the bat, was a good fielder and was prepared to work hard at my game. With the help of Micky Stewart, I corrected a tendency to fall to the off side. My footballing single-mindedness and competitiveness was a big help.

I'd cast my eye down the first XI and thought it would take a big effort to break in, but during the winter Monte Lynch broke his leg playing football and was ruled out for most of the 1989 season. I wasn't called into the championship side for about a month as Jonathan Robinson and Paul Atkins, who like me had made their debuts the previous year but had been on the staff longer, were tried without success.

After that, I didn't look back. I scored an unbeaten half-century in my first championship innings and, two matches later at Basingstoke, batted all day for my maiden championship hundred. This was a huge stride forward because Hampshire's attack was led by Malcolm Marshall, who was still playing for the West

Indies and was still one of the best bowlers in the world. It helped that I'd played on the ground before in youth cricket, and the wicket was slowish, but Marshall was frighteningly quick and good. I made a horribly nervous start. I had still not got many when Marshall smashed me, via the glove, on the helmet. The ball ballooned up for a catch but, as I began to trudge off, I saw the umpire signalling no-ball and wave me back. Great. So I got to face him some more!

Being small, Marshall's trajectory was different from most other fast bowlers and he could do everything with the ball, though one of the hardest things for me was coming to terms with the fact I was playing against a guy I'd seen on TV so many times. He was like a god. I'd even pretended to be him in my back garden, for heaven's sake! That innings made a lot of people sit up and take notice. It showed I was mentally resilient which, I'd later learn, was quite rare for a young player. I'd booked myself in as Surrey's No 4 and my medium-paced dibbly-dobblers took a back seat for good.

Although I was coping pretty well on the pitch, I found life in the dressing-room difficult. I didn't have a great relationship with Ian Greig, the captain. I think he was trying to impose a bit of discipline on a side that had seen a few changes in personnel, but he behaved like a headmaster and had a lot of rules which brought out the worst in me. The most intimidating thing was that the dressing-room at the Oval had a wall down the middle, one side for those who had been awarded their first-team caps, the other for those – like me – who hadn't. You had to knock on the door if you wanted to go in to speak to the senior players. They'd say stuff like, 'Oi, remember, I was capped in '85 . . .' or 'Just watch what you say' and 'Remember who you're talking to . . .' Sometimes it was done in a jokey fashion but it felt like I'd joined the army. I definitely felt some senior players didn't want to give out much advice in case you'd take their place. This regime survived a few more years, and contributed to our continued lack of success.

Greig called me in for words many times. I'd drive in to the Oval, which was two hours from home, grab a sandwich, sit on the balcony eating it and he'd walk in and say, 'What have we said about eating food here?' I might have been a bit lippy and sulky at that stage – I was very much still learning about myself – but I had this bloke breathing down my neck from first thing in the morning. It was like he was saying, 'This kid's a bit precocious, maybe if we give him a kick now and then he might learn a thing or two.' But my view was that, if anything, speaking to us like kids made us behave like kids, and it certainly didn't bring out the best in me.

But there were some decent people like David Smith, who had a fearsome reputation for pinning people against the wall but was actually a good guy, Grahame Clinton who seemed to have seen everything on the county circuit, including every local casualty department, and Monte Lynch, my benefactor, who was a wonderful guy. They gave me a lot of advice. Then there was the young Keith Medlycott, our future coach but then a left-arm spinner who'd been in the first team a few seasons and had seen enough to know he didn't like what was going on with the dressing-room hierarchy. He'd say to me, 'This is a load of bollocks.' I naturally became a Medders supporter. He wasn't in awe of anyone and just wanted to get the job done, which I liked.

This was perhaps the start of my lengthy tussles with authority. Players are very different people and yet I didn't often see much flexibility in the way they were handled. It shouldn't have been that difficult for someone to tap you on the shoulder and suggest you did something in a particular way, while offering some quiet words of encouragement. But more often I simply saw – and felt – whacks on the head which made me think, '*Fuck you.*' Especially Ian Greig.

Despite all that, I had a very good first full season with the bat. I scored 1,132 runs at an average of 45, and found myself being written up as one of the up-and-coming England stars. What had made the situation even more exciting was that, for the first time, England were sending an A-team on tour that winter. I knew next to nothing about it but hit decent form at the right time, taking fifties off Lancashire and Essex in the build-up to the announcement. It came during Surrey's second-last match, over the tannoy at the Oval. First, the full England side to go to the West Indies: Stewie and Medders were in that one, chosen for their first tours. Then the A-tour to Zimbabwe: Darren Bicknell was going, so too Martin Bicknell. And so was I. Brilliant!

I couldn't believe it. It was a dream to be playing for the Surrey first XI but this was something else. This was major. I must have been on a high and celebrated by playing my biggest innings so far against Kent, scoring 154 and sharing a big stand with Monte, who'd finally returned to the side after his long lay-off.

I had a good tour. The pitches in Zimbabwe were slow and the attacks not very menacing, and I scored runs most times I batted. Scoring is hard work on slow pitches, but I refused to be shackled. I was even on the verge of a century in the final A Test when I was stumped via the wicket-keeper's pads. Right at the end, news came through that Graham Gooch had broken his hand in Trinidad, and there was a buzz that one of us might be sent to the Caribbean as replacement. In the end, none of us went, but it seemed bizarre that not long before I'd thought breaking into the Surrey team would be hard, and now people were talking about me joining the England squad.

My cricketing horizons broadened in other ways on that tour. I was coached by Keith Fletcher, a former England captain, and played alongside guys like Atherton and Derek Pringle who'd played for England the previous summer. I also roomed with Athers. He was only a year older but as a player was on a different level altogether. I'd played youth cricket against him a few years earlier, and even then his wicket was easily the most prized.

I went home being written up as the next rising star but soon came back down to earth. I had an absolute shocker with Surrey. I don't know why. It was a batsman's summer and people were scoring mountains of runs left, right and centre. Maybe people had worked out my game. They say your second season is difficult. I don't think I'd changed but maybe I had put too much pressure on myself.

Surrey stuck with me, but after I was out for a pair twice in three championship matches, Greig told me they were sending me back to the second team. I spent the last month of the 1990 season there. I was pretty level-headed but found it a confusing experience. I had gone up and come down so quickly that I started to doubt myself. I wasn't in the habit of dwelling on failures, but I dwelt on them now. If there was a point in my career when I could have slipped into obscurity, this was it. But amazingly, Keith Fletcher – who may have been a quietly spoken, undemonstrative bloke but knew his mind when it came to judging a cricketer – stuck his neck out and got me on the A-tour of Sri Lanka that winter. I was a bit embarrassed. I knew my stats didn't really add up. Later, England often backed people who were out of form, but back then it was far more unusual. Keith said later that he had been certain, from seeing me play as a 15-year-old, that I would play for England. Boosted by his encouragement, I got back in the runs on that tour. It taught me not to lose faith, and never to get carried away.

Little did I know it at the time but I was now set upon a life of regularly spending winter on tour. In fact, I would be chosen to tour with either the full England side or England A every winter from then until I retired 15 years later, although I pulled out of a couple of tours for personal reasons. I still had to wait another two years to play my first Test though, but once I was in the side I was only ever left out for one spell purely on grounds of merit – until the end came in 2005. I'd be taken to some fantastic places and experience some great matches, from Barbados to Brisbane, from Karachi to Colombo. But I was also stepping onto a treadmill. My life had taken a new direction.

SIX

Learning From Lara

IF YOU ARE going to have a career in professional sport you have to accept you're going to have a public profile. There's no escape. But I always disliked publicity. I didn't want it, and I didn't need it. I was reluctant to accept I was public property, and for years my way of dealing with the public side was to pretty much ignore it. As a kid, I'd admired Ian Botham and Viv Richards, but I have always known I wasn't a showman like either of them, or like Darren Gough or Kevin Pietersen. I wasn't the least bit outgoing.

In fact it took me a while to be confident enough to speak up in England team meetings – perhaps one reason I wasn't a natural captain – and knew there was no point trying to be what I wasn't. As Alec Stewart once said, 'Thorpey will decide whether he'll get to know you or not.' I liked to think of this as a strength. I played up to the dour image; like Steve Waugh, I didn't see why

I should give much away on the field. I had little time for show because I preferred to see things as they were. Perhaps because I'd had to make my own way in the game, I sought no excuses. If I failed, it was because I'd played a poor shot; if I succeeded it was because I'd played well. I don't think at any stage I thought, '*I've cracked it*'. There was always another hurdle to clear. When I was growing up, I'd sometimes fantasise about succeeding as a sportsman but I always reminded myself of the work required to make it happen. And I knew if I scored a century there was every chance I might be out for nought next time, so I was careful not to have big expectations or make rash predictions. I was always suspicious of media hype.

During my separation and divorce, I hated my private life being splashed all over the papers but came to learn there was not much I could do about it. Not many people can handle reporters pushing their cards through their letter-box offering money to tell their story, or photographers lurking in bushes outside their house, and I certainly wasn't one of them. I wanted to ask them, '*What the fuck's any of this got to do with you?*' But I came to realize that it *had* got something to do with them. I was an England cricketer and, more importantly, my wife had just sold a tabloid story on me. Of course the papers were going to be interested. I was a story, like it or not, and was going to remain one as long as I remained an England cricketer.

In my early days, I thought life was great when I played well and read all the complimentary things written about me, but when things went badly I took care not to pick up the papers. Back then, I'd want to shut the door on the bad things and forget them. This pretty much typified my character during my mid-twenties. It was pride. Avoiding criticism was actually quite a good mechanism for maintaining the self-belief you needed to perform well, but I was ducking the reality of my position. It took me a long time to realize that there were people in the media prepared to tear you down.

Looking back, I can see how naive I was. I was a shy, quietly confident lad who just wanted to play his cricket. When the press first started taking an interest in me, I didn't have the skill to deal with them in a confident manner. There was no media training in those days. Before my first game for England against Australia in 1993, I was just thrown out to do press interviews after nets. It was like, 'Now, can you just be interviewed by that lot over there?' The press seemed to know more about me than I did. It wasn't in my nature to talk up my ambitions. I reckoned I'd only make problems for myself.

But everything changes when you enter international cricket. Before that, you've just played seasons of county cricket usually watched by a few hundred spectators when the pressure was relatively tiny.

Just the occasional one-day county match was shown on TV, but these matches did have an impact. They were good tests of character, being regarded by selectors and players as especially important. You found that some people performed and others didn't. I tended to do well. In 1991, I scored 91 in the NatWest Trophy final against Hampshire and just before I was chosen for England, I played in a televised Benson and Hedges Cup match against Lancashire – an amazing game which we lost after our last nine wickets fell for 18 runs – and scored 103. Although I was partly responsible for the collapse by getting out when I did, that innings helped my cause because I'd showed an appetite for the big stage by scoring runs against a strong attack including Wasim Akram and Phil DeFreitas.

Although I never craved attention, I certainly enjoyed the thrill of doing well when the stakes were high. That was not a concern. I wanted to test myself, and the toughest environment meant TV cameras and large crowds. You might think everyone feels like that but they don't. I think it was one of the reasons Graeme Hick didn't do as well as he should have done in Test cricket. He wasn't the kind of bloke who was comfortable with public expectation, and in his case there was plenty of it. It just wasn't in his nature. I could accept it because, as far as I was concerned, it was a test of me as a cricketer; what I didn't like was when the focus shifted onto me as a person. Doing well in those circumstances was an incredible feeling, a feeling which I know I'll never get again outside cricket.

In the Test arena, the pressure is intense and everything you do is subject to scrutiny from armies of TV, radio and newspaper pundits. When you are out, your dismissal is up on the big screen for everyone to study. It was difficult adjusting to all this, and I certainly wasn't at ease with the goldfish-bowl existence. Suddenly, everybody knows your job, and when you've had a good or bad day. You have to learn to handle everything that goes with the successes and failures if you want to survive. What I realized towards the end of my career was that the nearer you got to retirement the greater the debate about your right to be still in the team.

Try as you might to escape hearing criticism, you can't block off everything. You only have to bump into a mate and he'll pass on an opinion some commentator has given on how you played. You say, 'Oh really?' while inside you didn't want to hear it. Or some punter who days earlier had congratulated you turns round in a hotel lift and says, 'That wasn't a great shot you played today.' Yeah, thanks. It pays to develop a thick skin.

I remember before my first A-tour going to the nets at Lilleshall and finding our squad mixed in with the Test boys on their way to the West Indies. For a kid with one full season of county cricket behind him, I found it bloody terrifying having the likes of DeFreitas,

Devon Malcolm and Syd Lawrence trying to bomb the hell out of me at 90mph. It was a pretty harrowing experience and I took a few hits. Geoff Boycott had been brought along to coach the batters and afterwards came over to me and said, 'Your technique's not too bad, sonny, but you didn't hit many.' It wasn't what I wanted to hear.

Naturally I was anxious to gain the approval of such a great figure in the game. Although I was being talked about as an up-and-coming player, I didn't know if I was good enough to go any further in the game. A lot of people didn't like Boycs but, with time, I grew to like him, respect him and appreciated that he was upfront in his views. It was his honesty and forthright opinions that later made him such a good commentator. He wasn't always right but he was usually interesting. But you couldn't be sensitive about what he might say about you or you'd really struggle.

Some of Boycott's advice was easier to ignore than others. When we were bowled out by the West Indies for 46 in Trinidad in 1994, Boycott, who was commentating, urged us to get forward to Curtly Ambrose. It was the only way to keep him out, he was saying, especially after I was bowled by a shooter from Ambrose after a lot of hard graft for three measly runs. Well, yes, perhaps. But Curtly was about 6ft 7in tall and landing it just on a length, on an up-and-down wicket. Was I really going to lunge forward at someone bowling

90mph? I don't think so! I decided to keep taking my chances on the back foot.

Once a seed of doubt is planted in your mind it can be bloody hard killing it off. I wasn't good at it at first and got pretty intense about the whole thing. Stewie was a big help. He'd been in the England team a few years before I arrived. He was the most solid professional I ever met, and his attitude was that if you'd had a bad day you still had to get up the next morning and go through the same routine. 'Don't allow yourself to go down too far,' he'd say. 'Don't get too up or down.' Graham Gooch, my first England captain, was the same. 'You've just got to keep working hard at your game,' he'd say.

I think I started looking only at the good newspaper comments after reading Alex Ferguson, the Manchester United manager, say that he never read the press after a bad day. Much later, after I'd had my private life dragged through the papers, I was better at reading the bad stuff about my cricket. I was wise to the fact that some of the stuff written about you was plain rubbish. When I gave an interview, I would read the piece to see how it came out and would instinctively categorize it as good or bad.

It wasn't just criticism you had to deal with but advice, with pundits and ex-players telling you how to succeed at Test level, how to remove those little flaws that everyone was so quick to pick up on. You wanted to learn, so it was hard not to listen, but so much stuff was thrown at you it could finish you if you didn't quickly sift what to listen to and what to reject. You only had to take in a well-meant few words from one of the TV boys out on the field before the start, and you could find your fears multiplying when you walked out to bat. Robin Smith went through a bad time with his problems against spin, and Graeme Hick and Mark Ramprakash would probably have loved to turn round and tell a few people where to go. I viewed batting for England as a box into which I could fit only a few pieces of advice that suited my game. Boycott's mantra that you can't score runs unless you occupy the crease was one of them. And I also worked out for myself that you had to take some risks to score runs, which built confidence.

Things changed quite a bit during my career. By the time I retired, players could call up a video of themselves within moments of walking off the field. For some, this was a big help because it gave them a better chance to sort out their problems themselves, rather than searching for advice from anyone who happened to be around. I tended not to overdo that side of things. I just kept a few tapes of myself playing well. My attitude was that you could guarantee seeing your dismissals plenty of times when you got back to the dressing-room, and I was more interested in positive thoughts than negative ones. If you were out to a crap shot, admit it and move on. Besides, I didn't know how to work the laptop!

An interview I gave in *The Cricketer* magazine in 1994 reflected my attitude towards playing international cricket. 'You need certain mental qualities,' I said. 'At this level everyone has to have ability, so what separates them is the extent to which they apply it to pressured situations. The more you play, the more you learn and the more people try to talk to you. But if you can enjoy it and keep it as simple as possible by playing on instinct, then you're halfway there: it's not an easy game, but at the same time you can't afford to make it too complicated.'

In the end, it all came down to the individual. You had to be strong. No one could hold your hand when you were batting. Once you crossed the rope, you were on your own. You just had to look into your soul and see what you could produce.

IF I THOUGHT the step up to first-class county cricket was big, then the jump to Test cricket was no less of a culture shock. The cricket was so much more intense, more a searching examination of your game than anything I'd dealt with before. Of course, those going into the England side in those days were less well prepared than the likes of Andrew Strauss and Geraint Jones were when they made their Test debuts in 2004. Nowadays, the management go to so much more effort to tutor you about what to expect. And it also helps if the England side you join is in the winning habit, a luxury I certainly didn't enjoy.

When I made my debut, against Australia at Trent Bridge in July 1993, we were already two-down in the series. England were in quite a bit of disarray, and before the series finished Graham Gooch resigned as captain and Ted Dexter as chairman of selectors. I was one of five players brought in for the match in Nottingham, and four of us were making our debuts; me, and Mark Lathwell, Mark Ilott and Martin McCague who'd win only 10 Test caps between them. Nasser was brought back after a long spell in the wilderness.

The press had been doing their stuff on the selectors, piling on pressure for change, and the response had been sweeping. It was a huge gamble but, with the likes of David Gower, Mike Gatting, Graeme Hick and Mark Ramprakash unfit or out of favour, there seemed to be a general feeling that it was time for some fresh batting. It was a pretty typical state of affairs, being in the middle of an Ashes series.

I knew by then that, if there were changes, I was in the frame because I'd played in the three one-day internationals before the Tests. By now, Keith Fletcher had been promoted to England coach. After our three A-tours together, perhaps he had put in a word that it was time to give me a go. Fletch didn't survive long in the job – less than two years – and to me he always seemed under pressure.

Although I was slightly overawed in the one-day series, it was a good place to get a taste of international cricket and I was fairly satisfied with how I performed. I made twenties or thirties each time, and shared a big stand at Edgbaston with Robin Smith who did most of the scoring on the way to a record one-day score for England of 167 not out. However, I got out a couple of times to poor shots when we were in sight of victory, and we ended up losing all three games. I thought I should have gone on and won the match at Old Trafford, but I played like the inexperienced kid I was. I thought, '*Wow, I'm playing against Steve Waugh and Craig McDermott. I've seen them on TV*.' It was the first time I'd played on the big stage and boy did I recognize it.

So, when the Test call came, I felt excited and nervous at the same time. And very proud. I was a bit anxious that I wasn't in better form, as I was only averaging around 25 for Surrey that season. My fee was £2,300, which I viewed as a fortune – as did my parents, who told me I must save it!

Things were so different then to how they are now. There was no great analysis of the opposition beforehand, no studying of videos. I can't even remember a team chat. We just had dinner the night before the game at the hotel, a three-course meal, with the seniors having a glass of wine and the juniors like me sitting there trying hard to hide our nervousness. This strange ritual survived for a few more years. We might be joined by the chairman of selectors and the chief executive and committee-men of the club hosting the game, who'd inflict a lot of small-talk on you when all you wanted to do was think about the game ahead. Everything was so much more formal then. I remember there was even a rest day during the game because the Sunday was the day of the Wimbledon men's singles final!

I was extremely nervous going out to bat late on the first afternoon at Trent Bridge. I remember pulling on my head-band and helmet and thinking, '*Just don't let yourself down . . . Don't mess up.*' You so want to do well but you've no idea what's going to happen. And the not knowing was terrible. I can distinctly recall crossing the boundary line and telling myself, '*Breathe, breathe, breathe . . . You'd better take some of this in . . . fast.*' I could feel myself shaking.

Allan Border had been Australia captain a long time and, in his drive to make them the best side in the world, encouraged them to be pretty uncompromising in the field. They had a few roughnecks and they were a pretty abusive bunch, although sledging never greatly bothered me. I don't remember the slip cordon saying anything as I took guard, but they'd given me a fair bit of unprintable abuse in the one-dayers so there was every chance that they did. Maybe I was too nervous to hear them. But Merv Hughes, who could dish it out better than anyone, was soon right in there working me over with the ball. His first delivery had no sooner flown past my nose than he said he was planning to kill me.

I think Merv was carrying an injury that game, but he was still snorting and huffing, puffing and staring. In a way, it was like those Saturday afternoons I'd known on the football field, in which the game was played amid undercurrents of fear that someone would do you serious physical harm. Merv gave me a couple more bouncers which I got out of the way of nicely, but then he really let one go which tucked me up and all I could do was fend it off my glove to gully. *Shit!* What an awful way to get out! That's not good at any stage but in your first Test . . . 'Thorpe, you know what he's got? A weakness against quick bowling, that's what.' I knew what I'd get in my second innings. I couldn't have advertised it better if I'd painted a big red 'X' on my forehead.

Things didn't get any better. I dropped a chance from Michael Slater that was flying straight over my head as Australia built a small lead of 52 and, by the time we'd lost our top four, second time around, with me about to bat again we were only just ahead. Fortunately, the third day was drawing to a close and Gooch decided to send out a nightwatchman instead of me. To my relief, Andrew Caddick survived until stumps, and I was able to contemplate the second Test innings of my life over a family barbecue at home on the rest day.

Caddick frustrated Australia a while longer on the Monday morning and, by the time I walked out, the Australians were pretty eager to get stuck into me. They were very chirpy and one of the umpires, Roy Palmer, soon intervened to ask if I wanted him to stop all the swearing. I just said, 'No, I'm enjoying it. Just stop them if they spit at me!'

Steve Waugh and David Boon, both fielding close to the bat, certainly had a lot to say. When I pulled a ball past Boon, crouched at silly point and looking like a Viking with his droopy moustache, he threatened to kill me if I did it again. I kept my mouth shut and got on with the job. As I'd said to Palmer, their words didn't intimidate me but made me all the more determined to give it my best shot. It was just what I needed.

Predictably enough, they tested me out with more short stuff but, by now, the pitch was flat and I dealt with it okay and, eventually, Big Merv tried so hard to get rid of Gooch and myself he picked up a strain and hobbled out of the attack. My main memory is of Shane Warne and Tim May's bowling. They were an exceptional partnership, and I look back with immense pride at managing to bat against them for what turned out to be almost a whole day. I owed a lot to Keith Fletcher that I played spin as well as I did in those days. He'd given me a lot of advice with England A, and I always put a lot of value on what he said. This was certainly bowling on another level compared with anything I'd faced before, and I found it difficult to dominate in the way I had in county matches.

I actually found May the harder of the two. My technique against off-spin hadn't developed by that stage. Previously, my only plan was to run down the wicket and hit it over the bowler's head but that was unrealistic at this level, against someone with such good control of flight, and who varied his line of attack to an extent I'd never experienced. English off-spinners were very stereotyped by comparison.

Like me, Warne was in his early twenties and hadn't played a lot of Test cricket but he'd already played a big part in the first two Tests and, one reason I'd been picked, was that left-handers were reckoned better able to cope with leg-spin. I think it did give me an advantage, particularly once I'd got used to how far he was turning the ball into me. Often, he simply turned it too much and I was able to let it go through, and his googly was not that great. But he was incredibly accurate with his leg-breaks, and I've never seen anyone drift the ball as much as he did in his early days.

He also had a great flipper although, with time, I learned to pick it from the daylight that would show between ball and hand when his arm was at the top of its delivery. Even at this stage, it wasn't hard to work out that this fiery character, with his blond locks, white zinc cream on his face and confrontational attitude, was going to enjoy the celebrity side of the game more than me. Once you had played against him a reasonable amount, you knew what tricks he'd got but the first few times were difficult. He hadn't played in the one-day internationals and I'd only faced him once before, briefly during Australia's warm-up match against Surrey. I had tried to cut him and missed badly as the ball spun back miles, and he soon had me caught down the leg side.

Now, on a slow pitch, I used my pads to kick him away a lot. Otherwise, I swept him or went back to try tucking him away on the leg side. Once, I attempted a drive through extra cover but the ball spun straight back past me and I decided against a repeat. In my early encounters with Warne, I found I could stay in but not really dominate. At Edgbaston, later in the same series, and at Brisbane, the following year, I batted around four hours for 60s. In the first innings at the Gabba, I'd tried to take the initiative by going down the wicket but he did me in the flight, I checked the shot and ended up chipping back a return catch for 67, and it was not until much later in the series that I felt confident enough to take more risks against him.

In that second innings at Trent Bridge, it was made easier for me that Gooch was batting so well at the other end. He was the senior man and I just tried to stay with him. I didn't really know Gooch then. I'd only occasionally played against him in county cricket. He was constantly practising and couldn't understand why others weren't like him. When it came to training he was ahead of his time.

He carried a set of dumb-bells in his bag and, if he didn't get any runs, he'd go off for a run or to lift weights. We put on 150 together and he just kept encouraging me. 'Keep going,' he'd say. 'Keep going. Don't give it away.' A good partnership is often just about careful encouragement to keep going, battle hard and never throwing in negative thoughts.

We went a long way towards making England safe and, when Gooch was finally out, Nasser took over and kept me company for the rest of the day. At stumps I was 88 not out. On the last morning, Gooch told Nasser and I to score runs as quickly as we could before he declared. We were too cautious and ended up setting Australia 371 in 77 overs but, having spent the series being battered into the ground, it was natural, I suppose.

I got off to a good start by hitting a couple of boundaries. Then, on 97, I had a real swat at a bouncer from Brendon Julian, a future Surrey team-mate. I looked up and thought, '. . . *Oh, shit!*' as the ball sailed high in the air and I saw Slater running towards it. Fortunately, Slater dived but couldn't quite make the catch, and the ball bounced just in front of him and over his head for four. Though it didn't set up the win we wanted, scoring a hundred in my first Test was thrilling. For the first but certainly not last time, Nasser and I found ourselves together at a special moment in one of our careers, but what I remember most clearly was the congratulation of Border. Despite having been totally uncompromising throughout he shook my hand and said well played. Typical bloody Aussie!

This performance, of course, pushed me firmly into the public spotlight. I was the first England player to score a century in his first Test for 20 years. I felt like a shy school kid and cringe when I remember the TV and press interviews I gave after the game. As Peter Roebuck wrote about my post-match interviews, 'Here was a man out of his depth.' In the following days, I received lots of letters of congratulations, and gave a few more interviews, but thankfully didn't delude myself into thinking I'd made it on the back of one game. Apart from anything else, I knew what big Merv had done to me could easily happen again – and I wasn't wrong.

I was brought down to earth in the very next Test at Leeds. I was out for nought and 13, both times to Paul Reiffel, who darted the ball around like an old-fashioned English seamer. Soon after, my dad told me what Jack Bannister had said of me on the radio, "'He can't play the inswinger, he can't play the outswinger and he can't play the short ball." . . . He don't think much of you then.' That was the kind of comment that in those days could really hurt.

We took another hammering, and having Steve Waugh dropped by Athers in the 150s off a wide half-volley (the nearest I would ever come to taking a Test wicket) was no consolation. We were sitting in the dressing-room after the game when Gooch told us he was resigning as captain. He'd been England captain for four years but recent results had been poor. I was just a novice, but even to my inexperienced eyes it was obvious he was feeling the pressure. It was another indication of the unforgiving nature of Test cricket.

That series taught me some hard lessons. I was sledged out in the next Test at Edgbaston, Atherton's first as captain, and, as it proved, my last of the series because a guy called Peter Dickinson, who played for Farnham, broke my thumb in the nets on the morning of the final Test at the Oval. Personally I did okay, scoring 37 and 60, but England were again on the wrong end of things, although, in company with the tail, I dragged things out as long as I could in the second innings. I'd gone past 50 and we were eight down and leading by 97, not yet enough to give us any real chance, when I patted a ball back defensively. Ian Healy, the Australian wicket-keeper, turned to his team-mates and shouted, 'Hey! You know what? This guy's playing for red ink . . .', meaning I was only concerned with being not out.

God, I must have been raw. Healy must have read me well because the suggestion that I was playing for a not out hit its mark. Pride immediately took over. I thought, *'Fuck it. I'm not playing for myself. I'll show you.'* And I charged out of my crease at Warne, the ball hit the rough and I missed it by a mile. It was a sharp stumping by Healy but I suppose he was expecting it. It was the only time I lost my wicket to Warne that series.

There's always needle in Ashes Tests and you have to stand up for yourself, which with my competitive nature I didn't find difficult. I was warned by the match referee for excessive appealing at Birmingham, and in Australia the following year I dished out as good as I got. I launched into Steve Waugh in Brisbane, inviting to see him round the back of the stand, and had a bit of set-to with Warne in Adelaide. The Healy incident aside, none of this ever affected my concentration and it was apparent to several of the newer members of the side such as Athers, Nasser and myself that if we were to halt the defeats to Australia we needed a tougher frame of mind. The older and more skilful you get, the less you need to say, but at the time I needed to show I could look after myself. And I think it did help me focus.

LEARNING TO DEAL with fast, short-pitched bowling, of which there was plenty in my early days with England, gave me more concern than anything else. It was an area I was weak in, as Merv Hughes had so brutally shown, and had I not worked out an effective method I don't think I would have survived. I owe much to Brian Lara.

I'd been given an insight into the challenge awaiting me on an England A tour of the Caribbean in 1992, when I'd faced Courtney Walsh, Tony Gray and Kenny

Benjamin, but those matches lacked the intensity of Test cricket. By the time I left home for my first full England tour, back in the Caribbean in 1994, I knew I'd be getting plenty of 'chin music'. I wasn't wrong, as Curtly Ambrose, Walsh, Kenny and Winston Benjamin showed. In each of my first four innings at Sabina Park and the Bourda I was bowled, either playing across the line or done for pace, and I didn't get past 20 in any of them. An experiment to bat me first wicket down was abandoned after one innings.

It was at this point that I appreciated the size of the task. I'd simply been blown away by pace and, with two days before the third Test in Trinidad, feared I might be dropped unless I made some runs there. But what do you do against a barrage of bouncers? Take it on or get out of the way? It is a dilemma every batsman faces, and my decision was that if I wanted to score runs I had to take it on. If I was going to go down, at least I'd show some fight.

But deciding on an approach and carrying it out is very different. I decided to make some fundamental changes to the way I played. Up until this point, I'd been quite a static batsman, with little foot movement. Nor did I lift my bat back much. I lifted it a few inches and brought it down. It didn't flow. And often, when I was out of form, my back-lift became even shorter because I was less confident it would come back down straight, and that only made things worse.

I now resolved to increase my foot movement and back-lift, and got the idea from watching Lara bat in that series. I'd not really seen him play before but he was another man, like Warne, approaching the peak of his game and I now had plenty of opportunities to watch him bat. He scored 83 in the first Test, 167 in the second and, before the series was out, would add a world-record 375 in Antigua. Here was a guy I could learn from.

His footwork and back-lift – the biggest I'd ever seen – got him into positions to play shots all around the wicket, which was something I couldn't do. I reckoned that if I was going to score against 'steepling' bouncers – Ambrose and Walsh were both over 6ft 5in – then my bat had to be higher if I was to make room to cut and pull. The way I'd been playing, I'd next to no chance. I had a good eye and good hands, and playing on the bouncier pitches at the Oval, I already knew about hitting the ball on the up. Time to take some calculated risks.

This was one of those decisions I took myself; I didn't go to Keith Fletcher for his approval, I just did it. I took myself off into the nets in Trinidad and began to experiment. To be fair, Lara was not the only inspiration. I'd watched the way Michael Slater batted too. I liked his footwork and aggression, and Alec Stewart, too, had encouraged me to think of the short ball as a ball to be scored off. I could see how well Stewie was cutting, pulling and hooking in that series. 'If you're going to take it on, take it on 100 per cent,' he said. That stayed with me.

There wasn't much time before the third Test in Trinidad, and I continued experimenting as the tour went on, but the results were almost instantaneous. In the first innings I scored 86 – easily our top score in a game which ended with our humiliation of 46 all out in the second innings – and battled away for four hours, sometimes taking on the short ball, sometimes not, before Ambrose produced a great delivery I could only glove to slip. Thankfully, the pitch was quite slow.

My confidence boosted, I stayed positive in Barbados where the surface was quicker and, although I fell to an extravagant stroke in the first innings, I got 84 in the second, playing shots I couldn't have imagined playing at the start of the tour. Alec's game was bearing fruit too: he scored two hundreds in that Test, which reinforced his no-nonsense philosophy. I tasted a win for the first time as a Test player in Barbados, a place which came to hold many special memories for me.

Ironically, I was dropped when we got home. I missed all three Tests against New Zealand. At first, I wasn't too concerned. Gooch, who had missed the West Indies tour, now returned and Ray Illingworth, the new chairman of selectors and coach, wanted to play an all-rounder rather than a sixth batsman. Illy told me I wasn't yet in the best five batters in the country and that when I was, I'd be picked. I felt a bit frustrated when

John Crawley was chosen ahead of me to replace Robin Smith in the first Test against South Africa. By now I was short of runs and suspected Crawley's Lancashire connections had gained him favour with Athers, but I was soon back anyway when Craig White, the all-rounder, went down with an injury.

In my comeback at Leeds, I was given a lot of short stuff from Allan Donald, Fanie de Villiers and Brian McMillan – a big bear of a man who was always growling at you – and just took it on with the cuts and pulls that were now my forte. I made 72 and 73, and added a third seventy at the Oval. Six months later, I was scoring a Test century against Australia on the fastest, bounciest track in the world in Perth. I was back in the side for good and playing a totally different way now. I accepted I might have lost some elements of my defence, which played a part in my struggle to convert fifties into hundreds, but reckoned it was worth it to be more aggressive. In spite of what Merv Hughes did to me on my debut, I stuck with the hook stroke and was very rarely out to it in Tests again.

One spin-off was that I finally gained the respect of Athers, who could be hard to please as England captain. He didn't panic – one of the reasons we won the next Test after the debacle in Trinidad was that he didn't hand out bollockings, and just accepted Ambrose had produced an incredible spell – but he knew that you needed certain qualities to be a successful Test cricketer.

Until he was convinced you possessed them he could withhold his full support. I had been a bit wary of him until now. He was always pretty cool and it was difficult to read his mind – apart from at the end of a Test match when he would go out and get completely slaughtered – but we now began to develop a good relationship. I think that, in the end, I played in more of the Tests when he was captain than anyone. I came to like his company, and looked out for him as someone to socialize with.

I might have been a nudger and nurdler in one-day cricket, but in Tests I was going on the offensive. It suited my character, and the team's needs, to play the role of middle-order, back-foot counter-attacker. I had come to realize that you need different styles for different situations. You could play off the front foot in county cricket to an extent you never could in Tests. It had taken a bit of time, but I'd now got a clear picture of the type of player I wanted to be. As I said, you're on your own out there, in cricket as in life.

SEVEN

Pulling Out of Australia

WHILE I WAS out of cricket in the summer of 2002, I looked back on all the effort and time I had put in to turning myself first into a professional cricketer, and then into a capable international one by the age of 25. When I reflected, I realized the sacrifices my family and I had made, but also how much the sport meant to me. I didn't want it to spoil my family life, but I didn't want to be without it either.

In August 2002, about a month after I dropped out of cricket, I received a phone call which made me think that everything was going to be okay again, that I'd get all the parts of my life back.

I occasionally still spoke to Nicky, usually when it came to arranging when I might see the children. One day she stunned me by hinting that, after all, she might be willing for us to get back together. This, of course, was what I still desperately wished for. As far as I was concerned, if we got back together, everything would be all right again. I would get my family and my life back. And if I was with Nicky and the children, I could face playing cricket again. I could face anything.

I was at a barbecue at my parents' house when she phoned. She wanted us to meet and, when I asked why, she said, 'Oh, you know. I want to talk about us.'

When I came off the phone someone said, 'You look happy. Like you've just won the lottery.' I suppose that shows how extreme, and evident, my moods were.

I wasn't sure quite why Nicky might now regard the time right for us to get back together, but to be honest I didn't care either. I wondered whether now that she'd been with Kieron for about a year the novelty of the relationship was wearing off. Maybe all of a sudden she was thinking that perhaps she didn't want to be with this bloke after all, thought she'd taught me a lesson and got the revenge she'd said she wanted for my infidelity in New Zealand, and was in no doubt that I loved the kids. I didn't know what she was thinking and could only guess. In my fragile state of mind, I was still happy to cling to faint hope rather than have no hope at all.

A few days later, I went round to the house that Nicky and Kieron had bought together – which I'd paid for – in Epsom Downs, about five minutes from 'Colditz'. It seemed that she had sent Kieron off for the night and while I was there she said, 'Maybe one day we will get back together again . . .' *Fucking hell!* Then I told her I was thinking about playing cricket again and she said, 'Yes, good, it's a good idea.'

And it was true. I was thinking about playing again. My dad, who knew I was in a mess, had been urging me to do so. He probably thought getting back on the field was the only way I could get my life back in order. He said to me, 'You've had a month off now. What are you going to do? You've got to make some decisions. If you're going to go away on tour this winter, you've got to play again.' I hid from my parents what Nicky seemed to be proposing, but her words had given me a lift and to my dad I eventually said, 'Okay, okay . . . I'll go back and play.' And there was a part of me that wanted to get back into the team and perform, and not let people down any further, but it was what Nicky had said that encouraged me to believe I could actually go through with it.

I wasn't really in a fit state to play. I'd done little for six weeks bar abuse my body, and was scarcely less of a zombie than at the time of the Lord's Test. Nicky may have offered me some hope, but I was still wrapped up in my problems and struggling to concentrate on anything else. My memory of events around this time is as hazy as it is for the India game, a sure sign I was still an emotional wreck.

I spoke to David Graveney, the chairman of selectors, and told him how I was keen to be considered for the winter tour of Australia. We were approaching the end of the season and the selectors were starting to look at their options; they needed a definite answer soon. I told Grav that I was back in the right frame of mind to play for England again. On quite what basis I made that claim I can't imagine. I also phoned Nasser and told him, 'Yes, I'm okay. I'm up for it. I'm ready to go.' I could hear the scepticism in his voice when he said, 'Okay, but I think Duncan is going to want to have a talk with you.'

I was then using an agent called Graham Staples to put things out to the press and keep them off my doorstep, and I made it publicly known through him that I was planning to come back and play. I also phoned Keith Medlycott, by now the Surrey coach, and told him I wanted to play again for Surrey. I told him I was thinking of getting on the Australia tour. He didn't ask many questions and his attitude was pretty much, 'Right, if you want to play, you're playing.' It probably helped that Surrey already had the championship in the bag. I phoned Micky Stewart and asked him to come down to the indoor nets and feed the bowling machine for me. I wanted to keep a low profile, and with the final Test match going on at the Oval, we held the session at Surrey's academy at George Abbott School in Guildford. There was no one else around, just Micky, me and the bowling machine. Fine by me.

As Nasser had suggested, Duncan wanted to see me and we met two days before the Oval Test match at the

Conrad hotel in Chelsea Harbour, where the England teams then stayed. The squad for Australia was due to be announced after the game. We gathered in a suite early in the evening and the meeting lasted about half an hour. There was me, Duncan, Nasser and Grav. I'd spoken briefly to Grav beforehand and he'd advised me not to sit on the fence. 'Give a firm answer, one way or the other,' he'd said.

The questioning was pretty aggressive. Nasser said they wanted me to tour, provided I could assure them I would buy into everything. They were conscious that the previous winter I'd hardly trained and not been well motivated. This was clearly very important to them. Duncan's attitude was the same: if I went, there could be no messing around. 'We can't have you the way you've been this summer,' he said. I'd been reminded before that, as a senior player, there were others in the team who looked up to me, and I was expected to set a good example. I assured them I wouldn't burden anyone by rambling on about my problems. I'd just get on and play cricket.

They also didn't want me suddenly leaving for home, like I'd done in India. 'What if you get another bad phone call, like you did in Ahmedabad?' Duncan asked. 'How are you going to be?' I had been rehearsing my lines and heard myself insist that everything was in control off the pitch, that I'd got more of a grasp of what was going on. I'd phone home once a fortnight to speak to the children and that would be it, I said. I didn't tell them the truth: that I thought I might be going back to Nicky and that this hope had given me the strength to carry on. Looking back, it was ridiculous but it showed how emotionally weak I was at the time. But my claim that I'd got to grips with things was probably believable to them, simply because it was almost a year since my problems began. It was high time I had got over them. But I hadn't. I was putting on a front. Knowing that the team was about to be selected, I knew I had to convince them I was over my problems if I was to have any hope of going. I had it all planned – I'd get back with Nicky, get back in the team, and everything would return to normal. Looking back now it's obvious: I was still in denial.

A few days later came the announcement of the next round of central contracts and the winter tour squad. As I'd feared as far back as my meeting with the solicitors at Lord's, the selectors had decided against awarding me another year-long England contract. No surprise there. But I was among the 16 names to tour Australia.

I remember making some sort of statement to the press about my delight and determination to repay the faith the selectors had shown me. I must have been living in La-la land.

THE NEXT DAY, I made my comeback at Southampton. The lads in the dressing-room gave me a warm welcome but, having just won their third championship in four years, they viewed the trip as an end-of-season jolly. They were primarily down on the south coast for a bit of nightlife. My mission was slightly different: I had to try to do something out in the middle. But I hadn't stopped drinking, and was in my now usual nervous, edgy state.

I'd never seen so many journalists turn out for a county game on which so little depended. The pitches at the Rose Bowl could be difficult to bat on at that time, but fortunately for me this one was docile and a lot of runs were scored over the four days. I can remember scratching around badly on the first day for not many before Shaun Udal bowled me, even though Ian Ward and Nad Shahid had softened up the attack during a long opening partnership, but my timing returned in the second innings as we pushed to build a big lead. It was a good pitch and an ordinary attack, and I stayed to score 143.

It was the same old story. If I got to 20 I started to feel I could get something out of the game, and would go into another little world for a short time. In the evenings, I could see the lads enjoying themselves but I couldn't get into it. I'd been on my own too much. My priority was getting through the game and that was hard enough.

Naturally the press wrote up my hundred in a buoyant way. They drew the obvious conclusions: 'Thorpe's back. His life is sorted out and he's in form. Now he's ready to take on Australia.' I infuriated myself with the rubbishy soundbites I spouted to the press about how I'd been through a difficult period but was now feeling fine. I'd go back to my hotel room and think to myself, 'How the fuck could you say that? When clearly, inside, you are not all right?' But I was trying to portray an image of my professional self as being back on my feet. Perhaps if I said it enough times it might actually come true.

We finished the championship season against Leicestershire at the Oval, but I can remember next to nothing about the game or my performance. *Wisden* records that Surrey won by 483 runs, the biggest margin in their history, and that I scored 44 and nought. I clearly recall what happened after the game, though. That evening, a Saturday night, I went down to Nicky's house. I felt a mixture of trepidation and hope: hope of her agreeing that we should, indeed, get back together; that Kieron was an episode in her life she was prepared to put in the past; and that we could resume our life together with the children. I was there about an hour, I suppose. At first it went well. Interestingly, Kieron was again not around. I saw the children, bathed them and put them to bed. It was just like the old days when we were a family. To me, deprived of so much contact with Henry and Amelia, it felt wonderful.

Then I sat down and talked to Nicky. When she said

she wanted us to get back together I couldn't hold back any more. If that was the case, I wanted it to happen there and then, and like an excited kid suggested I move back in straight away. 'Okay, if you don't want to be with this guy any more, fine, why don't we just get back together?' I said. 'And we can make a statement to the press.'

But Nicky didn't want that. She said she wanted to take things slowly, and needed more time to decide. I couldn't understand her at all. I was about to go away on tour again and wanted it all fixed before I went. Surely I could move back in and we'd work at it then. I explained that if I had the backing of my family I'd be able to face the world again and in particular Australia, the world's best team.

We'd only been talking about half an hour when Nicky suddenly said, 'Maybe it's not right after all.' As soon as she said that, what little control I had was gone. I got down in front of her and started crying and pleading. I'll never forget what she said next. She told me that it was *unattractive* to beg, that we'd never get back together and that I should leave. It was a knife through the heart.

I fled in tears. I remember getting home in a daze, staring at myself in the mirror and saying to myself, 'Can't you see? She'll never have you back. It's over.' But still I just couldn't accept it.

It's clear now that Nicky had been dangling me on a

string. She knew how much I loved the children and that she could play me pretty much any way she wanted. She'd had me jumping at her command. I still to this day have no idea what she was playing at.

Anyway, I had no time to think. The next day I was due to play in Surrey's final match of the season, a one-day league match against Gloucestershire. Don't ask me how I got myself to the Oval or through the day, let alone scored another century. I played pretty well, so I can only imagine I operated on some sort of auto-pilot. We needed to win to be sure of the runners-up spot in the second division, and my runs teed up a match-winning score. But all I can recall going through my head as I was scoring my runs was, 'What am I going to do? And what on earth am I going to tell the selectors?'

I was in a real dilemma. I was due on an Ashes tour the next month but, emotionally, was pretty much back where I had been two months earlier, unable to face cricket, unable to face life. I knew there was no way I could go. My flimsy plan was in ruins. Scoring some runs for Surrey only made the situation worse.

'I can imagine how this looks,' I thought. 'I've just come back and got two hundreds in three games. Everyone's going to be thinking I must be really bloody raring to go.' But, as Nasser and Duncan had said, if I was going to Australia, there could be no room for weakness. Quite apart from the fact I was short on practice, I couldn't afford to be mentally off the mark one bit. I wasn't so naive as to think the Aussies, given the chance, would pass up on an opportunity to serve me a few choice words about my domestic problems. Just thinking about that convinced me I could not go. But if I withdrew I'd look a complete idiot. It just shows how unstable I had been – one word from Nicky and I'd felt able to conquer the world, but when that was withdrawn I was at rock bottom again. I was completely incapable of making a decision.

I phoned my parents the next day and told them all that had happened, that I didn't think I could now go on the tour, but that I was afraid how I'd look if I pulled out. Dad's advice was typically practical. 'If you can't do it, what's the point in going?' he said. 'If you go and mess up you may never, ever play again. Repeat what happened last time and you're probably stuffed for ever. Be honest now. Tell them you can't do it.' I knew he was right. It was what I had been thinking myself, but the thought of speaking to the selectors filled me with dread. Still, Dad's advice was good and possibly helped save my career.

The next day I decided I had to speak to Duncan or Nasser. By this time, England were in Sri Lanka playing in the one-day ICC Champions Trophy. Nasser was unavailable but I spoke to Duncan, and remembering the phone call still makes me cringe.

'Duncan? It's Thorpey here . . .'

'Oh, hello, Thorpey. How you going, mate . . .'

'Er, I'm in a pretty fucking bad way actually, mate. I've got something to tell you. I'm not going to be able to tour Australia. I'm sorry I'm letting you down. Things have happened back here I need to get my head round. I need to sort them out . . .'

He was quite short with me. He just said something like, 'Are you sure?'

'Yeah, I am.'

'Okay, boy. I hope you can sort it out. Just take care and try to look after yourself.'

And that was it. It was awful. When we'd spoken on the Lord's balcony, Duncan had been quite concerned about how I was going to cope. He wanted to make sure I was going to be all right. Now, he'd less to say, though I think he appreciated that I'd at least picked up the phone to speak to him. I hoped he was prepared to draw a line under it, but he must have been very disappointed. Nasser told me later how he and Duncan had spoken not long before I rang, and Duncan had said to him, 'You know, Thorpey's got another hundred.' They must have been really hoping I could do something for them in Australia.

I made a statement to the press through Graham Staples announcing my withdrawal from the tour, putting out some line about how I'd been struggling to focus on my cricket since my return. My comeback hadn't even lasted two weeks.

THE FIASCO put the journalists back on my doorstep, shoving their cards through my letterbox encouraging me to tell my story. My over-riding emotion was anger: anger at Nicky for manipulating me, and anger at myself for being so naive. We all have to make decisions in our lives and by saying I'd tour Australia when I was in no position to carry it out, I'd just made a wrong one. The episode showed just what a pathetic figure I still was.

As I tried to get to grips with my situation, I consoled myself with the thought that by pulling out of the tour rather than trying and failing to stumble through it, which I know is what would have happened, I still had a shred of a chance of playing for England again. Most people were writing me off completely, and some newspapers called me a disgrace who should never be allowed to play for England again, and a part of me actually agreed with them.

I was lucky not to be sacked by Surrey around this time. About three weeks after my withdrawal, I was called into a meeting by Paul Sheldon, the club's chief executive. Richard Thompson, the chairman of cricket, was also there. Thommo had worked for a computer company that had sponsored some Surrey players, and I'd got to know him pretty well. In his professional capacity, he had encouraged me to take counselling but I had decided not to. Surrey had been very supportive but I now discovered with a painful jolt that their kindness also had its limits. They couldn't keep paying someone behaving so erratically, and I only had one year left on my contract.

Sheldon asked me straight out, 'What's going to happen? Do you not want to play cricket any more? Where do we stand for next year?'

Sheldon was a nice man, and looking back I totally understand his position, but at the time what he said shocked me. I insisted I was getting my private affairs sorted out. I pleaded with them, 'Give me time . . . Just give me time . . .' But the truth was I had no plan to sort myself out, or any expectation of doing so. I was hoping some magic solution to my problems would drop out of the sky. In fact I wasn't ready to rule out playing cricket again because it was the only thing bringing in an income, and that was all I knew. I clung to playing cricket as it was the last shred of normality in my life.

I can imagine how unconvincingly I came across, but thankfully Sheldon allowed me the rest of the closed season to get myself in shape. I walked away thinking, 'Christ, if I haven't pulled things together in about four or five months, and I fuck up next season, it's the end. I'm finished.' I knew precious time was ticking away, but that meeting still wasn't enough to drive me back down to the gym or to the nets. I couldn't motivate myself because the old motivation – supporting my wife and children – had gone.

Once again, I wanted to leave England and escape

abroad. I had made a fool of myself and all I could think of was: '*Just get on a plane and go . . . run away and hide.*' But deep down, I knew it wasn't the right way to deal with anything. It was all pretty sad really.

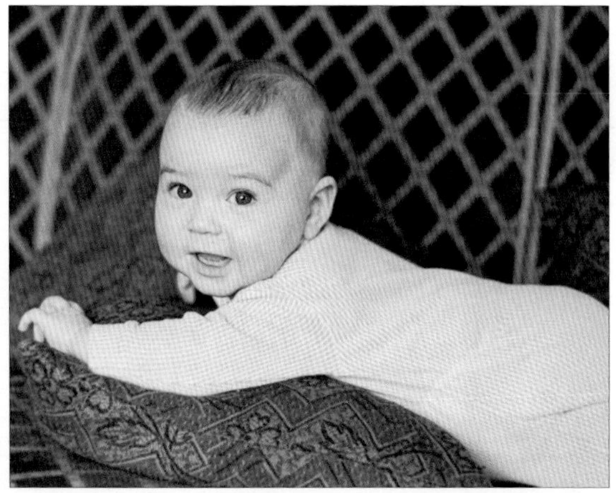

LEFT: At four months.

BELOW: On a family holiday to the South Coast with my mum Toni and dad Geoff.

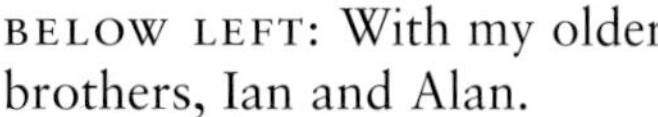

BELOW LEFT: With my older brothers, Ian and Alan.

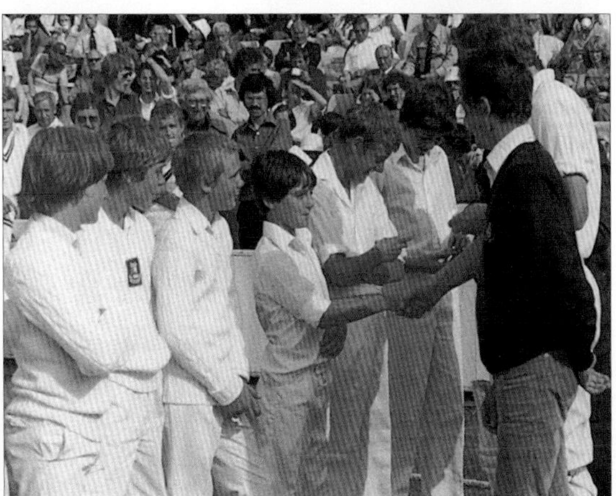

ABOVE: At the Oval, playing with the Wrecclesham boys team and shaking hands with Surrey captain Roger Knight, aged eleven.

RIGHT: Football played a large part in my early life, and I represented England schools in the Under-18s team.

My first tour: batting in Zimbabwe for England A, 1990.

Graham Gooch douses the Man of the Match in champagne after my century on Test debut, Trent Bridge 1993.

Batting with Gooch during my first Test. 'Keep going,' he kept saying. 'Don't give it away.'

With Nicky on our wedding day, September 1995.

Arriving home from the ill-fated tour to New Zealand in 1997, to be greeted by Nicky and Henry at the airport.

I'm out to one of the worst umpiring decisions of my career in a crucial World Cup match versus India in 1999.

I chiefly remember the 1999 World Cup for a pay dispute and a £1,000 fine.

Meeting Her Majesty The Queen with captain Alec Stewart.

Surrey celebrate our 1997 triumph over Kent in the Benson & Hedges Cup final at Lord's.

In the second half of my career, I played less often for Surrey than I would have liked.

At long last. Under Adam Hollioake's inspired leadership in 1999, Surrey won their first championship for 28 years.

ABOVE LEFT: Courtney Walsh celebrates dismissing me with a brilliant slower ball at Old Trafford in 2000.

ABOVE: Facing Walsh during that 2000 series was one of the sternest tests of my career.

LEFT: I rated my century against Muttiah Muralitharan in Colombo in 2001 as one of my best.

RIGHT: Asia was a great place to play cricket – and a great place to visit.

LEFT: We were up against the clock in Karachi in 2000, but I was confident we could win.

RIGHT: Running back to the dressing-room with Nasser Hussain, ecstatic after hitting the winning runs in the Karachi gloom.

ABOVE AND RIGHT: My double-century at Christchurch in 2002 was one of Test cricket's fastest – but my life was falling apart.

Mark Butcher was not only a Surrey and England colleague but also one of my closest friends.

I often fielded next to Graham Kersey, who tragically died in a car crash in 1997.

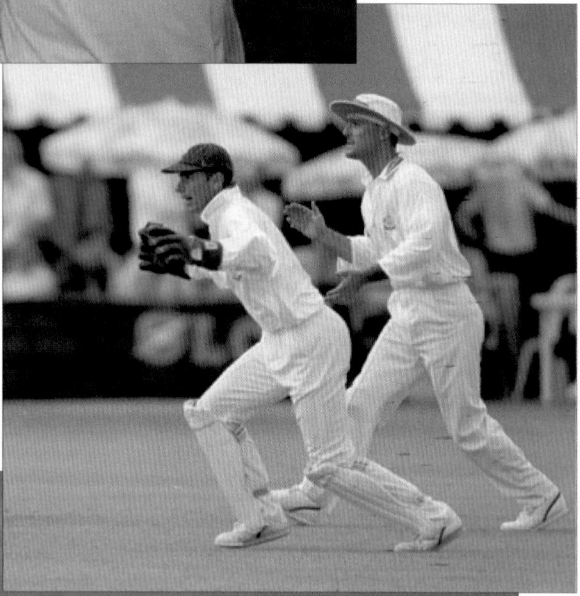

Over and out. I lose my off stump against India at Lord's in 2002, a nightmare match that persuaded me to withdraw from cricket.

EIGHT

No 1 Rebel

DUNCAN FLETCHER must have thought I was more trouble than I was worth. When he first took over as England coach I had to assure him at our first meeting that, contrary to some reports, I was not a paid-up member of the awkward squad. Yet for years that was my reputation: to many, I was a rebel. But, to my eyes, there was plenty to rebel about because before Duncan Fletcher's time English cricket was not well run. If I had been running a business, I certainly wouldn't have run it like that. So, if I occasionally spoke out of turn, I make no apology, because the way England's top cricketers were sometimes handled in the early days was scandalous. We were underpaid and treated like school-children. We were at the top of our profession yet I got the impression the management didn't always care for us. By the time Duncan came along, however, I had mellowed and, in any case, many of the problems that had created my bolshieness had been sorted out, or were in the process of being addressed.

I'd carried the 'rebel' tag since sharing England A tours of Sri Lanka and the West Indies with two other up-and-coming batsmen, Nasser Hussain and Mark Ramprakash, and the press boys had labelled us English cricket's 'brat pack'. This was slightly misleading. I suppose we'd all acquired reputations in county cricket, rightly or wrongly, for being talented but difficult. It's certainly true that we were all pretty intense about our cricket and were inseparable, so perhaps it was inevitable we'd be described as some sort of 'pack'. But I don't remember us doing anything notorious. We were competing to see who'd be first to break into the full England side but it was a healthy competition among mates. We'd been coming across each other since we were teenagers, and were young and ambitious, but I don't think we did anything on the tours to suggest that we were difficult to handle.

I don't think professional sportsmen are generally unruly towards authority. The nature of the job means we are basically insecure types. We don't want to rock the boat because it might give people an excuse not to pick us, and even if we never step out of line we don't know how long our careers might last: it could be one year or 15. All it takes is a brief loss of form or injury. In fact my career lasted 15 years, but I'd no idea that would be the case when I set off on my first tour with

England A in 1989, or when I met Nicky the following year.

I saw a lot of players who simply kept quiet and accepted their lot, even though I know some of them privately agreed with me. But I felt that the way we were treated simply wasn't good enough. If some of the gripes were over apparently petty issues, like sticking to the dress-code, there was a serious underlying point: given that we were supposed to be at the top of our profession, how well were we actually being treated? Did we get a fair deal?

A lot of the time I didn't see supposed managers doing a lot of managing, and something in me just wouldn't take things without questioning them. I have to accept that there were times when I was wrong and out of line. For some reason I always found it very hard to wear the right shoes, or put on the approved jacket and tie at official functions. Later, when things had improved under Duncan, I managed to toe the line better, so I think it must have had something to do with my lack of faith in management. It wasn't premeditated and I didn't mean to be disruptive.

What the management didn't like – and this went for Duncan as well, to an extent – was that sometimes I would put my family ahead of cricket, and even preferred to spend a winter at home with my wife and children rather than go on tour. They actually seemed to find someone who didn't always put their job first more subversive than someone else who might do the usual thing like occasionally break a curfew, or get up to some high jinks. Phil Tufnell, who was good company and who I got pretty close to, was labelled a bad boy by the press but his disciplinary record on tour was pretty good and, when he was asked to play, he did. No one was more insecure than Phil, yet the management seemed to find me harder to read and, for that reason, I became the No 1 rebel. I made my feelings plain on several issues but, Tuffers aside, I wouldn't say I was much more insecure than the next man. Maybe my insecurity just manifested itself in other ways.

Tuffers spent a lot of time worrying about what figure he cut. Often after he was out, he would return to the dressing-room and ask: 'How did that look?' He was afraid he'd looked scared. 'You looked fine, Tuffers, don't worry, you're a No 11.' I can vividly remember during a nail-biting run-chase in Trinidad in 1998 Tuffers sitting in the dressing-room, wearing the full body armour, smoking his way through a whole packet of cigarettes as we edged to a two-wicket victory without him being called on to face a rampaging Ambrose and Walsh.

One way a lot of sports people, including myself, dealt with the insecurity was to live with someone, get married and start a family when still quite young (Tuffers was first married at 20). That gave you some stability. After all that travelling it was nice to have someone to come home to, someone who gave you a taste of normality.

But the downside is marrying young can mean marrying wrong and, looking back, I think that happened to me.

I should have moved away from home when I joined Surrey, and lived in a house with a bunch of cricketers and found out about a few things. I ended up making some big decisions at a young age, too young. Nicky should have chosen to follow her own life too, but she chose to stay with me.

We met in Dubai when we were both 20. Surrey were on a pre-season tour there, and when we were invited to a party all the squad went. There, Nicky and I passed in the room, our heads turned, and that was that. She had a big hairdo, a pretty face and good figure, and we clicked straightaway.

Her mother's boyfriend piloted a private jet for the Maktoum family, and she was on holiday in Dubai for the summer staying with her mother. She came back to England that summer, and between games I drove down to see her in Bournemouth where she was staying. About a year later we were living together in Aldershot, about five miles from my parents' home. Nicky had a succession of short-lived office jobs – in a recruitment agency, with British Gas, and a travel agent. At one point she gave up work to do a sports therapy course, but this also lasted only a few months before she changed her mind and gave that up too. She stopped working once we were engaged.

One brief separation apart, we lived together for

about four years before marrying, by which time she knew about the ups and downs of life with a professional cricketer. She'd come out on tour for a couple of weeks each winter in the early days, although obviously this became more difficult once the children came along. We moved into a house in Ewell soon after we got married in September 1995.

If playing cricket all-year round didn't teach me how to cope with real life, it certainly taught Nicky. Being married to a sportsman who is away from home a lot is very difficult. I remember when Nicky had two small children on her hands she found it really hard being a full-time mother. But with time they get into their routines without you, and I think that in the end Nicky was strong enough to say to herself, 'I've got through 10 winters without Graham, and he's away a lot of the time in the summer, I reckon I can live without him. It'll be a bit tough on the children, but I can manage.'

I think she decided that she'd had two kids, done all the hard work while I'd been off having a ball playing cricket, and now it was her turn to have some fun. She said she was unfulfilled. And she'd fallen for someone else. The bottom line was that it wasn't that difficult for her to make the break, while for me it was like a bomb had been dropped.

THAT SAID, I think I made more effort than most to balance sport with family life. I wanted Nicky to be happy and would have done anything for her. Cricket never completely drove my life: I wasn't obsessed with how many runs I scored or what I averaged, and wasn't even that desperate about playing for England. I suppose what changes for you and your partner is the money. Tour fees got bigger the longer you played, and the more established you were the more likely you'd pick up extras like bat sponsorships or newspaper contracts. This was the up-side for both of us. Once we were married, my priority was earning a living and doing well for my family, something Nicky really encouraged. But if anything was my life, it was my family, not cricket, and I think my attitude towards the game changed for the better once I had children. When I got a duck, it was disappointing, but I knew it wasn't the end of the world. There were more important things.

When playing cricket for 10 months a year, serious things are inevitably going to happen when you're away, and my attitude was that I had a duty to go home when they did. Not every cricketer I played with shared this view, but I was someone who had always been controlled by my heart. If some crisis occurred, I didn't often have to think too long about what to do, which was why I later found it difficult when Nicky accused me of selfishly pursuing my career. I made a lot of sacrifices for her and the children, and there were times when I put my career on the line for them.

The first incident that really brought home to me that

things didn't stop happening at home just because I was away on tour, was when Nicky suffered an ectopic pregnancy shortly after we got married. I immediately flew back from South Africa to be with her. She had been eight weeks pregnant, and although we suffered the trauma of losing the baby at least Nicky came through okay. I stayed at home for about 10 days before she assured me she was okay to be left, and that I should rejoin the tour. I struggled to switch back into the cricket and had a poor Test series, not reaching fifty until the final Test in Cape Town.

Two winters later, I cut short my tour of West Indies by a week because my grandfather was dying. My dad had phoned after the first one-day international and told me that granddad, who was well into his nineties, had only a few days to live. I was close to him. He was a lovely old London boy who lived in Hammersmith and used to get everybody's name wrong. He'd call Atherton 'Appleton', stuff like that. I was so glad I made the decision to go back. I only just made it. I went straight to see him and spent about half an hour by his bed; he died the next day.

It was the first time I'd experienced the death of someone close and it was very upsetting, although I was also inspired by the strength my grandfather showed. Even though he knew he was dying he didn't seem afraid. It was a bright sunny day when I saw him and the light was pouring through the window. He was lying on his bed and asked me if I'd had a good tour. 'I haven't got long left now,' he said. 'I've had a good life. I think I'm going somewhere else now.'

The reason given for my return home was a recurrence of the back trouble I'd experienced during my century in the Barbados Test, and it was true that my back was playing up, but the real reason I went home was my father's phone call.

Fortunately, neither of these incidents created difficulties with the management, but this was not always the case until a more sensitive approach to handling players was brought in by Duncan and Nasser. Like me, Nasser had been tagged awkward. He'd occasionally kick the ground or throw his bat, but to me that showed he cared. When he became captain in 1999, he calmed down of course, because as captain you're under pressure to, and I think he told Duncan that the likes of myself, Tufnell, Andrew Caddick and Darren Gough were not difficult people.

Before they took charge, things were far less well organized. In fact, it was often a complete jumble. We didn't have structured team meetings of the kind we had at the end of my career, when we'd have the names of our team and the opposition up on a board and we'd talk tactics. But the truth was that back then we weren't really a team. They were more like representative matches. Yes, on tour, you might spend enough time together to start bonding and find something that might pass for team spirit, but it was a fragile thing. Selection strategy was flawed, with players never quite sure whether they commanded the support of the management and could expect to be around in six months, let alone a year.

Most of us lived in fear of being dropped in favour of some bloke who happened to be scoring a mountain of runs in county cricket, should we have a couple of bad Tests. The selectors thought nothing of swapping people over when that happened. It was an irrational way of trying to build a side, and hardly created an environment in which people felt able to play their natural game or learn about Test cricket. It was naive and shortsighted.

The fast bowlers had it worse, though. These were the days before central contracts, and they were expected to play regular championship cricket between Tests. The injury toll was severe, the turnover phenomenal – I played with more than 20 fast bowlers in my first four years in Test cricket – and the whole process totally counter-productive. A number of fast bowlers might have had longer careers if the system had been different – Devon Malcolm, Angus Fraser, Dean Headley, and Chris Lewis, for example. It was obvious to most of us that central contracts were the way forward – we could see how they'd benefited the Australians – but it took until 2000 to bring them in.

Once they'd come in, we soon saw the benefits. Gough and Caddick, who'd had a brief spell together in 1997, became the first settled new-ball partnership I'd known and consequently results began to improve. They were hugely different bowlers and hugely competitive against each other, which was a good thing. At the beginning I was unsure whether they actually liked each other, but there was always mutual respect and an understanding that they had to work as a pair, feeding off each other.

By the end, I think they had a good, healthy relationship and enjoyed bowling together. Caddick had more natural attributes for the job, but Gough had the bigger heart. Caddick sometimes felt the pressure, although he was not alone in that, but once he felt more comfortable in the team, and knew that we liked and valued him, it wasn't such a problem. Nasser did a lot to make him feel wanted and, once he'd achieved that, was able to be a lot firmer with him. He and Gough led the attack without a break for almost two years and played a huge part in the series wins against the West Indies, Pakistan and Sri Lanka in 2000 and 2001.

I think the uncertainty helped form the character of the few of us who remained regulars in the Test side during the mid-nineties, i.e. myself, Nasser, Athers and Alec Stewart. All of us were dropped at various times and this, and the failure to win many games during that era, helped make us the scrappers we became. Typically English backs-to-the-wall fighters, I suppose.

The team was often in disarray and when things went badly, we could go down quickly and little factions would develop among senior players and youngsters. This was perhaps most apparent at the World Cup on the subcontinent in 1996. Tactically, we were miles behind the opposition. We weren't as flexible or as well-prepared as they were. We only caught onto pinch-hitting halfway through the tournament, and then in a half-hearted fashion. We had little experience of playing in Asia, and thought we'd score our runs at the back end of the innings when run scoring was actually at its hardest against the Kookaburra ball (the type used overseas, and which tended to swing more when it was new than the Duke's ball, the one used in England). We didn't beat any worthwhile opposition, and went out to Sri Lanka in the quarter-finals, pulverized by Sanath Jayasuriya in the first 15 overs.

We were caught cold in our first game against New Zealand in Ahmedabad, although I was in no position to complain as I dropped both openers inside the first five overs, including Nathan Astle, who scored a hundred. The games started very early because of the early dusk, which meant we were getting up around 6am and running around practising our fielding before 8am. It clearly didn't do me any good. This was my introduction to World Cup cricket and I'd messed up almost before I started. It was an awful game. There were flies everywhere, and we spent the day spitting them out of our mouths. With no videos, I knew very little about the New Zealand bowlers. I hadn't faced Chris Harris before, and hadn't a clue what he was up to with his medium-pace all-sorts. What a shambles.

By this point, near the end of two years together as captain and coach, Atherton and Illingworth were struggling to work with each other or formulate a clear game-plan. I heard from Athers that he found things with Illy difficult. I don't know if it affected his relationships with the players, but Illy was not very comfortable with the public side of his role. I often heard him complain how much the media had changed for the worse since his days as a player.

Athers, who hadn't played that much one-day cricket, had his run-ins with Dermot Reeve, who'd had a lot of one-day success captaining Warwickshire. Illy – whose plain-speaking I liked – clashed with Stewie and Robin Smith. Alec's attitude was 'either it's my way or the wrong way', and he was left with a bit of egg on his face because Illy was too powerful not to get the last word, and a few months after the World Cup Illy was ready to end both their careers. They were dropped from the Test side, but Stewie was soon back because of an injury to Nick Knight though Robin never reappeared. I don't know what Illy's problem with Robin was; maybe Robin liked to enjoy himself a bit too much.

Robin had made me welcome when I first got into the Test side, and his attitude was like mine. The previous year, in 1995, when he'd been under pressure for his place during a home series against West Indies, he'd said, 'If they're going to drop me, I'm going to play my shots,' and he'd responded with two fifties. I think he was dropped far too early.

One of the main problems was that the captain, whether it was Atherton, Stewart or Hussain, found himself having to do so much more than lead the team on the field. He was also expected to represent the interests of the team in discussions with the board over pay and conditions. It added immensely to the burden of the job. Nowadays, if an England player has a grievance, there is a representative of the Professional Cricketers' Association he can speak to and who will take up his case with the ECB. I can remember as recently as 2001 a group of us sitting down at Lord's with Tim Lamb, the ECB's chief executive, and the chairman of the finance committee to tell them we weren't being paid enough. It was all done in such an amateurish way.

Until 1996, we were also still sharing rooms. The management said it brought the team together and maybe it did help first-time tourists, but everyone needs their own time and space. I can remember rooming with Devon Malcolm in South Africa, and I was waiting half an hour for him to finish using the shower on the morning of the first Test. My issue wasn't really with Devon but why we were put in that situation. We were meant to be professional sportsmen and should have been able to have a shower when we wanted.

Marginal issues seemed to take priority over the

cricket. On my second tour of the West Indies, Bob Bennett, the manager, devised a dress-code committee and put me on it, which may have been his way of getting me on-side because he'd recently fined me for coming down to breakfast at the team hotel wearing an official England cap (I'm not joking). So we wasted valuable time in team meetings deciding what to wear and, get this, making sure we were clean-shaven because Lord MacLaurin, then chairman of the ECB, was coming out to watch the Test. When this was mentioned, I just put my hand up at the back and said, 'Please. Can we cut out the shaving issue? It's not high on my list of priorities this morning. I've got to think about Ambrose and Walsh.' I was called in for a few words of admonishment from Bob after that. He'd worry like hell. He wanted to make sure Lord's would say he'd done a good job, and if that meant us losing 3–0 but being clean-shaven, so be it.

Duncan's style was so different to David Lloyd's, his predecessor, who replaced Illy as coach in 1996. Lloyd made some important changes – he brought in Steve Bull as psychologist and got rid of the eve-of-Test dinner – and always had England's best interests at heart, but some of his ideas were a bit mad. In his first series, against India, he tried motivating us by playing recordings of Winston Churchill's speeches. I think he was a cricket coach who really wanted to be a football manager. All the latest stuff that was coming out of

Manchester United, he'd be quoting at us, and we always knew what he was going to say to the press because he'd say it to us first. His infamous remark about us 'flippin' murdering' Zimbabwe in Bulawayo, when we actually drew the match, was made to us in the dressing-room before he went off and said the same thing in a press conference. He made me laugh a lot, but usually inside. I wouldn't have got away with laughing out loud.

He thought I should have bowled more than I did and once announced, 'If Nathan Astle's a better bowler than Graham Thorpe, my arse is a fire-engine.' Maybe he was right, but while Astle went on to take around 150 international wickets for New Zealand with his medium-pacers, my haul for England stopped at two. Both were taken during a one-dayer against India at Old Trafford during Lloyd's first series in charge. Athers put me on because the ball was swinging, and my victims included Sourav Ganguly stumped off a leg-side wide. Given the troubles I had with my back, it was probably best for me – if not Lloyd's reputation as a pundit – that I didn't pursue a career as an all-rounder.

Lloyd was probably a bit unlucky that my most awkward, rebellious phase coincided with the later stages of his time with England. My inability to dress as required drove him up the wall. He wasn't best pleased when I turned up in the Caribbean for a function on John Paul Getty's yacht wearing jeans. 'He's not part of your team, then?' our host apparently said to him. Oh dear. Sorry.

I think Duncan had a better idea of what he wanted than Lloyd and was more clinical about getting it, though perhaps he knew he could be; he was given more power than David Lloyd or Keith Fletcher ever had. For a start, he had overall charge of the team so the Bob Bennett role – filled by Phil Neale during Duncan's time – was less intrusive.

Duncan would just have a quiet word in your ear or fine you under the system we used to fund an end-of-tour booze-up. That way it became a bit of fun. And he dealt with people who were thought difficult by giving them responsibility. On my first tour under him he put me on the general management team. I loved that. In retrospect, it was exactly the right way to deal with me. But he would come down on you if you weren't trying or if you constantly broke one of his rules. Occasionally I would still break our dress code, but I don't think he thought I was being deliberately awkward.

THE INCIDENT that most upset me occurred in the build-up to the 1999 World Cup. It not only distressed me at the time but its repercussions shaped the next two years of my career. It all could have been handled so much better and, under today's regime, undoubtedly would have been.

A few months earlier, I'd come home early from a

tour of Australia with the back problem that bothered me throughout my career. I'd been afflicted by back spasms since my early twenties, and had previously got by on injections and painkillers, but in 1998 the problem had resurfaced with a vengeance. It caused problems in the West Indies (I had to stop for treatment during my Test century in Bridgetown) early that year and made me miss the Texaco Trophy one-day series at home in May.

Then my back went completely during the third Test against South Africa at Old Trafford in July. Although I batted twice in that game, which we hung on to draw by the skin of our teeth, I could barely shuffle to the wicket and didn't score a run. I feared pretty much the moment I felt it go, when I bent down to pick up my socks on the Saturday morning, that it was serious. Sure enough, I required surgery and took no part in the second half of the season. I underwent an operation to shave a facet joint and remove a cyst near the base of my spine.

In Australia the following winter, I spent the first month of the tour trying to get fit. My rehabilitation programme hadn't worked out, and my back seized up on the eve of the second Test in Perth. If we'd known more about how to build up the strength in our lower back in those days, I might have avoided a lot of trouble, and not missed seven Tests in seven months. Subsequently, daily pilates exercises largely kept trouble at bay, although I still regularly took painkillers because my back would often stiffen up, especially once I resumed playing after several weeks off, as happened on my last tour of South Africa and at the start of the 2005 season.

Anyway, I was told by the England management that if I didn't prove my fitness during our 1999 World Cup preparations in Lahore and Sharjah, I would not be selected for the final squad. I had no quibble with that except that our second child, Amelia, was due to be born while we were out there and I was basically being told that I had to choose between being at the birth of my child or taking part in the World Cup.

It was all done in very heavy-handed fashion. Just before we left for Lahore, I was called to a meeting at the Oval with David Lloyd, David Graveney, Simon Pack, an ex-army officer who then oversaw all England team affairs, and Philip Bell, the team doctor. They said, in effect, 'Look, this is the decision you've got to make. We know your baby is due soon, but if you don't go on this trip, we will not select you for the World Cup squad.' They suggested I should go away to think about it for a few days, which I did.

Nicky and I talked about it and, in the end, we agreed that I should play the cricket and miss the birth. We reasoned that if I didn't play, it would have a long-term impact on my career. Given that we had begun planning things like private school education for the children, we decided that this was not the best time to take risks. It was an agonizing decision, and one I should not have had to make. Basically, I was being asked a crass question: would you rather hit the winning runs in the World Cup final or be at the birth of your child? My real, unspoken response was, 'I'd like to do both, thank you very much.' I didn't see why that shouldn't be possible. For some reason, the England management thought otherwise.

Amelia was born on 2 April at midday (7am in Pakistan). Funnily, I'd just had a dream about Nicky having the baby. Then I was woken by the phone ringing with Nicky on the other end saying, 'We've got a baby girl.' It had been an easy birth. I was exhilarated but sad because I hadn't been there. Later, I went down to the hotel pool and told some of the lads. There were plenty of congratulations but soon everyone was back to putting on their Factor 15 and carrying on as normal. I felt flat when I shouldn't have done, and it made me ask, 'Is this really worth it?'

There was more trouble on that trip, for all of us. It was the start of perhaps the unhappiest period for the England team in all my time with it. The whole squad was very unhappy at the pay we were being offered to play in three warm-up matches back in England, and for the first phase of the 1999 World Cup. We agreed to make a stand, and Tim Lamb had to come out and meet us in a hotel in Sharjah. I was among the most belligerent but we had to stick together for anything to happen. We talked about not playing the warm-up matches, but although negotiations continued, back in England resistance crumbled. People were picked off and, at one point, our captain Alec Stewart said that although he wasn't happy about the money, he'd play in a World Cup for nothing, which wasn't the right message to send out to his squad. In the end, we agreed to go ahead and play under the original terms. We'd got absolutely nothing to show for all our trouble. And we hadn't made ourselves look good in the process. Relations remained fraught between the players and board for quite a while, but that dispute did help pave the way to central contracts and new ways of handling pay.

All this was the background to perhaps my most well-publicised misdemeanour, refusing to go to a dinner in Canterbury, where the team were based on our return home in the lead-up to the World Cup. This was just one of several functions we were expected to attend as a team, even though they were not covered by our contracts and came at the end of hard days of preparation for one of the biggest events of our careers. Again, most players accepted their lot even though they were gravely unhappy, but I couldn't bring myself to do that. Whether I would have been so belligerent had the board been more understanding over Amelia's birth, I don't know, but I was boiling up inside. When the time arrived for us to get on the team bus, I told Nasser, with whom I was rooming (we went back to sharing rooms for this tournament for some reason), that I wasn't going. 'Tell them I'm unwell if you want,' I said, 'but I'm not going.'

The management took my no-show very seriously, and I was hauled into a meeting the next day to explain myself, which I did. Perhaps if I'd apologized I would have got off more lightly, but I wasn't prepared to do it. They fined me £1,000, and David Lloyd told me some years later they came close to kicking me out of the World Cup.

But despite everything, we felt we might still achieve something in the tournament. We were on home territory and the early season conditions suited our bowlers. We beat Sri Lanka, Kenya and Zimbabwe, but South Africa gave us a hammering and showed how far ahead they were in fielding and attacking bowling. Going into our final group match against India at Edgbaston we were confident of qualifying for the second phase, until Zimbabwe surprisingly beat the South Africans, the form team, and left us needing a result in our game, which went into a second day because of rain. India had the upper hand – we were three wickets down – but I felt that with a couple of good partnerships we could still get the 160 needed in the 30 overs left. I resumed on about 31, and knew I needed to stay there if we were to win.

A few minutes into the second day, all hell broke loose. Bowling at me from around the wicket, Javagal Srinath hit me on the pad and appealed for leg-before. I wasn't worried because I was sure the ball was going to miss leg stump. But to my utter astonishment the Pakistan umpire, Javed Akhtar, raised his finger. I was incensed. How on earth could he have given me out? I couldn't suppress my anger and, as I walked past him, I gave him a volley of abuse. 'You fucking cheat!' I shouted. We lost the match to India by a decisive margin, and went out of the tournament.

The TV replays confirmed my first impression that it was a terrible decision, but my outburst was an instant reaction and I feared hearing from the match referee. Normally, you wouldn't get away with calling an umpire an effing cheat. But, on this occasion, I did.

The following year, Hansie Cronje's exposure led to a spate of match-fixing allegations, including some directed at Javed Akhtar's decision-making in the Leeds Test of 1998, a game I'd missed because of my bad back. No evidence was found and he was cleared of any wrong-doing. In his defence, I would have to say that for an official from the subcontinent with little experience of cricket outside his own country, as was the case with Javed Akhtar, having the ball seam around on an English pitch must be very challenging. For his part, he denied that he acted improperly during the World Cup match at Edgbaston.

Shortly after the World Cup was over, Stewie was replaced by Nasser as captain after only a year in the job. I'm sure his initial role in the pay dispute did not help his cause because the board would certainly have been displeased.

It was Nasser injuring his hand in his second game in charge that led to me falling out with Butch over the captaincy. Looking back, I can see that, given all that had happened, there was really no way that they were going to make me captain, even on a temporary basis, although it didn't stop me having a go at Nasser for suggesting Butch be his replacement when I next saw him. Once again the board had created trouble that could have been avoided had they officially designated a vice-captain, something they were curiously reluctant to do in home Tests. I couldn't for the life of me understand why. Surely whoever was to stand in if the captain was injured deserved some warning, but they preferred to keep everyone guessing.

My mood wasn't helped around this time when Mike Gatting, a former England captain and one of the selectors, publicly questioned, 'what Graham Thrope brought to the table except his runs'. At the time, I found it a mystifying and hurtful attack, but I came to notice a pattern in Gatting's behaviour. He had always been pretty hostile towards me in Surrey-Middlesex matches, and he laid into Nasser after he resigned the England one-day captaincy in 2003, accusing him of selfishness in wanting to play on in Tests. It was the old Thorpe-Ramprakash-Hussain 'brat pack' triangle come to life again, except Gatt seemingly wanted to show his loyalty to Ramps, his protégé, whom he claimed was the most talented of the three of us. And he was probably right. But I suspect that the real reason he was not my No 1 fan was that when I made my debut he was dropped from the team. Personally, I could not understand his attitude because, as far as I was concerned, it'd be good luck to whoever took my place when they finally threw me out.

Part of my problem around 1999 was that I was worn out. At the end of the summer I announced my unavailability for the millennium Test series in South Africa. There were two reasons. One was that after 10 years of playing cricket summer and winter I was stale, and badly in need of a break. My game had lost its edge and I needed to regain my enthusiasm. I hadn't done much at the World Cup and the home Test series with New Zealand, which we lost after being 1–0 up, had been one of my least successful. I had only found my best touch for Surrey a couple of times, during match-winning centuries at Northampton and against Hampshire at Guildford that at least made me feel like I'd contributed to our first championship title for nearly 30 years.

My other reason was that so soon after Amelia's birth I felt I owed it to Nicky to spend time with her and our young family, helping out in the way most dads do as a matter of course. So I stayed at home and, for the only time in my married life, devoted several months solely to my family. I really enjoyed it. But my decision only made me more unpopular with the management, whose first reaction was to reject my offer to play in the one-day matches in South Africa. It meant I was to have nothing to do with the tour.

It was not just my decision that upset them but the way news of it came out. I'd been mulling over pulling out of the Tests for several weeks, and had still done nothing about it come the final New Zealand Test of the 1999 summer at the Oval. I should have told someone sooner, and I think had there been a better management structure at the time I might have done. But the England team didn't have a full-time coach and the authority of Graham Gooch, who ran our practice sessions, had been undermined by his removal as a selector the previous week. Affairs were largely in the hands of Nasser and Graveney. My own state of mind certainly played a part, and I was too wrapped up in my own disenchantment to remember that the tour squad was being chosen straight after the Test.

In the end, most people learned of my decision through a report in a Sunday newspaper. It was only the newspaper asking me what my winter plans were that reminded me a selection meeting was due, and jolted me into telling Nasser on the Saturday night. We were in the middle of a tight run-chase against New Zealand in that last Test. Athers and I had finished the day not out, but we were both out next morning as England suffered a horrible collapse, a fitting end to a miserable few months.

In principle, though, I can't understand why anyone should object if a seasoned player takes off a tour to recharge his batteries. Surely, he should know what is best for him. Graham Gooch opted out of tours to be with his family but, for some reason, it didn't seem to be held against him in quite the same way as with me, perhaps because he didn't do it until he was a few years older than I was (I was then 30). Some people thought I was wrong, others thought I was gambling with my career. But the rest left me refreshed and, I believe, helped lengthen my career. The following winter in Pakistan and Sri Lanka I not only played perhaps my best-ever cricket helping England to two historic Test series victories, but I also approached my cricket in a more mature, relaxed manner. That new outlook was the cornerstone of much of my later success.

I think the criticism from former cricketers was down to a culture clash. Previous generations of players had gone away on tour for months on end and they just got on with it. Basically, in their eyes I was a soft-arse. They didn't seem to have noticed that society's expectations of what men did in the home had changed. I noticed, for example, that Micky Stewart, who had played and then managed, brought up Alec to hardly miss any cricket in his entire career.

However, my timing was badly out, in that the tour I had chosen to miss was Duncan's first as England coach. We didn't know each other at all and, from the outset I needed to convince him that, despite appearances, I remained fully committed to England's cause. Even before I'd met him, Fletcher and the rest of the management decided to leave me out of their first batch of contracted England players, which hurt my pride, not to mention my wallet. I even briefly feared I might not get on any better with this new England regime than with the old.

Early in the 2000 season, though, Duncan came down to Surrey to see me. I don't suppose at that time that either of us was the type to waste words, and he was pretty blunt. 'I've heard a few things about you,' he said. 'Does England have to come to Graham Thorpe, or does Graham Thorpe come to England?' I was slightly taken aback. I said, 'Look Duncan, if I'm good enough to get back in the England team I don't think you'll have any problems with me. I'll give you my best and that will be it.'

We had a good chat and Duncan seemed to go away happy. But the selectors kept me waiting until July to recall me. Ramps, Hick, Knight and Michael Vaughan were all called back into the Test side before I was. I knew I was hardly in a position to make demands and Duncan was naturally keen to establish his authority, so I suppose I understood why it happened, but I was unhappy at any implication that I had acted selfishly. There had been newspaper speculation that I'd chosen to miss the tour so I could concentrate on my benefit season at Surrey, a ridiculous allegation but one not easy to refute. The delay did have one positive effect, though. Once I got back my Test place, I was desperate not to let it go again. Nicky agreed: 'Go and play for as long as you can.'

Even so, I continued to wonder whether I'd got the balance of my life right, and toyed with retiring from one-day cricket. I spoke to Duncan about it in Sri Lanka early in 2001, but he persuaded me to keep going and even made me captain for the one-dayers when Nasser returned home injured; I was again fully committed and it showed that he had forgiven me for taking time out. It was the only time I lead England. I was honoured to be asked but am not unfulfilled that I didn't do it more times. Maybe the job meant more limelight than I really wanted.

Being confident of my position in the Test side, I didn't have too many qualms about how I did the job or what I said to the lads, but privately I doubted how competitive we'd be against Sri Lanka on their own soil, where they had a great record. I was right to be concerned. We had a sniff of a chance in the first match but, after that, they took us apart and we lost the series 3–0. But nothing could take the gloss off a fantastic winter for me and the team.

NINE

One-Night Stand

ONE OF THE worst decisions the England management ever made was to have a massive impact on my life. It all went back to the defeat by South Africa in the New Year Test at Cape Town in 1996. We gave a poor performance, lost the match in three days and the series with it, and Ray Illingworth laid the blame squarely at the door of our families joining us over the holiday period. It was felt the team lost focus at the climax of a close-fought series.

It's true that there were many family members on that tour over Christmas and New Year. There were mums and dads as well as partners, and it was a bit of a bunfight with the team bus in the morning loaded up with relatives. So it wasn't unreasonable to question what had gone on, and say that changes had to be made to the way tours were run. But to respond by imposing a complete ban on families joining tours at any stage, which was what the management demanded the following winter, was a major over-reaction. Athers, the captain, naturally wanted his players on the ball but at that time he was a single man. Most of his players were either married, like me, or had girlfriends, and I'm not sure he had a great deal of sympathy for our positions.

We were due to be away for three and a half months in Zimbabwe and New Zealand the following winter. I think that long before the tour was over, Atherton and David Lloyd realized that they'd made a big mistake. The ban was never imposed again. In fact, as the years went by, steps were taken to make it easier for wives and girlfriends to join tours, to the point where things were never so relaxed as they were on my final England tour. But having said that, when we lost in Cape Town, in January 2005, the debate about the unhelpful influence of partners on tour was heard again.

From the day the announcement was made that wives and girlfriends would be barred during the winter of 1996–97, the grumbling started and I was certainly among those hostile to the idea. Touring wasn't something I much enjoyed or was good at. I wasn't one for venturing out of the hotel to explore local culture and found long tours hard going. I felt such a ban would have an adverse effect, both on me and the team. I think later experience showed that having partners around made you more content, less likely to stay out late, and gave you a welcome escape from thinking and talking solely about cricket. But after my previous run-ins with the management I was not inclined to say things straight out to them. I'd bottle up my feelings and simply give off an air of grievance without explaining exactly what my problem was, though I guess during that winter it was pretty obvious, and the management were able to draw their own conclusions as to the reason for my being morose.

In my case, being forcibly separated from my family seemed all the harder to bear given that Henry, our first child, was due to be born in the early days of the tour. In the end, I was allowed to leave home a few days later than the rest of the team in order to be at the birth – a privilege not extended, of course, when Amelia was born three years later – but even then Nicky was induced so that I wouldn't be delayed.

To be a good tourist, you had to force thoughts of home out of your mind, but I was always reluctant to do that, fearing that it might have some sort of permanent effect. There were players who simply grew away from their families. For all his efforts, Graham Gooch was one. We all learned to cope in our different ways. There were those like Tuffers who would go out and have a few drinks, sometimes to excess, and others, like Stewie, who channelled all their energies into their cricket.

The team didn't have a good mentality from the outset. The facilities and hotels in Zimbabwe were inadequate, and we were unhappy at an itinerary which had us staying in Harare over Christmas. We felt that with a bit more planning we could have returned home over the holiday period between Zimbabwe and New Zealand. This was one of my biggest grumbles with the authorities in those days. I thought it was wrong that we spent so much time away from our families and that the tours could have been shorter, as they became in later years.

We had a point, but I can't imagine an England team undertaking a tour with such a negative attitude nowadays. A siege mentality took hold and it was reflected in the poor way we played on the first leg of the tour, when we failed to win a match of any consequence. Athers was out of form and feeling the pressure of the captaincy, while I really struggled to motivate myself and scored only one half-century before they decided to drop me – not unreasonably – from the last two one-dayers in Harare which we lost. We sank to an unexpected but deserved 3–0 series defeat. I think if I ever set a bad example to others, it was in Zimbabwe that winter. Had I carried on like that under a later regime, I would have been told in no uncertain terms to buck up my ideas or not play for England again.

Things got worse as the tour went on. While we were in Harare over Christmas, news came through one night that Graham Kersey, our young wicket-keeper at Surrey, had been badly injured in a car crash in Australia. He died a few days later. I'd known Graham very well and he was a very popular lad. I'd stood next to him at slip and roomed with him many times. His death hit me really hard. He was just 25, a couple of years younger than me. It completely took the wind out of my sails, and made me feel that I just wanted to get the tour over with and get home.

Thankfully, we played much better cricket in New Zealand and won the Test series 2–0, and drew the one-dayers 2–2. I managed to get back into things, and made something of a personal break-through by scoring centuries in the first and second Tests in Auckland and Wellington. Since my debut against Australia, I'd experienced real difficulties in playing the type of long innings required at Test level. I'd reached fifty 20 times and, during one period of 13 Tests, I'd passed fifty in 11 of them and made an unbeaten 47 in another, but I'd gone on to complete another hundred just once, at Perth in 1995.

These statistics became etched into my mind because it was a problem I knew I needed to rectify. I'd come within striking range of a hundred several times, so I knew I was good enough, but my aggressive instinct had made me the master of the counter-attacking 70 rather than the hard-fought century. I'd also been brought up on 20-overs cricket, and three-day cricket, in which hundreds were not the be-all and end-all. To be fair, we had also been up against some good attacks. I had to wait almost three years to play against a side other than Australia, the West Indies or South Africa, who all had bowlers who could produce balls that you could get out to at any stage, and frequently that happened. Looking back, I wouldn't say there were too many times when I threw away my wicket.

The only way to stop the talk was to reel off a few hundreds, which was what I now did. I batted almost six hours in both Auckland and Wellington on this New Zealand tour and within a few months did so again against Australia for my third century in five Test innings. I'd often batted through two sessions before, but rarely much longer. The innings in Wellington, where I had another lengthy partnership with Nasser, was especially sweet because it was the first time I'd scored a century for England to help win a game.

We ought to have made a clean sweep of the New Zealand Tests but were held to the most ridiculous draw I'd ever played in. In the first match at Auckland, when Danny Morrison, the New Zealand No 11 and a batsman so bad he was famous only for making ducks, held out for more than three hours with Nathan Astle. With New Zealand effectively 11 for 9 early on the final afternoon, someone unwisely had champagne and beer sent to our dressing-room, where it sat, preying on our minds, as Morrison and Astle inched their side's lead ever further towards safety. After that, whenever anyone started talking about a celebratory drink before the last ball was bowled, I'd tell them to back off. 'I once played in a game,' I'd caution, 'in which you wouldn't believe what happened . . .'

But the New Zealand tour was not remembered purely for the cricket. After the hardships of Zimbabwe, the team felt it had finally been let off the leash and we happily indulged ourselves in golf, fishing trips, go-karting and a few glasses of wine in New Zealand. The sense of liberation was heightened by the fact that Lord MacLaurin had decreed that the outdated practice of room-sharing must finally end. I felt it was one of the earliest blows against those who seemed to want to treat us like children.

In our excitement, we should have reminded ourselves of one important thing. The media was on our case in a big way after our farcical failures in Zimbabwe and Auckland, and the arrival on tour of Dominic Cork. Cork, the most colourful character in the team, had been struggling to handle fame and the recent failure of his marriage, and had joined the tour late. Dom was good company and a brave cricketer who should have achieved more, but he could get over-excited and on this tour was almost sent home for misbehaviour. He brooded on the break-up of his marriage (something I could relate to) and had running battles with the Kiwi players that the management weren't happy about. And he would pull his shirt over his head after taking a wicket, which didn't go down too well with Lord MacLaurin.

It ought to have been no surprise then when, about two weeks from the end of the tour, Tuffers found himself being accused in an English tabloid of smoking dope in a restaurant in Christchurch. The charge proved false, but the fact the story surfaced at all showed how things stood with the media. And being the naive young fool I was, I'd failed to grasp that anyone might be interested in anything I did off the field, although with 30-odd Test caps I was now one of the higher-profile members of the squad. Just as I was showing signs of maturing as a player, I was about to show that I'd still got a lot to learn in life.

ON THE EVENING of the second one-day international in Auckland, several of us went out to celebrate a victory that had put England two up in the series. There was quite a group of us – a couple of Kiwis, Chris Cairns and Dion Nash, joined myself, Nasser (who was on his first full England tour for a few years), Athers and Tuffers. Management-wise there was nothing off-limits about this particular evening and we all intended to enjoy ourselves, including the skipper, who'd missed the game because of a bad back but like me was in better spirits after returning to form in the Tests. We ended up in a small bar somewhere in town that was absolutely heaving with people. I don't know about the others, but I got completely plastered very quickly.

There was a theory, and one to which I originally

subscribed, that the local student I met in that bar had been encouraged by a tabloid newspaper to go in search of a cricketer and a story. I don't know whether that was true, but whether Olivia Martin had planned what happened that night or not, the result was the same. She ended up coming back to my hotel and staying the night in my room. I remember waking up in the morning with the girl in my bed, as the previous night's events came flooding back to me. I felt sick.

The details of exactly what had happened were sketchy from halfway through the night, but even though I was sure we hadn't had sex – I was frankly too drunk – something had obviously gone on. I was already wracked with guilt even before the phone rang and I heard Nicky on the other end of the line. What I'd done sank in there and then. I heard myself telling Nicky that I'd got a heavy head after going out with the boys the night before for a few celebratory drinks. I thought, '*You fucking idiot . . . What have you done?*' I was disgusted and disappointed, and all the more so since I had succumbed in a three-and-a-half month tour with only about 10 days to go before we left for home.

I lived in blissful ignorance of what a disastrous mistake I'd made for a couple of weeks before the details of my one-night stand were splashed all over the *News of the World*, on my first Sunday back home. Looking back, I think what happened was that as Olivia Martin left my hotel she was approached by a local New

Zealand freelance and a *News of the World* reporter. They asked if she'd been with a player and if so, who was it and was she prepared to sell her story for a few thousand pounds? I learned later that there was also a reporter from the *Daily Mirror* hanging around on the lookout for stories too.

The first inkling I got of the impending story was the day before it came out. I was leaving the house to nip down to the shops when I was met by a couple of blokes jumping out of a car parked at the end of my drive. One had a camera, the other just said to me, 'Hey, Graham, I'd just like to ask you about this affair you had with a girl in New Zealand . . .'

My first reaction was, 'What affair?' At first, I genuinely didn't know what he was talking about and said so. But when he said, 'Well, we're running a story on it in the *News of the World* tomorrow,' alarm bells started ringing. I got in my car and drove off on my errand, but by this stage I was seriously worried. I'd worked out what they must be talking about, knew I'd done something wrong and knew I was going to have to confront Nicky with it. The fact I'd only been back home a few days made things all the more uncomfortable.

A warning Nicky had once made came back with a jolt: if ever I misbehaved, she'd said, that would be the end of our relationship. All I could now think was, '*What's going to happen when I tell her? We have a small baby. What's she going to do?*'

We'd arranged to go to the pub for lunch but, feeling physically sick with nerves, I could barely eat anything. My mood was not helped by the two reporters having followed us to the pub. I could see them having a laugh around the other side of the bar, smiling and apparently happy at what they'd achieved. They'd got a photograph of me coming out of the house and got a reaction from me, of sorts. I was trying to sit there with Nicky and Henry as calmly as I could, and make conversation with her, but inside I was reeling. It was lucky those guys didn't try and pull a camera and take a photo of me and Nicky together, or I don't know what I would have done.

I think it was then, while caught in their lair, that it finally dawned on me that my long-held hopes of playing my cricket and keeping my privacy had been an idle fantasy. *I was public property.*

I told Nicky in the car on the way home. It was a pretty short conversation. There was not much I could say other than the basic facts, that a girl I'd met in New Zealand was doing a story in one of the newspapers the next day. I admitted that I'd got drunk, that something had happened, but that it was nothing like as bad as she might think. I told her that we'd not had sex, but didn't admit that she'd stayed the night with me. Inside I was scared of what I might lose and was trying to play the whole thing down. Nicky was naturally pretty upset and disappointed. There were lots of tears. The next day –

the day the paper appeared with my story plastered over it – was Mothering Sunday. Not the greatest present I could have given the mother of my new child.

Naturally, this incident had a huge impact on both of us. It made me realize how important my family was to me and I was determined that nothing like that would ever happen again. Things were difficult at first, but Nicky soon saw how much I regretted the incident, and for a while it actually brought us closer together and made us stronger. But it also pushed us inside the four walls of our home. We were both less trusting of outsiders.

Although I knew what had happened was my fault, my attitude towards the media changed. I began to realize that there were people out there willing to do what they could to ruin people's lives, which angered me, and these fears proved justified when Nicky and I split up. The involvement of the newspapers then just brought more acrimony to the break-up, with many things printed that simply weren't true. Unbelievably, when I returned to New Zealand in 2002, the same local journalist who'd done the Olivia Martin story was on my case again, trying to persuade an Australian girl I went out with on that tour to write her story too, even though by then Nicky and I were apart, and I was trying to convince myself that things between us were over. Thankfully, she refused to cooperate.

One of the decisions Nicky took after the incident was to have nothing more to do with cricket, players or their wives, which was understandable but hard given my profession. She later told me that she'd wanted everything in her life to be perfect, and what happened in New Zealand had punctured the dream. I'd wanted everything in my life to be perfect too, but as we both discovered the world isn't like that. Perhaps we weren't very mature.

She didn't kick me out of the house, but nor did she properly draw a line under the incident. Over the next few years, until we began to break up, what happened in Auckland was perhaps only mentioned half a dozen times between us, and I always told her how much I regretted it, but she still found it hard to accept. She doubted my account and became suspicious about what might have happened on other tours. It is so easy to imagine and exaggerate all kinds of things. To make matters worse, Nicky had once said to me that she didn't see the importance of the father's role in the family anyway. Her own father hadn't been around and, according to her, she'd coped fine and it hadn't done her any harm – something with which I would certainly beg to differ. The whole thing put a strain on our marriage and my inclination to bottle things up intensified. We needed to talk things through properly but weren't capable of doing so. Perhaps because I'd spent so much time away we'd grown apart, and weren't as frank with each other as we needed to be. When you're so often away from home, it's easier to avoid facing up to things and that makes trust that much harder. When I look back, I wish I'd said more.

In contrast to what would happen later, I didn't allow this incident to affect my cricket. I had one of my best seasons that summer, in 1997, scoring heavily for Surrey in the championship and the Benson and Hedges Cup, which we won and, having seen England home in two out of three wins over Australia in the Texaco Trophy series, I finished as our leading batsman in the Ashes series, scoring most runs and topping the averages. I played a big part in the victory in the first Test at Edgbaston that gave us a rare series lead over Australia (one that predictably didn't last), Nasser and I sharing a record-breaking fourth-wicket stand of 288. Glenn McGrath was having difficulties with his rhythm and Shane Warne – who had a shoulder problem – didn't get the drift I always associated with him (that didn't last long either). We took full advantage to pave the way for a massive win.

Off the field, however, I did change. I became more protective towards myself and my family, and totally altered my behaviour. I became more insular and didn't socialize that well. When I was away from home, as Nicky wanted I made sure she knew my every move. I was very conscious of her feelings, that I'd publicly embarrassed us both, and that I needed to do the right thing by her. I wouldn't say I lived a dull life for the next four years, but I did stop going out with the lads to celebrate a win. I think in a way I was trying to make things up to her, to fix the mistake I'd made. I think it affected the way other people came to perceive me, too. I'd never been a huge socializer, but now if there was a party going on, they knew not to look to me to be its life and soul.

Part of me wanted to deny what had happened but I'd also been forced to face up to what was really important to me, and I was determined not to mess up further. With time Nicky and I were able to move on to another stage in our life together, and two years later Amelia was born.

When Nicky started her relationship with Kieron, she started going on about what happened in New Zealand and how she hadn't yet got her head round it, or forgiven me, even though it was five years in the past. She started asking whether I'd got a girl in my room when I was away again, things like that. I thought, *'We've moved on from there. What is so bad about our lives now?'* I think she was trying to make me feel guilty to excuse what she was doing. She tried to portray our marriage as having been terrible for ages, but in fact until Kieron came along things had been fine. I don't think people who knew us at that time would have said Nicky was unhappy either. Basically, I think, she wanted to change her life and take her share of the spoils.

If these were her tactics, they worked well. I was left trying to justify things I'd done years earlier and blaming myself for what had gone wrong.

TEN

Salvation

ONE SUNDAY EVENING in October 2002, a few weeks after I had pulled out of the Australia tour, I lay back in my bath in the deserted family house in Epsom. I had just dropped off Henry and Amelia back with Nicky. At this stage, my access to the children was not much of a problem and Nicky was allowing me to see them most weekends.

Always, at times like this, I felt very emotional and very down. I could not help thinking back to what Sunday evenings used to mean during my married life: putting the children to bed, reading them a story, kissing them goodnight. Now, what did I do? I said goodbye to them, got into my car and fought a losing battle to hold back tears as I drove home, whatever home now was. Opening the front door, there was nothing to look forward to. But this particular evening

I felt lower than ever. Emotionally, I think, I'd reached the end of the road. I had hit rock bottom.

I decided to run a hot bath and take with me a bottle of Scotch. And there I lay, allowing my feelings of frustration and despair to be gradually anaesthetized. I started to think to myself, '*How much longer can this process go on? Nicky and I have been apart for a year and I've shown no sign of improving my mental state. I'm so weak, I'm never going to be able to haul myself out of this situation, or stop feeling sorry for myself. I am going to be unhappy and alone for the rest of my life.*'

I was trapped. I was tired of looking back but didn't know how to move forward. How could I build a new life? If I had not been a public figure with a public profile, it might have been easier. I might have been able to recreate myself. I could have gone to night school, done classes or something, met some new people and made a fresh start. But being a well-known England cricketer, with a face some people would recognize and a career I couldn't pretend had never happened, it felt near-impossible to do anything. No way forward, no way back.

And so, with nowhere to go and no one to turn to, I started talking to God. I started talking out loud, saying a kind of prayer. I was asking for help more than anything. It was the first time in my life I'd openly said a prayer.

I was not a particularly religious person. My visits to church were pretty much confined to weddings and christenings, and one of the last times I'd been inside one was for Amelia's christening three years earlier. But I'd never been a disbeliever. I might not have actively worshipped God, but then I wasn't convinced that He did not exist either.

In fact, during the course of that year I'd become more convinced than ever that He did exist. That March, Ben Hollioake had been killed in a car crash in Western Australia. This was a terrible tragedy and, for those of us at Surrey who had been so close to him and Graham Kersey, who had died in similar circumstances five years earlier, it came as a doubly hard blow to take.

The news came through one morning while we were playing a Test match in Wellington. We were batting and I didn't actually hear about it until I was out and back in the dressing-room. I walked in, sat down and was just about to take my pads off when I saw Butch, in tears, come over from a corner of the room. He sat down next to me and said something like, 'I've got to tell you something . . .'

I was in tears for much of the rest of the day, numb with disbelief. I was lost for the rest of that game and so were most of us. We had to carry on – there were a couple of days still to go – but for the likes of myself and Butch, who had known Ben better than most, there seemed no point. Of course, I was in a pretty bad way mentally anyway, trying to come to terms with my divorce. It was a very tough few days, especially as I was unable to go to Perth for the funeral because we had another Test to play in Auckland a couple of days later. There was a lot of debate about whether the whole team should go but, in the end, only Nasser, as captain, made the journey. Instead, Butch organized our own memorial service to coincide with the funeral.

Ben was somebody I'd spent a lot of time with. Even though he was eight years my junior – he was 24 when he died – we'd enjoyed each other's company a lot. We naturally got on but I'd also taken a kind of paternal interest in his development. Ben had struggled to live up to the enormous expectations created by his brilliant start in international cricket when, while still a teenager, he'd smashed fifty in a one-day match against Australia in front of a full house at Lord's. He'd had a reputation as a hugely talented cricketer who was perhaps a bit too laid-back for his own good and Adam, his elder brother and our captain at Surrey, often asked me to talk to him because he didn't want to appear to be the one banging his little brother on the head. Perhaps he thought Ben would listen more to me, and I think there were times when he did. I had no doubt that, as a player, Ben would get there in the end and I encouraged him to do the things necessary to improve his game.

Ben had recently got back into the England one-day side – he'd been with us in New Zealand only a few weeks earlier – and I think the penny had finally dropped. Like Andrew Flintoff, another gifted all-rounder, Ben had taken time to grasp what international cricket was all about and, like Fred, would have gone on to shine on the big stage. To me, his being cut off when the big breakthrough was so close made his death all the more cruel and inexplicable.

As a person, Ben had very special qualities. If he'd taken time to grow up on the field, he was years ahead of himself off it. He gave so much. When I was going through bad times he was always so attentive, taking time out to try and make sure I was okay. I was never that thoughtful when I was his age. Most young men are wrapped up in their own lives and absorbed in getting to the next base, but perhaps the reason Ben's cricket took a while to mature was that he didn't want to overlook other things in life. He was a lad who seemed to be saying, 'I'll get there at my own pace. It may not fit in with everybody else's plans, but I'll get there in the end.' Perhaps that was why so many of us liked him, because we would have loved to have his refreshing attitude. He could live with success and failure just the same. Everyone loved Ben. He could walk into a place and light it up.

Death is bad enough when it hits the elderly – I lost all four of my grandparents in the space of 18 months and was very affected by that – but it is especially tragic when such young people as Ben and Graham are taken away. There seemed no rhyme or reason. I think

Graham's death, in particular, contributed to my irritation at the pettiness of authority; life and death were important, not whether you wore the right tie or shoes. These were two of the most popular lads in the Surrey dressing-room. You shouldn't lose people at that age. One of the hardest things for me was that I'd roomed with them both and had those sort of chats you have when you are away from home and bored, about what you might do when you stop playing and the deeper meaning of life.

At the time of Ben's death, my life was already in a mess. His loss seemed like just one more cross to bear, but also one more reason to question whether there was not more to our existence than just the here and now. I couldn't imagine that Graham and Ben, who gave so much, just didn't exist any more in some capacity. It didn't seem right then, and it doesn't seem right now. There had to be a reason why we were all put on this earth. To me, there had to be a pathway for each of us and there had to be somewhere our souls went when we died.

Their deaths had a massive impact on me. It was not something I was able to rationalize straightaway but, when things in my life improved, I thought about them a lot and my outlook changed. I started to appreciate how quickly life can be taken away from you. Obviously, I still cared about what I did as a sportsman but, once I'd resurrected my England career, I no longer felt that if it was to be gone the next day I would be devastated. Too much had happened to me. I remembered, too, the strength my grandfather had shown on his deathbed and that he felt confident he was going to a better place.

So, lying in my bath that autumn night, perhaps I was more inclined to believe that Someone might be listening if I called on God for help than I had been, say, a year earlier. Even so, I had to fight back the fear that praying out loud confirmed I was going crazy.

What I said to God was this. I know I have never spoken to You before, but if I have really been such a bad person, if I have really been so terrible, then fine, I accept everything that's coming next. But if I have not, and You are out there and You are listening, then all I ask for is my happiness back again. I will give up every penny I own, and hand back every great day I've ever had on the cricket field, just to have some happiness back again. Please, God, I ask only for one thing.

WHEN I PULLED out of the Australia tour, it had occurred to me that, by staying at home through the winter, something good might come of it. I didn't know what shape or form that 'good' might take, but I clung to the belief that something beneficial might present itself. It was a bit like when I left school and told my parents that I felt sure something would happen, and that if it did not, I'd make it happen.

Equally, I hadn't a clue how. Like I say, I felt trapped. But I knew things weren't going to change if I continued to stay in my house. By this stage, even I knew that. If I stayed at home, nothing was going to happen. It was up to me. It was my choice whether I went out the front door and faced up to a few things. It would be a very slow process but I felt it had to be done. I was still very much embarrassed in public because I knew I was still a topic of conversation. I'd met people who'd been through divorces of their own and who wondered why it was taking me so long to get over it. But that was just the way I was. I had a broken heart and a broken mind.

Then, one night Ally Brown asked me to go along to one of his benefit functions. I'd never been the best at turning up to such occasions and, in my state, would almost certainly have ducked out but, this time, I steeled myself to say yes. I felt I owed it to myself and to Brownie, who thoroughly deserved a big pay-day and had been such help to me in my troubles, to turn out. It was a fundraiser at Wimbledon dog-track, and I agreed to join his table and present one of the night's prizes. It was mid-November, and the first time I'd gone out socially in quite a while.

Unbeknown to me, Richard Thompson (the Surrey chairman) had invited along a Wimbledon neighbour of his called Amanda Duncan, who was in her early thirties and whose husband had recently left her for someone else after the birth of their first child. Like me, she was emotionally in a pretty fragile state.

Having arrived at the track, I'd gone over to the bar, picked up a drink and gone through to the dining area. I saw Thommo, went over to say hello and ended up talking to Amanda. We didn't know who each other was. I asked her what she did. She said she was a law student. 'Oh,' I said, 'you should talk to my wife about the law,' meaning divorce law. 'Don't talk to me about your wife,' she said, 'I'm in the middle of getting a divorce.' 'So am I,' I said.

At which point, we were off. People who are getting divorced can talk about it for ages and that's what we did. I think we were both trying to prove to the other that our circumstances were the more horrible!

I'd no idea that Amanda was alone. I thought she'd come along with a friend of Thommo's, Giles Fox. But when the time came for us to sit down for the meal, and Brownie came over and tried to usher me to his table, I said I was quite happy sitting with Amanda and so we sat together at her table for the rest of the evening. We laid a few bets and had several drinks, but I don't think we got round to eating much. At one point, I had to go up and present a prize, and I think it was then that Amanda found out who I was, although she wasn't much into cricket and my name didn't mean anything to her. I found out that we'd got a fair bit in common beyond the basic fact that we were separated; we had both been with our partners for about 11 years, and had both split up late the previous year. We'd both been on anti-depressants and, if she'd not quite had a breakdown, Amanda had been pretty close to one. She later told me how unfit I'd looked that night, how grey in the face I appeared.

At last, I'd found a soul mate. Amanda was a regular at a gym in Chelsea and she persuaded me to go along a few times over the next few weeks. Perhaps she was a bit shocked at the poor physical condition of a man supposed to be a professional sportsman. My dad had been going on at me for ages to train properly again, and now I really tried. Amanda and I had lunch together and started speaking a lot on the phone in the evenings. We spoke a lot about our respective predicaments. Well, mine mainly.

I think part of the attraction for Amanda was that she had found someone who was actually in a worst state than herself. She was able to throw her energies into helping me. She forced herself to be upbeat and tried to pull me out of my despair.

When she met me, I was really down; emotionally, I was still that broken man, lying in the bath, praying to God for salvation. When Amanda first asked me what I was going to do with myself in the future, I told her I didn't have a clue. I told her that I hadn't really done anything with my life. I'd played a bit of cricket, but what was that to anyone? I hadn't done anything else; I'd had no other training.

After I'd mentioned cricket, she'd gone onto the internet, looked me up and sent me a text message saying something like, 'It seems you've been rather clever with your bat.' Later, she tried to make me feel proud about what I'd done in sport. 'Surely, playing cricket for England has got to be a special experience . . . Not many people have done that . . .' But I didn't want to know. I told her I definitely never wanted to play for England again. I think she thought I was quite bitter about it.

I think fear lay behind a lot of my remarks. I'd had everything kicked out of me, and no longer had the energy to put myself back into the glare of publicity. I wanted to forget about international cricket. I could cope, I thought, with county cricket. That would be fine. But nothing more than that. I was simply too bruised.

Meeting Amanda was the first glimmer of light in my life for a long time. I went round to see my parents about a week later and told them I'd met someone. They could see I was quite excited. My dad was understandably pretty cautious. He was, like, 'Okay. This is really good. Maybe if this works out for a period of time, and helps you move on, then that's great.' One of the most important things was that as our relationship developed it made me think that perhaps I couldn't be such a bad bloke after all.

I'd been asked to do some TV work with Sky Sports, acting as a studio summarizer on their Ashes highlights programme presented by Ian Ward, a team-mate at

Surrey. It wasn't difficult stuff. Fortunately, it wasn't necessary to sit up through the night watching six hours of play because I couldn't have managed it. It was the first time I'd ever done something like that. It was good because it gave a purpose to my day, but it was also hard because I was being asked to show my face in public again, even if only in quite a controlled way.

To be honest, I was still play-acting at being a normal human being. All I had to do was put on a suit, be chauffeured across London to a studio and then sit there and spout authoritatively on a topic I didn't have to think too hard about. It probably gave the misleading impression that my life was in some sort of shape. In fact, I'd often only managed to drag myself out of bed shortly before leaving home.

I hadn't a clue where things were going to lead with Amanda. Little did I know how much she would help me move forward and revive my career. I had met somebody who made me happy, and gave me the strength to fight on if I had a bad day. To her I would owe everything.

Now disbelievers will say that my meeting Amanda was just one of those things, part of life. Maybe they are right, but maybe not. All I know now is that, by whatever means, that prayer I offered up in the bath was answered.

AT FIRST, I had no idea Amanda was religious. In fact, she was a Catholic, but had become quite cool about the whole thing after her husband, who was also a Catholic, left her. Understandably, that had seriously challenged her belief. But as we got to know each other better she encouraged me to take a relaxed approach to religion, to take the good bits out of it that might help me.

A couple of years later, I began to go more deeply into the whole thing. Amanda's older sister, Caroline, was more religious than she was. She prayed every day. Before the tour of South Africa, the three of us began going to our local church in Putney every Sunday and I began to learn more about Catholicism. I also began to visit our priest. At first I was a bit embarrassed and Caroline came along for company. Had you told me several years ago that Graham Thorpe might want to pray, I would have laughed at you. It turned out that the priest, who was a man in his mid-fifties, had converted to Catholicism in his late-thirties, about the age I was now. He made me realize that in religion badges are not handed out to you when you are born, allocating you membership to one sect or another. Religion can come to you at any stage of life.

I'm still treading quite carefully. I'm still studying and still learning and doing it at my own pace, but my faith has helped me cope with bad things, appreciate the good and decide how I want to be as a person and how I want others to view me. When bad things happen to you, you want to understand, and sometimes this makes you turn to another source. And that source for me at the moment is faith. But there's still plenty to be understood. It takes time and work to say, I believe in this, this and this. Caroline gave me my own Bible which I took away with me for the first time to South Africa. I still have a lot to learn but I think religion has now become an important, integral part of my life. When Nicky started making it difficult for me to see Henry and Amelia, it helped me come to terms with why she should want to do something that I found so hard to understand.

When I look back on my cricket career, I see someone who struggled to grasp life's bigger picture. I was aware that there were other considerations, such as family, and tried to put them first, but I was young and the demands of playing at the highest level were great. Despite my attempts to maintain some balance in my life, these demands consumed me. I got to know all about Wasim Akram's inswinger, Saqlain Mushtaq's doosra and Shane Warne's drifter, but my outlook was very shallow. I found out the hard way, I suppose, but I eventually came to realize that while cricket had rounded me in some ways, it had also led me into things I wouldn't do now. It led me down some paths that I now look at, and I know that they were wrong.

ELEVEN

Clearance

THE BIG PROBLEM is that a path that helps you succeed in sport doesn't always improve your life outside the game.

Sport is all about self-belief. Before a match, you have to keep reminding yourself how good you are, how you've been successful against this opposition before, and why you can do it again. Negative thoughts can creep up on you unawares, and you must be ready to stamp on them. Always think twice before opening a newspaper or switching on the TV sports channel in case some pundit has decided it's time to have a go at you. The fear of failure is something you don't even want to admit exists. You need to be single-minded and almost a little self-absorbed. As someone once said, top-level sport is not for well-adjusted people.

Batsmen need their confidence building up more than most. Typically, we survive many more balls than we get out to, and when we play well we rarely lose our wickets. Convincing yourself mistakes are things you simply don't make is not an easy state of mind to get into. What you are always trying to avoid is a minor flaw creeping in that starts to throw out other parts of your game as you try to correct it; otherwise, before you know it, you've completely forgotten how to bat.

But I also learned that to play well I had to be content with other aspects of my life. If my mind was distracted by personal problems, it was almost impossible to play consistently well, and the realization that my marriage might be failing eroded my self-confidence. Cricket was sometimes an escape, but never for long, and in the end the stress wore me down. Batting is incredibly mentally demanding, and you have to be extremely focused to play match-winning innings in Test matches. At the best of times, I found Test cricket mentally and emotionally draining. In my darkest days, it was a challenge I simply could not meet.

For almost two years, from 2001 to 2003, my self-esteem took a battering and, hard as I tried to tell myself I was still a top player, I simply couldn't maintain the pretence. That was why I returned from India, why I dropped out after the Lord's Test, and why I pulled out of the Ashes tour. Visualizing success is a big part of making success happen, but I just couldn't envisage myself doing well any more at those times.

Looking back, there are four main things that got me

back on track. Amanda and religion, and an attempted 10-day reconciliation with Nicky (which I'll come to) when I finally realized that Nicky and I could never be together again, and that our marriage was a wreckage that wasn't fixable. The moment that became completely clear, I became a totally different person and almost overnight my cricket improved. In 2003 I came close to playing as well as I knew I could. I was fluent and focused, and it was a long time since that had happened. The fourth factor was Adam Hollioake.

I was lucky to have Adam as Surrey captain at this time. Ben's death had forced Adam to look at life afresh, as it had me, and it brought us closer. We chatted about the bad things that had happened to us and, although I can't compare divorce to death, I knew what Adam meant when he said that you have to get mental clearance before you can move on. He had felt guilty at how he'd sometimes treated Ben, telling him he wasn't working hard enough at his game and things like that. His determination after Ben's death to enjoy his cricket and not get too uptight about it struck a chord with me. When I went back to playing in 2003 I too knew there were more important things in life.

With my mind wiped clean of so much pain and confusion, coming back and playing for Surrey that summer felt like going for a walk in the country on a beautiful morning. It wasn't like going back to how I'd been two years earlier; I was actually miles further forward.

Mentally, I was a much stronger player. I could enjoy the good days for what they were. As for the bad days, they meant nothing.

WHEN I LOOK back on that roller-coaster summer of 2003, it so nearly never got off the ground. Under a different captain and in a different era, Surrey would probably have run out of patience with me far sooner than they did. Keith Medlycott, the coach, was especially understanding. But even they could not indulge me forever. They had asked me to sort myself out the previous autumn, I'd had all winter to do it, and yet when the season began I still seemed to be tangled up in my personal problems. It was not long before the club felt they could not allow the situation to continue.

By this stage, Surrey were a very strong team and not even those fully committed to their cricket could be guaranteed a place in the side. Mark Butcher, who had scored a century in his last Test in Australia three months earlier, was left out of the first game against Lancashire and I didn't escape the axe for long. It must have been obvious to Adam and everyone else in the team that when the season began I was still struggling to concentrate. I played poorly against Lancashire, and seemed totally distracted for our first National League match at Chelmsford. Adam was the one who sat me down and told me I was to be left out.

I had to sit out the next three championship matches,

and the fact I'd gone back to Nicky certainly played its part. There were those at the club like Adam and Richard Thompson who knew my having gone back to her meant I clearly couldn't be properly focused. Thommo had seen me with Amanda over the previous few months and thought I was moving in the right direction. Now I'd done a U-turn. I learned later that the club had discussed my situation in the light of this news and viewed me as unfit to play four-day cricket, though they allowed me to stay in the one-day side.

I wasn't at all happy about this and worried about what it might mean for my career. But, as Surrey were aware, other things were dominating my thoughts. Had I been in the right frame of mind, I would have been bashing the doors down, demanding to know what was going on and telling the club I needed to play first-team cricket if I was going to get a place in the England side – behaving just like Butch did when he was left out against Lancashire. But I didn't.

Going back to Nicky. This was all I had wanted for the previous 18 months and yet, when it finally happened, it was nothing like I'd hoped for and almost immediately felt wrong. I quickly discovered that simply too much had happened for it to work, and that we could never get back together.

Although Nicky was living with Kieron, her attitude towards me changed as soon as she got wind of Amanda. Until then, perhaps she thought she could get me back whenever she wanted, but Amanda's arrival on the scene threatened to change all that. Maybe it made Nicky really question whether she wanted everything between us to be over, although it seemed a bit late in the day for that considering she had bought a house with her boyfriend, and had been living with him for over a year. When she first sent me a text message saying she wanted me back, I'd been working at Sky on the New Year's Test in Sydney. By the time I'd reached Amanda's house, she said I looked like I'd seen a ghost. It's certainly how I felt.

That was to be the start of a four-month process of me being drawn back towards my family by Nicky, culminating in my going back to live with them in early May. Nicky tried everything to get me back – she said she was unhappy with Kieron, she could never love him, and, worst of all, she used the children to make me return by starting to make it hard for me to see them while we were living apart. It was a very hard situation to deal with. I now had serious reservations about whether Nicky and I could ever work anything out as a couple, but felt I had to try for the sake of the children. Give me a smidgen of a chance to go back to them and I had to try it, even if it was to the detriment of everything else. To that extent, Nicky still had me on a string and she knew it.

It was the children I went back for. For the first time since we split up, Nicky had begun giving me less access to Henry and Amelia. Before then, there had been a few ups and downs but, generally speaking, access had not been a major problem. Before Christmas, I had seen them most weekends and had taken Henry to his first Chelsea match. We saw them beat Manchester City 5–0. Once, when I told Nicky all I wanted was good access, she warned me to be careful – 'behave yourself or you know what could happen'. I took this to mean that she might go and live in South Africa with Kieron, and take the children with her. She never made this threat directly, but I think she wanted to remind me who was in control. By the time I finally went back to her, I had not seen Henry and Amelia for three months. It was a strange way for Nicky to get me back, but it worked. By then, my head was totally screwed up.

Leaving Amanda was traumatic. I'd finally sold the old family house in Epsom a few weeks earlier, and had been staying with her since then. Now I was leaving her to go back to my wife. It was totally the wrong way to treat her, but I felt I had to do it. It was as though I had to try going back to Nicky just to prove to myself it wouldn't work, and that I had at least tried to do the right thing by the children. As I packed my things into the car Amanda told me Nicky would chew me up and spit me out – she'd finish me off this time. She was very hurt, but also felt afraid for me too. She told me it would never work. Of course, she was right. Although the times during the day when I saw the children were fine, it hit home in the evenings once the children had gone to bed how crazy the situation was. I didn't even like Nicky! I realized it was impossible for me to be happy with this woman again. I thought, *'You've shown me no compassion. I just don't have any love left for you. You've taken it all away.'*

It was a situation that gave me no pleasure. I knew then that I was never going to live with Henry and Amelia again, which was heartbreaking. But even as I drove away from Nicky's, having stayed for barely 10 days, I knew that I'd released my demons and could now get to grips with things.

Everything was suddenly clear. For a start, I knew I had done the right thing. I knew, too, that Nicky would never have any emotional pull on me ever again. Nicky was furious, and I knew there would be a backlash with the children. Sure enough, there was: Nicky ensured that from now on I saw them much less often. I didn't know what would happen with Amanda but I said to myself that I would try to win her back. We'd just about stayed in contact but I didn't want to jump to conclusions. I took out a six-month rental on a flat in Wimbledon to be near her.

I knew, too, that I could finally get back to thinking properly about my cricket, which I'd been unable to do even though the season was well into its second month. Mentally, I was a totally different person from that day onwards. I felt free. My recovery had finally started.

ONE OF THE reasons I grew impatient with the way the England team was run before Duncan Fletcher's time was that I'd seen how well things could be run at Surrey, and what could happen when players were treated like grown-ups and given responsibility.

Everything changed at Surrey when David Gilbert, a former Australia fast bowler, came in as coach in 1996 and Adam Hollioake, who'd grown up in Melbourne and already led the side a lot as Alec Stewart's deputy, took over the captaincy the following year. I viewed them as the perfect match, two Australians at heart with a positive attitude and willingness to take a fresh look at things and cut the crap out of the dressing-room. As had sometimes happened with England, peripheral things sometimes assumed more importance than the winning and losing. But Dave and Adam put an end to that. They ripped down the wall in the dressing-room between capped and uncapped players, and dismantled a few other silly traditions. There had been administrative problems too, but a new committee came in that was fully behind the players.

The way they ran the side was exceptional. They brought an honesty to our team which I loved. They created a team that governed itself, at least in terms of discipline. For example, if you were late – something that could happen in London traffic – you weren't punished the first two times but faced a hefty fine the third time. Adam, who'd had his problems under earlier regimes like I had, once said that the last thing he wanted was to be bollocked by the coach for being late. He already knew he was late and had apologized to the team; was it really necessary to punish him further? Not if it was a genuine accident. It was an attitude thing. You know if you are letting us down, he would say; just make sure you don't carry on doing it. Surrey were often described as a team of difficult players but that wasn't true under Adam, who was extremely competitive but didn't want to add to the pressure we were under. There was enough of that already, he reckoned.

Chris Lewis had a reputation as a difficult player but was handled well by Adam and, in return, gave Surrey his best years. He was a flamboyant character, but could relax with us in a way that he was perhaps unable to do at less cosmopolitan clubs. Like me, he wasn't the world's greatest timekeeper but he never really let us down, and no one threw the book at him. Even so, he was a huge talent who should have achieved more. On the one hand, he tried to protect his body so he could play longer, and on the other he sometimes got bored spending eight hours a day playing cricket.

People often say anyone can captain a strong team and Surrey were obviously strong. But I don't necessarily agree with that. Things didn't work that well before Adam came along. There was little continuity in those days: like me, Stewie was often away playing for England, but for about five years he was still officially club captain. And, for some reason, before Adam got the job in 1995, there was no officially designated deputy and various people tried their hand at leading in Alec's absence.

In 1994, when I was briefly out of the England side, I had a go and took to it quite well. I'd done a bit of captaincy in schools cricket, but then you often got the job simply because you were one of the best players, but now there was more to it; you had to handle people. It was a good thing for me to do at that time. I was about 25 and had the respect of the dressing-room because I'd played for England. I enjoyed talking to bowlers about our plans, and could be quite ruthless. I remember being warned by the umpires at Trent Bridge for ordering Cameron Cuffy to go round the wicket and bomb Tim Robinson with short balls, but I didn't see what was wrong. After all, Robinson had opened the batting for England. Unfortunately, Robinson ended up retiring after Cuffy hit him on the forearm.

Stewie didn't really want to relinquish the captaincy, and came up with the honorary captain tag, but having an England player captaining the side didn't really work. There was a time when Stewie and I played in a Test against the West Indies in Birmingham that finished early, and he told me I needn't turn up for a Sunday league match against Essex the next day – except he didn't realize that Grahame Clinton, then the coach, was expecting me. Before central contracts came in, England players felt under great pressure to perform for their counties. We felt a loyalty to our clubs, but often were so drained after a Test that we might have been there in body but not in mind. Dave was one of the first to understand this and, after the Edgbaston Test in 1997, gave me a few days off to recover. When I came back, I scored 100 not out against Yorkshire to win the game and he said, 'That's the benefit of rest.'

We'd had a strong group of players for a few years but needed a strong personality to run things, and that's what Adam did. We were desperate to do well. What he did was stop us making excuses about losing players to England, and made us focus on putting the trophies in the cabinet we knew we ought to be winning. We all grew up a bit under him, and perhaps learned to express ourselves a bit better. Under him we were county champions in 1999, 2000 and 2002, and also won the national league twice, the Benson and Hedges Cup twice and the Twenty20 Cup. That was an impressive haul. But I think we should possibly have won even more.

If Adam provided the inspiration, Dave – and later Keith Medlycott, who took over as coach in 1998 – made sure we were up to speed with the latest technology to make sure we didn't squander our advantages. At a time when the fixture list was even busier than it is now, Dave got us using videos to analyse our games and those of the opposition. When we beat Kent in the first of our Benson and Hedges Cup victories in 1997, we spent the night before watching videos of their batsmen and bowlers, and came up with game-plans which we executed to perfection. Another massive factor behind our three championships was the signing of Saqlain Mushtaq, the Pakistani off-spinner, who Dave snapped up after spotting him bowling in a one-day tournament in Australia. Armed with one of the best mystery balls around, Saqlain gave us the ability to finish off games quickly that once would probably have slipped out of our reach. He took more than 50 wickets in each of our championship-winning seasons at an amazing rate of about six per game.

But it was Adam's team. If people were being petty, or talking rubbish, he'd tell us to shut up. If anyone had a suggestion, he'd listen, but he'd make the final decisions. He was also very good at admitting to his mistakes. If we lost a game and he thought he'd made the wrong bowling change, he'd say so. And because he'd said it, he could still do the same thing again and you'd still follow him, and the next time it might work. The team drew a lot of strength from that. I look back on some one-day games and wonder how on earth we won. The opposition would need something like 20 off five overs with five wickets left, Adam would run up and bowl these bloody loose-cannon deliveries with split fingers, get in the batsmen's faces and get a bite out of them. That's all we'd need. He'd created something and, before you knew it, we'd won the game. He was a true leader. And he was big on celebrating. Whenever we won, he made sure we celebrated together and, when we won the first of our championships, we partied all night in the dressing-room. I played about half Surrey's matches that year and about the same the next, so although I wasn't a regular I felt I'd played a part.

Perhaps my best innings was a big hundred against Hampshire, our main rivals, at Guildford in 1999. Adam came up with a team song that had all our names in it, and ended with a line about the opposition, 'Who the fuck are you?!' He built up a great camaraderie, and it brought us all very close.

I didn't play much for Surrey in 2002, the season following Ben's death, but when I did I went into games trying to draw inner strength from Ben's memory, and I tried to view him as a friend who was still alongside me in spirit. If I wasn't around any more, I wouldn't want people to make too much of a song and dance about it and I'd still want them to enjoy their lives, and I think that's what we tried to do. We won the championship at a canter.

After Ben died, Adam became even bigger on making sure we enjoyed our cricket. He was still determined to win, but if we didn't he didn't mind as long as we'd tried our best. Adam had always liked to do things differently, but now he was keen we didn't just do things for the sake of it. If we wanted to play football for 15 minutes to warm up then we would, and if we wanted to wear tracksuits to the ground we could, just so long as we went onto the pitch totally committed to winning. But by the end of Adam's captaincy, he was looking tired and things had perhaps become a bit ragged, but I loved his attitude and it was just what I needed at the time I made my comeback.

I think it was because of this enlightened outlook that I was allowed back after being left out for those three championship matches early in the 2003 season. They could have pulled the plug on me altogether, in which case things would have turned out very differently in my career, but thankfully they didn't.

In my new mood of determination after I left Nicky, I made sure I was quickly on the phone to Adam and Medders to tell them what had happened. You may have heard this before a few times, I said, but I'm clear of everything now. This time, I *am* clear. Earlier regimes might have taken a bit of convincing, but this set-up trusted you to be honest, and they gave me another chance.

Fortunately, I'd somehow managed to get a few runs in the one-day team, so they reckoned if it was true that I'd sorted out my domestic affairs, then I might do something in the championship.

There was also an opening because Butch and Stewie were going off to play in the first Test against Zimbabwe at Lord's. Surrey had such a strong squad that they could have found decent replacements without me, but as I was claiming to be okay they obviously thought it was sensible to give me a go. I was brought back at Essex and scored fifty in my first innings, although perhaps equally significant was the fact that I was a lot chirpier on the field and in the dressing-room. It must have been obvious from my mood that I'd got my enthusiasm back, and that I wanted to be out there. And with a bat in my hand I felt good. I could feel my game coming back. I was actually enjoying playing and looking forward to what was going to happen, rather than brooding on the past.

Within the next week, I'd scored two hundreds, one in a televised game at Somerset in the C&G Trophy and the other in the championship against Sussex at the Oval. The innings at Taunton was a big moment. It won us the game and I played really well; *Wisden* described it as an 'exquisite' performance. It was the first time Amanda had watched me in a game on TV, and she was struck by how happy I looked.

In the dressing-room afterwards, as our celebrations began, Adam stood up and said he wanted to say a few words to me. Why Adam had so much as a captain was that he was prepared to wear his heart on his sleeve. He wasn't afraid to say what he thought, whether it meant handing out criticism or praise; in fact he saw it as an essential part of his job. He said that I'd been through some very hard times, for quite some time, and that he just wanted to welcome me back and say Thorpey, really well done. It was quite a special moment.

TWELVE

England Again

MAYBE I can still do it . . . really do it.

This was all that went through my head after I'd followed that hundred at Taunton with another against Sussex in the early weeks of the 2003 season. After all I'd been through, and my determination only a few months earlier to box up any thoughts of myself as an England cricketer and bury them somewhere deep in the back of my mind, it seemed an outrageous and dangerous idea. But I couldn't stop it surfacing.

Part of the problem was the timing of this sudden remembering of how to really bat. The day after the Somerset match, the England selectors were announcing their first team of the summer – the one-day squad for the NatWest Challenge against Pakistan and the triangular NatWest Series with South Africa and Zimbabwe. Of course, I'd very publicly retired from international one-day cricket the previous year but, at the start of the season, I had said to a few enquiries from reporters curious to see me shambling back, that if ever England were interested in me again I would be available for both forms of the game.

But two things need to be said about that. First, I said this because I sincerely felt that after pulling out of the Australia tour I was in no position to pick and choose which games I might play for my country. If they decided they wanted me for one-dayers, who was I to insist it was Tests or nothing? Second, at that time I didn't believe for a minute I'd got a future with England because I was still in a very distracted state, being on the verge of going back to Nicky and putting very little into my cricket. But now, after making several reasonable one-day scores for Surrey culminating in a top innings to win a televised C&G Trophy game, the case for recalling me didn't seem quite so ludicrous. Maybe they'd remember my words to the press, go with a gut instinct and just name me.

Of course, they didn't.

When I went out and took 156 off Sussex the very next day, I was far from being the only one wondering what it might mean for me and England. That was a Friday, and on the Saturday the selectors were announcing another squad, this time for the second Test against Zimbabwe. The Saturday papers speculated whether England would be recalling the formerly wayward but now in-form G P Thorpe, and I must admit I got a bit sucked in by all the talk. I'd gone back to Amanda on the Friday evening and said to her, 'Right. I want to get back in . . . I want to give it my best shot and get back into the England side.' I couldn't remember the last time I'd said those words and really meant it. Scoring those two hundreds had made me realize I'd still got the energy and, from that point on, I started training harder than I'd ever done.

Deep down, I knew they wouldn't pick me that Saturday. I'd come up on the rails too late; the selectors had not had time to sound me out properly. I'd had no contact with any of them. Four days earlier, I might not have even warranted a mention in their phone calls. And England had trounced Zimbabwe in the first Test at Lord's the previous week; why should they want to change a winning side? The most obvious candidates to make way for me, Robert Key and Anthony McGrath, did not really deserve to be dropped.

I wasn't surprised that I hadn't been picked but, though I didn't want to admit it to myself, I was disappointed. The fact that no one had been in touch made me realize I was some distance from a return. I actually found the whole thing a bit unsettling. It was one thing for me to rule myself out of ever playing for England again, but another for the selectors to come to the same conclusion. I'd always had faith in the Duncan Fletcher regime. It wasn't petty and not in the habit of holding things against people. I knew my circumstances had changed totally in the past few weeks, but perhaps the selectors didn't know.

I took the plunge and phoned Duncan. During my darkest days, I'd remembered his words to me on the Lord's balcony the previous year. 'What are you going to do?' It had taken me a long time to find an answer, and now I had it. Cricket was what I wanted to do. And now here I was, back again, knocking on his door and this time really meaning it. I told him I'd seen the press were starting to connect me with the England side again, and wanted to state my position in case anyone asked him about me. And, to be honest, I wanted to make sure he knew how keen I was. I explained to him what had recently happened with Nicky, and how I'd now got complete 'clearance'. I was playing good cricket again. Hopefully he could see that from my scores. I asked him where I might stand with the selectors.

He told me that they were not going to consider me for one-day cricket – no problem there, as far as I was concerned – but the door was firmly open to me in Test cricket. 'You score runs, and prove that the ability and hunger is still there,' he said, 'and I'll be considering you.'

I was relieved. He seemed prepared to judge me purely in cricketing terms, and I couldn't really ask for more. But it was also very clear I was in a queue, and not necessarily near the front. Drop out of the picture for even a short time and things move on. You are indispensable one day, surplus to requirements the next.

THE SUMMER turned into one of mounting frustration. There was a gap of several weeks before England picked their next Test squad, for the first match in their five-match series against South Africa, the showpiece of the season.

I needed to do what Duncan had said and score runs in the championship. The first problem was that the new Twenty20 Cup – which Surrey won – took centre stage for most of June and, by the time we got back into four-day cricket, I'd lost a bit of rhythm. I made 46 against Middlesex and 68 and 46 against Kent, but at Warwickshire in our last match before the England selectors met, I didn't score many and felt a bit scratchy.

I don't know whether it affected me, but some of the selectors came to see me play during that match at Edgbaston. I think Grav, Rod Marsh and Geoff Miller were all there at various stages. Miller came and had a chat. I got the distinct impression that they were unsure about me. I'd spoken to Grav before, and he'd assured me he'd tell the rest of the panel that I was adamant my troubles were behind me, but despite what Duncan had said about assessing me on my cricket form I felt some of his colleagues still needed convincing about my state of mind. Miller wanted to know everything about my situation. 'We've heard it all before about how you are okay,' he said. 'What's changed? What happens if something goes wrong?' All I could do was fully explain how my personal life stood and assure him I was on the right track. I think there was also a feeling that I'd ballsed up with England once too often, and should serve penance or even be written out of plans forever. I was only a month away from my 34th birthday and suspected I was going to have to go the extra yard just to get a sniff of a chance.

Although I could sense their scepticism, I also felt that they wouldn't have bothered to come and see me if they weren't at least thinking of picking me, but rather than fill me with confidence this thought only made me ridiculously nervous when I batted a second time, for what turned out to be a terrible innings of nought. I was angry with myself for getting into such a state. I thought, '*How many times have you played in front of England selectors?*'

But, in a sense, I was right to be anxious because the selectors were split over whether to recall me. Much later, Duncan told me that he personally would have had me back in the side earlier, but I heard on the grapevine that others had voted against me. I feel sure that Rod – who had a reputation as a no-nonsense Aussie – doubted me most. I think he'd got his own agenda.

He'd been head of the England National Academy for two years, but this was his first summer as an England selector and he was keen to push forward his young players. That was fair enough, but his philosophy was very different to Duncan's, and my case was only one of a number over which the two of them clashed.

Duncan didn't want to casually discard experience; the view he often expressed to me was that as long as you were committed to the job, it didn't matter how young or old you were. Which, as far as I was concerned, was great to hear.

Sure enough, I wasn't chosen. The only change to the batting was Andrew Flintoff, fit again after a shoulder problem, who came back in for Rob Key, although Grav publicly said that the matter of McGrath versus Thorpe had been 'well debated'. But now things started getting more complicated. After an awful England performance in the field in the first Test, Nasser suddenly resigned the captaincy on the last day of the game. He'd been in charge four years, which is a long time in such a demanding and high-profile job, and I suspect he felt he'd taken the side as far as he could. He had dragged us from a pretty low state, and certainly helped us become a tougher, more organized side. That he'd given up the captaincy of the Test side only a few months after resigning as one-day leader suggests he'd run out of energy, and it turned out that Michael Vaughan, the new leader, had to give him a pep talk to get him focused on his future in the side as a batsman. Nasser was feeling disillusioned, and it might not have taken much to persuade him to give up his place altogether.

Marcus Trescothick, meanwhile, had chipped a finger and the selectors needed to call up someone as cover for Lord's. Amanda and I were having lunch in Wimbledon when Grav rang, and told me they'd decided to go with the uncapped Middlesex opener Andrew Strauss. At least they'd phoned and told me. In the end, Tres passed himself fit to play and Strauss was not needed, but England were outplayed and lost by an innings.

Naturally I didn't want to see England lose, but this result raised the possibility of changes to the batting for the third Test because the top six certainly hadn't done much at Lord's. McGrath was looking the most vulnerable. Just as Strauss was a logical choice as cover for Tres, so I might be a logical replacement for McGrath in the middle order.

Time for another twist. Over the very weekend the selectors were meeting, my creaking back decided to go into spasm. When Grav called to tell me they were thinking of picking me, and ask me how I felt about it, after a lot of soul-searching I decided I had to tell him I was struggling to be fit. I said that if I could delay a decision for a few days, the spasm could well have passed, but if they wanted a decision now, I would have to say that I couldn't guarantee my availability. Maybe I should have just tried to ride it out – said I was experiencing a bit of back stiffness but was sure I'd be okay – but I could imagine how it would have gone down if I'd hobbled into the nets at Trent Bridge barely able to hold my bat. They really would have shipped me off to the knacker's yard. And I suppose, too, I didn't want to go into what was probably my last chance with England only half fit.

If I was going to play again, I wanted to be fully fit, not winging it.

So they went with Ed Smith instead. Smith had not played for England before, but he had been reeling off one century after another for Kent so he deserved his chance. I knew England were bound to give him a decent run in the side. The days of dumping people unceremoniously after one or two games were long gone, and I reckoned Smith was in for the remainder of the series, which proved to be the case. I feared my last chance had gone.

Of course, sod's law dictated that the spasm subsided and I was able to play for Surrey in their championship match at Whitgift School that overlapped with the Test. I know a few critical remarks were passed in the press questioning how I could be fit to play for my county but not my country, but that's just the way things went. I couldn't have done anything about it. Maybe I didn't help myself by scoring 99, but what had turned into a roller-coaster ride around the margins of the England side seemed to galvanize me back into form. I followed up with 87 and an unbeaten 52 at Grace Road. And then it happened.

Nasser broke a toe during the fourth Test in Leeds, or rather a ball from Andrew Hall broke it for him. By now, he'd got himself mentally back and had helped England level the series with a battling century on a difficult wicket in Nottingham. Even after the break he was unwilling to give up his place without a fight. He talked about playing in a specially made cast for the final Test against South Africa at the Oval – which England needed to win to draw the series after losing at Headingley – but was overruled by England's chief medical officer, Peter Gregory.

It was a Saturday afternoon when the phone rang. I was in Leeds. Surrey had just finished a championship game in Manchester, and we were due to play Yorkshire in the National League the next day. Amanda had come up to join me for the weekend, and we were having lunch at Harvey Nichols when the phone rang.

'Hello, Thorpey? . . . It's Grav here . . .'

'Oh, hello mate, how are you?'

'I'm fine . . . Look, we've picked you for the last Test match . . . you're in the squad. It's a like-for-like replacement for Nasser . . .' There was a silence as I tried to take in this astounding news.

'Oh, okay . . .' I muttered. Now that I'd heard the words I'd long dreamed about, I wasn't jumping out of my box the way I thought I would. Looking back, I can imagine what Grav was thinking. '*Christ, we've picked him and he's gone flaky.*'

'That's good news?' he asked.

'Yeah, right. That's really good news . . . Brilliant. Thanks.'

I WAS EXCITED, really excited, but the trouble was I was bloody scared too. It wasn't like the previous year, when I could no longer stand the public spotlight, although the thought of the close attention of the media in the build-up to the game made me feel sick to the bottom of my stomach. What really worried me was whether I was actually still good enough to play for England. I'd been out for 14 months, a long time in international sport.

I knew you could lose it in no time because I'd seen it happen. You could score runs in county cricket, but at international level the eyes and feet were simply no longer up to speed. I'd seen it happen to Gooch and Gatting on my first Ashes tour. They'd wanted to go out on a high but it had proved a tour too far.

For two months, jostling with the thought 'Maybe I can still do it' was the chilling fear, 'Maybe I can't.' Those two hundreds in three days in May had made me desperate to get back my England place, but I still remained wracked with doubt. An inner pessimistic voice kept saying, '*Have you still got it? Do you really want it? I know how focused you have to be, how stressful it is . . . I'm enjoying things at Surrey, why not stick to that? At least I can't fuck up again.*'

When I'd pulled out of the Australia tour, I'd looked finished and reasonably enough many people had written my sporting obituary. I remember a piece by Simon

Barnes in *The Times* in which he'd said something like, 'Sadly, I don't think we'll ever see this man play for his country again. But at least he's got a perspective on life . . .' At the time, I pretty much accepted his verdict. I thought, '*Maybe he's right. I'm not sure I'll ever get back up there again.*'

Amanda grew exasperated at my negative attitude and tried to prod me out of it. She'd actually start agreeing with me, saying that I was right, I *was* too old to get back, *especially* considering the state of my back. Then my pride would kick in and send me off in the opposite direction. 'I've played for England for 10 years, I know what it takes . . .' Amanda was being very clever. She knew my playing again would remove a lot of the bitterness, guilt and frustration locked inside me. Caroline, her sister, was the same. 'Ah, you're going to play for England again,' she'd say. And I'd mumble something like, 'Er, well, maybe . . .'

I was a bag of nerves for the next few days. I didn't get many against Yorkshire and was out to Anthony McGrath, as it happened. I went down with the shits, I was so nervous. A friend of Amanda's came round with some herbal calming tablets for me when she heard the state I was in. Although I'd still got my flat in Wimbledon, I was by now spending most of my time at Amanda's.

By this stage, Amanda was cheerfully optimistic. 'What if you get a hundred?' she'd say.

'Don't . . . don't even *say* it,' I groaned. She didn't know much about cricket in those days.

Caroline gave me a good-luck chain to wear round my neck. 'Wear this when you're batting,' she said, 'and I'll pray for you . . .' I was slightly reluctant. I wasn't a superstitious person. Unlike some players, I didn't put on my kit in a certain order or follow precise routines before I went out to bat. Didn't really believe in luck. Wasn't in the habit of clinging to things desperately in the hope they'd get me through. But something made me say, 'Okay, I'll put it on. I'll wear it . . .'

By the time I left on the Tuesday for the Oval and the team hotel, Amanda was pretty glad to see the back of me. I'd become a nightmare to live with. Those close to me assured me they'd love me whether I scored nought or 100.

I was called to give a press conference in the Long Room. There was quite a lot of interest in my return, as you'd imagine. Typically downbeat, I took the line that simply getting back in the side was enough. To an extent, after how low I'd sunk and how much I'd had to deal with, this was how I felt. I *was* happy just to be picked again. But I also felt that this was the best way to deal with all the hype. The last thing I wanted was to pump up people's expectations.

Someone like Darren Gough would have talked himself up because he's that sort of character, but not me. Maybe I was a little too low-key. Amanda was driving in the car and heard a radio report that Graham Thorpe was saying he was unsure he had still got what it took to play Test cricket. She called me later to say, 'What did you say that for?!', and she was right, it wasn't a thought I should have shared with the world!

Although I did regard my selection as a victory in itself, I knew it couldn't really be as simple as that. England hadn't picked me to be a passenger. They wanted me to do something and help them win a must-win game. My biggest fear was that I would make a fool of myself, and my anxiety was hardly eased by the memory of my last big comeback. In 2000, I had been recalled to the England Test side quite late in the summer following my decision to stay at home with my family rather than tour South Africa – another case of my being made to wait and not walking straight back into the team – and naturally there was a fair bit of interest when I finally returned for the third Test against the West Indies at Old Trafford.

Of all the ducks I collected in my career, I can honestly say that in that instance I was probably most blameless, because the first ball I faced that Friday afternoon was among the best I ever received. Batsmen should never make excuses but it was a bit dark – it often is in Manchester – when Courtney Walsh ran in with his arms wheeling all over the place as usual. All I saw was his action and thought he must have been having a bit of a joke. Maybe he was treating it like one of those benefit games when the bowler runs up and just before delivery slips the ball into his pocket . . . I didn't know where it had gone. I looked for it but never found it. All of a sudden it hit me on the foot. Courtney had bowled me a superb slower ball and I'd lost it in the darkness of the hospitality boxes above the sightscreen. He told me later that he and Brian Lara, standing at slip, had come up with the idea separately: they'd both worked out that his hand was coming up over the sightscreen, and out of the dark windows of the boxes above. G P Thorpe lbw Walsh 0.

I'd trudged back to the dressing-room feeling pretty stupid, and was just putting down my bat when I caught sight of Athers in the corner. He would sometimes see the funny side of people falling on their face and was sniggering away. I couldn't help smiling, 'That was a good comeback, wasn't it, Ath?' He just pissed himself laughing.

I'd never seen Courtney use that ball before, but he did me with it again at the Oval two games later, this time when I'd got 40 to my name. By the time I went out to face him in the second innings, for perhaps the only time in my career I didn't have a clue what to do. I started lunging forward to avoid getting trapped by a slower ball I couldn't pick up, but then he began bouncing me, so I had to drop back. I didn't know whether I was coming or going. I hung around for more than an hour for ten runs before tamely pulling Walsh to square leg.

If I was to be out first ball this time, again at the Oval, now in 2003, I wasn't sure I'd be able to smile again. I just kept thinking back to that India match at Lord's. I so much wanted that humiliation not to be the end. Now I'd got my chance. But I certainly didn't want to replace one humiliation with another.

THIRTEEN

Resurrection

WHICHEVER WAY I looked at it, I was now facing the biggest challenge of my career. Any big match always brought pressure and I was used to dealing with it, but sometimes it was easier than others. To me, the key was getting relaxed to just the right extent, which was tricky. Even the best sometimes got it wrong. Crave success too much and you ended up taut as a drum, and unable to do yourself justice; too casual, could be equally disastrous. It was a delicate balancing act.

But for me the 2003 Oval Test against South Africa was pressure of a completely different kind. I was trying to prove so many things to so many people. I wanted to show my team-mates that I was still a good player, and that I still wanted to play for the team. I wanted to prove the selectors right for picking me for a match England needed to win to draw the series. I wanted to show everyone I'd overcome my problems. And I wanted to rewrite the end of my Test career.

After all my to-ing and fro-ing of the previous couple of years, I owed everyone a performance – myself, my team and the public. Just to add to the mix, I knew that if I failed England might well not take me on the winter tour and I might never play Test cricket again. I was not usually a nervous player but I was nervous now, probably more nervous than at any other time in my career.

I was very conscious of looking keen during practice in the two days before the game. As was more usual, I also started fussing over my choice of bat in a major way. I just couldn't make up my mind which one to use. Which bat do you use after you've been out of Test cricket for a year?

Like Nasser, I was a great one for tinkering with bats. I needed to be sure that the one I was using was okay, and when I got my hands on a new one I would take off the rubber grip and cut bits off the handle to mould it to the shape of my hands. It was a habit I picked up after starting international cricket, probably because it was only then that you started to get a bigger choice of equipment, with manufacturers offering to make you bats to order. All of sudden it became very important that the handle was just so, and the blade. I would often worry about the feel of my bat handle in the early part of an innings as I searched to feel comfortable with it. It was a crazy habit really, and drove a lot of people in the dressing-room up the wall, but I think I was trying to reassure myself this was a bat I could lift back and then bring back down straight. No two bats ever felt the same and if you'd just given up a good one, you wanted the next to be exactly like it. I would carry around anything from two to six bats with me at any one time. Once a bat broke or was to be discarded, I'd write the Test hundreds I'd scored with it high up on the back of the blade and put it away.

I tried various bats in the nets but couldn't settle quickly on one. After much agonizing, I plumped for one I'd used once before that summer. It was far from the best bat I'd ever had. It had one little sweet spot in the middle, but to me the rest of it was pretty ordinary.

Getting the right bat was one thing, getting into the right mind-set another. So much international cricket is played in the head. The doing is far less than the thinking. For me, the 24 hours before a Test was all about getting into a good state of mind, with the right mental information to hand, but not so much of it that you were overwhelmed. I tried to net well and get an idea of the problems I was likely to face. If I was playing a leg-spinner such as Shane Warne or a left-arm spinner like Daniel Vettori, I'd like to get a leggie or left-arm spinner in the nets two or three days beforehand so I could practice against the action. Then I'd have a quick look at videos of the bowlers I was up against, although I didn't like to overdo this. The night before the match,

I'd try to recall the times I'd played against them and visualize what they'd be trying to do. And then I'd pack these thoughts away, into a box in my mind, and try not to think about anything much at all until the time came to bat.

That was the plan. But in truth as a game approached, thoughts could pour into your mind like marauding armies. That's why international cricket can cut into you so deeply and why, if you are not to be mentally exhausted before you bat, you have to find ways to cope. One of the problems is that you never know when you're going out to bat – it could be in five minutes or five hours. Batting is a strange business. And your preparation for facing some bloke hurling the ball down at you at 90mph is to sit on your backside for an hour or two, knowing that the instant you got out there, your mind has to switch straight into over-drive. It's no wonder your thoughts sometimes run riot. I found listening to music on my iPod was a good way to try to relax before going out to bat.

I only slept well about 80 per cent of my Test career. I didn't often have bad dreams, although occasionally one would recur in which I wouldn't have my kit on in time. If it was a batting day for England, I would sometimes wake early and be unable to get back to sleep. My mind would be buzzing. *What about my form, their bowling attack, and that bowler?*

Going into the match at the Oval, I certainly spent

time thinking about how to deal with Shaun Pollock, who gave me more problems in Test cricket than any other fast bowler. I found him difficult because he bowled so close to the stumps and had the ability to get my head out of line with the bat and ball and trap me leg-before. He'd got me out like that a few times, and if there was one bloke I'd rather not have faced on my return it was him.

My view was that you only had so much mental energy to expend and that not sleeping well, or dwelling too much on what lay ahead, threatened to eat into your performance. For a long time I didn't really have a plan for dealing with this problem. I used to just believe my game would see me through and, if it didn't, I'd just be impatient for my next innings so I could make amends. I was too wrapped up in the whole business for my own good.

In the end though, during a nail-biting series in Sri Lanka in 2001, I found a way of keeping things in perspective; wanting to do well, but not wanting it too much. Some people may find this bizarre. I don't know if anyone else has ever used the same thought-process. What I did as I sat there waiting to bat was imagine that, after the day's play had finished, I'd go home and learn that both my children had been involved in a bad accident. As brutal and simple as that. 'Now what are you worrying about?' I'd ask myself. 'Do you really care if you go out there and fail? Remember what really bad things could happen.' And I found this violent, shocking thought worked. It helped me relax about the job I had to do. I was able to convince myself that what I was doing in this cricket match, important though it was, was not that important in the scheme of things and that I ought not to fear the occasion, but enjoy it and just try my best to make something happen. If it didn't work, so be it.

I first used this technique during a Test in Kandy when we were 1–0 down in the series, and 25 for two in the second innings, chasing 161 to win on a pitch doing all sorts. Murali was bowling at one end, and Chaminda Vaas at the other. Next man in, I was sitting in the dressing-room on the edge of my seat. All of a sudden, I broke off, got up and went for a wander round the back of the room and told myself that there was no way I was going to perform in this state. I was wanting to do well far too much for it ever to happen.

After a few minutes, I went back and sat down, put on my headphones and asked myself how I'd feel about this match if I got back to the hotel and learned that Henry and Amelia, both then under four years of age, had been hurt in an accident. That made me take a step back and put my innings in perspective. After that, I went out and scored a quick 40 and got the team into a position from which we were able to win. Afterwards, Duncan told me that, given the context, it was one of the best innings he'd seen me play.

I remember old-time players like the Bedser twins saying that younger generations like mine didn't know what real pressure was because we hadn't fought in wars. I suppose they were right. The great Australian all-rounder Keith Miller, who had been a fighter pilot in the Second World War, once explained his carefree approach by rejecting the idea he was ever under pressure on the field. 'Pressure is a Messerschmitt up your arse,' he said.

For that 2003 match at the Oval, the big thing for me was to go into the game ready to accept failure if it came. I was desperate to do well, but knew how easy it was to get out early; anyone can nick one before his eye is in. I think it took a lot of courage to accept this, and I'm not sure I could have done it without my religious faith to calm me. I don't think I could have coped with all that pressure unless I had told myself that, to an extent, what was about to happen was in somebody else's hands.

The evening before the game, Nicky helpfully sent me a text message. It read, 'Henry's favourite food is biltong [South African sun-dried meat]. Hope the South Africans break your head.' If she was hoping to put me off, she failed. It didn't even annoy me, I just laughed. I'd started to feel quite focused.

THE FIRST DAY of the match turned into a waiting day. South Africa won the toss, chose to bat and batted well into Friday racking up nearly 500. To my relief, I didn't really make any mistakes in the field; in fact, not many balls really came my way and I didn't have any catches to take. But we faced a few hard days if we were going to win the game. To my mind, it was one more problem. And I'd got enough of those on my plate already.

As the time approached for me to bat at No 4, I began to believe that I might actually be able to do well. I wouldn't say I was quietly confident, but I felt so much more in control than I had during that last nightmare Test a few miles away across London the previous year. I certainly wasn't thinking I was going out to fail, like I did then. But I popped three painkillers so I couldn't feel too much, partly for my peace of mind, partly for my back. It was the back end of the season and I had been playing a fair bit for Surrey in the four weeks since the spasms. I didn't want them recurring now. I took off the chain that Caroline gave me and put it in my pocket.

I watched the first 20 minutes or so of our innings, then tried not to watch too much in case I became tired. Then Vaughan was out, which meant I was next man in, so I started watching again, but Tres and Butch had a bit of a stand together and when they'd put on about 30 I thought I'd give myself another break and went into the dressing-room to have a bit of a chat, fiddle with my kit and keep an eye on things via the TV. Then Butch was leg-before to Andrew Hall.

I'd been quite relaxed until then. All of a sudden, I was gathering up my kit, pushing on my helmet and those armies of thoughts were stampeding through my mind as I walked out of the room and down the steps of the Bedser stand . . . '*You've been out for a year, everybody knows you've been through hell, everybody knows about your private life . . . but this is your chance, THIS is your chance . . . just control the breathing . . . Right. Get out there. Get on with the job . . .*' By the time I crossed the rope, I think I had gathered myself pretty well considering everything I had to contend with. '*Christ, I really want to do well.*'

My view was that if you expected to do well you needed to feel relaxed and confident walking out to the middle. But then came a surprise. The crowd had realized I was next man in and gave me an incredible reception that gave me goose bumps. I had never walked out to a reaction like it before, or since, and I was at once overcome with a feeling of pride at having made it back into the England team. The crowd clearly felt for me after all that had happened. To feel their sympathy and support was very special. But it had taken me by surprise and briefly knocked me off guard. '*Shit. I'd better not get out first ball after that.*'

Hall's first ball was good, a big inswinger that hit me on my pad as I lunged forward. Fortunately, I'd only fallen across my stumps a bit and, although the ball had swung enough to beat me, it would have gone on to miss. His second ball was pretty much the same, and again I fell across, but this time it would have hit middle had I not got a thick inside edge which squirted the ball away for a single. I can remember listening to the commentary later – it's one video I don't mind watching again and again – and David Lloyd saying, 'Yes, a typical Thorpe shot to get off the mark . . .' I wish!

I was desperately trying to get into the right frame of mind as quickly as I could. I checked my grip on the bat to make sure it wasn't too tight, a sure sign of tension. Too tight and I'd probably end up jabbing at one. What I was striving for was that state of mind when your thinking is clear and concise, and you just keep sending yourself short memos that allow instinct to take over as the ball's delivered. Don't get overconfident. Don't relax. Stay focused on the ball. Keep a good shape. Stay sideways. Keep your hands close to your body. And for Pollock, don't get your front foot too far across. And with Ntini, who bowled wide of the crease and angled the ball across me, don't get opened up. As a partnership, they provided an interesting contrast – when you had time to think about it!

I remained very nervous for the rest of that evening through to stumps, but I began to feel really focused. Looking at the innings as a whole, I'd say it was the most focused I'd ever been ball after ball, but things didn't really click into place until next morning. That night, it was all really just about not getting out. Fortunately, the pitch was not that quick. I'd got to about seven when I said to myself that if I kept playing as I was doing, I wasn't going to get many and that I'd be better off trying to do something. Basically, I'd started off reluctant to take risks but didn't feel I was settling. I reasoned that breaking the shackles might calm me down. Steve Waugh used to say he liked to get to 20 quickly and, after that, felt like he was 'in'.

I took my chance against Pollock of all people, twice square-cutting uppishly off length balls. Both flew for four over backward point where Herschelle Gibbs was fielding. They went past him at head height but however athletic he was he wasn't going to get them, but I could see in his eyes he knew I'd taken a risk. But I felt better. '*Right. Now just get through to the end of play.*'

Gibbs tried to gee up his team by saying something about how I was desperate to get myself on the tour of Bangladesh, which must be one of the worst sledges I've ever heard! '*I'm not THAT keen, mate!*' The South Africans had a bit to say for themselves, as they usually did. I didn't mind a bit of banter; it was one of the things I'd missed about Test cricket. But interestingly the South Africans didn't give me any stick about my broken marriage or my children. I learned later that Gary Kirsten, who had himself found religion and was coming to the end of a long and distinguished career, dissuaded them from doing so.

Tres, who was always a very professional bloke to bat with, didn't show any sign that he thought I would need looking after on my comeback. He would have taken the attitude that I had been around long enough to look after myself. Besides, he'd been going through a lean patch and was in need of a score himself. It was perfect in a way. I was intensely focused on what I was doing and so was he. At stumps, we were 165 for two. Trescothick was on 64 and I was on 28. I'd been batting an hour and a half.

My parents had been at the ground that day, but Amanda had not. That evening, I drove back to Wimbledon to see her and stay the night. Normally, of course, I would have stayed in the team hotel, and for the rest of the game I did, but after all the tension of the last four days I wanted to be with her and relax; besides it wasn't as though it was a long journey – a 20-minute drive from Kennington to Wimbledon at most. I was more relaxed than the last time she'd seen me, thank goodness. We watched some TV and I tried to forget about the game, although I did say to her, 'It's all right now. Even if I get out straightaway, it's not nought. It's not a failure.' Amanda made some food, we had a couple of glasses of wine and an early night.

I drove back to the ground first thing in the morning. I didn't bother having a net. I just hit half a dozen throw-downs, and concentrated on telling myself not to be as tense as I had been the night before. Amanda and Caroline had come along with some of their friends, and were sitting about six rows in front of our dressing-room. I must have felt pretty relaxed because I waved my lucky chain at them with a big smile as I trotted down the steps with Tres. Then I put it back in my pocket. I think Amanda was more nervous than I was, while Caroline just kept praying all through my innings.

I *was* relaxed. I think I viewed every run I scored that day as a bonus. I'd got my platform and now I was building on it. I didn't know where it was going to end, and began to feel that this was one of those occasions when I could make mistakes – play and miss, and get an inside edge – but things were destined to go my way.

I got off to a good start, hitting some good shots off the middle of the bat – I think I'd found its sweet spot by now – and before I knew it was into the forties. I was feeling good but never got carried away. I reached 50 and thought, 'That's good.' I began looking at the partnership, something I often did to take my mind off my own innings, and that kept me going. I don't know why I enjoyed being involved in big partnerships the way I did, except that I liked encouraging the other guy and it gave me something to think about, and perhaps meant that I didn't fret if I went a while without scoring many. I would take a partnership 10 runs at a time; if you looked too far ahead, that was when problems might start. The stand became worth 100 early in the day; then 120, then 150, 170 and 200. Then it became a case of, this is a great partnership, let's see how big we can make it. I was playing well, we both were. The

South Africans didn't seem to have much to say for themselves.

In those situations the thing that often got in the way was one of you approaching your hundred. You would have a bit of a waft because you were anxious to get there, and get it over with. Tres safely got to his hundred first. Normally, I wasn't someone who got particularly nervous about such things and I was rarely out in the nineties, but the thought of making a century on this occasion, as I'd told Amanda a few days earlier, was simply too good even to dream about.

I remember getting to 80 – Amanda told me later that by this point she and Caroline had cracked open the champagne – and I also remember reaching 94 because it was at that point that South Africa took the second new ball. Almost immediately, Pollock found my outside edge but thankfully they'd only posted two slips and the ball flew through where third slip would have been. They'd been in the field a while by now, and second slip remained static and the ball ran away for four. That took me to 98.

I went on strike at the other end against Ntini, and thought to myself that wherever the ball landed I was going after it. Looking at the video of my next stroke, it looked like quite a controlled shot, but at the time it felt like I was having an almighty thrash. I didn't really think about where I was trying to hit it. I just wanted to get it over or through the off-side field. The moment

I saw the ball go wide of third man, I told myself to make sure I didn't fall over on the first run because I *had* to get back for the second.

Running that second run was the most incredible feeling I ever had on a cricket field. The whole innings had been about more than just a cricket match, although in the match itself the stakes were extremely high. It felt like I had played out my life through one innings and the reaction of a capacity crowd – my home crowd – told me all I needed to hear. They went mad and, by going mad, told me again that they were behind me and happy for me. I felt like a huge weight had been lifted from my shoulders. Maybe I wasn't such a bad person after all . . .

In that one moment, as I took off my helmet to acknowledge the applause, I felt fulfilled both as a cricketer and human being. I clawed back so much through that one innings. For that reason it overtook anything else I ever did as a sportsman.

Inevitably, comparisons were made between that century and the one on my Test debut 10 years earlier. But, in truth, they were totally different. In 1993, I was totally naive; I knew next to nothing about cricket or life. In 2003, my heart and mind had been through so much more, good and bad. Scoring a century in my first match was a great beginning and a great bonus, but when I ran that second run 10 years later I knew I had just achieved something absolutely incredible.

Wisden described it as a 'beautiful' hundred. I think to many on the outside, that's how it looked. Out of all the confusion and pain of the previous two years, I'd somehow managed to create something special. It was what I'd hoped for, but more than dared ask for.

WHEN I WAS out for 124, Amanda, Caroline and friends left the ground to carry on celebrating. They phoned Nobu – a restaurant you can't normally get into on a Saturday night for love nor money – and, cheekily using my name, managed to book a table for six. Even though it was the middle of a Test match, I let my hair down. We were still batting at the close, on around 500 for seven, so I knew I wasn't going to be required to do anything significant for a while. After the meal, we went on to a club, but I didn't get drunk. Frankly, I didn't need to. I was high enough on adrenaline.

The next day, England went a long way towards winning the game. Flintoff smashed 90 and gave us a crucial lead of 120, which the bowlers then built on. They finished the job on the Monday morning, and we ran out easy winners by nine wickets to draw the series 2–2. I didn't need to bat again. What a victory!

It had been a great match for the Surrey players on home soil because Stewie finished his career as the most-capped England player on a winning note, Butch completed a good series, while Martin Bicknell had shown what a skilful bowler he was by taking four for 84 in the second innings. It was extraordinary that Martin and I, so often team-mates for Surrey, should find ourselves appearing together for England again. He had last played Test cricket in my debut series 10 years earlier, and in the interim I had played around 80 times. He was one of those medium-fast bowlers who was perfect for typical English conditions. I think that as a youngster he tried to bowl too quick, but in the later stages of his career he really knew his trade. His partnership with Saqlain Mushtaq was crucial to Surrey's success.

At the end of the match, the South Africans came into a dressing-room to share a traditional farewell drink. Shaun Pollock asked why England hadn't picked me all summer, and admitted that every time they didn't see my name on the England team-sheet the South Africans had cheered. I didn't return the compliment by telling him what he sometimes did to my sleep patterns.

As time passed, the significance of my innings grew. Despite the controversy of my delayed selection, I am grateful things turned out as they did. What happened later made me realize that what that innings represented was the total resurrection of my life. All the good things that subsequently occurred might not have happened but for that game. But if I'd been told I wouldn't play cricket again after that match, I would still have walked down the streets 20 times taller than the week before. To think there was a time when I resented cricket for ruining my life. Now it had given me back my dignity.

When I look back on the slices of luck I enjoyed in that innings, it is hard not to think that divine intervention did not play a part. It is why I have offered prayers of thanks for the good things that have happened to me since.

Caroline's chain had come good. I have carried it with me ever since.

FOURTEEN

Boxing Days

ONE OF THE things I came to realize after playing international cricket a long time was that, while you might play in many matches with certain people, scrapping shoulder to shoulder with them and sharing many extraordinary highs and lows, it didn't necessarily mean you were going to socialize with them, or even be particularly close to them away from games.

Looking back now, such a conclusion ought not to have been such a huge surprise. After all, we had all been brought together to do a specific job. Ours were professional relationships rather than friendships. Dressing-rooms were places where people appeared, and then you mightn't see them again for months. It was that sort of environment. But that isn't what you think when you come into the game. The camaraderie of training and playing together, and shared trips away from home, create a misleading impression of togetherness.

Personally, I would be surprised if many people walk away from Test cricket and – provided they don't go into the media – stay in contact with more than half a dozen people.

So what's the difference between a professional relationship and a friendship? I would say a friendship is when you pick the phone up when someone you know is struggling away from the game, and check that they are all right.

When I was going through my hard times I was struck by the fact that it was chiefly the people I knew outside cricket who stuck by me. People like Jeff Banks, a guy I'd known since we were at primary school together and Ray Alikhan. I turned to them for advice more than anyone. It didn't upset me that many cricket people didn't call. When I saw them again, I knew that they cared and that they had been concerned about me, but their detachment highlighted the nature of my relationships with them.

After we'd won at the Oval, the lunchtime celebrations in the dressing-room continued into an evening party. Before we left, we staged a comical football match on the outfield with a huge Swiss ball – by this stage, as I'm sure you can imagine, most of us were well on the way to being thoroughly plastered. I think we even managed to get a couple of drinks inside Alec! I remember Butch – who later that night was sick in my shoes at the hotel – aiming a kick, completely missing and tumbling over. Afterwards, we went to a restaurant in town for an end-of-season dinner, where we had even more drinks before we sat down.

Although he'd not played in the match, Nasser joined us. It was the first time I'd seen or spoken to him since I'd been chosen to take his place. I knew what it was like to be around the team but not involved; you felt on the outside and I guess that was how Nasser felt that evening. I don't think that he'd had that much to drink.

The situation between us had become quite complicated, although I didn't know quite how complicated at the time. With the squad to tour Bangladesh and Sri Lanka due to be announced two days after the game, there'd been talk – which, even if I'd heard it, had gone over my head – that Nasser and I were competing for the same place. Only one of us would go. There was a feeling that Vaughan might not want too many old lags in the dressing-room. It turned out there was some truth in this because the incoming captain went to see some businessmen to ask them what he should do, given his new position of authority. One of the things they said was clear out as much 'old rubbish' as possible to establish control over the team.

This was an unfortunate situation, given how far Nasser and I went back together. I'd always liked Nasser's determination, and enjoyed batting with him and being captained by him. Of course, inevitably we'd had our spats; we'd played 50 Tests together. I remember one stand-up row we had in the dressing-room after I dropped a catch in a warm-up match in Pakistan, but it was really nothing other than our both letting off steam. Nasser was very honest in his views and it was good to be honest back. If you weren't, you could take it away with you and you were much better getting it off your chest. That was the way he was.

Frankly, the winter tours hadn't entered my thinking. Until Nasser's injury, I was outside the England squad and struggling to get back in. And I was aware there were people who might prefer me to stay there. The idea that I might feature in anybody's winter plans didn't seem worth entertaining. Then, once I'd scored my hundred, I was too ecstatic to give a damn about the future; the present was enjoyable enough. The winter could wait. In any case, I'd come to realize there were certain things I couldn't control, and being picked for England was one of them. I'd find out soon enough.

For Nasser, things were different. He'd had time to reflect on the way he'd left the captaincy, pretty much without warning, for his successor. Then he had been forced out of the side by injury and seen his replacement – me – score a century. I could well understand why speculation that only one of us might make the tour made him uneasy. Just as I'd not wanted to end my career after the way I'd played against India in 2002, he didn't want this to be the end of his. No one wants to end on a low.

I think things had been building up for him over a few weeks, and he was anxious enough at the dinner that night to try and find out what the captain was thinking. Apparently Ashley Giles, who was closer to Vaughan than any of us, confirmed to him that the captain held reservations about taking the two of us. In fact, Mick spoke to me that evening and told me I would be going on tour. At around 4am, I sent a drunken text message to Amanda saying something like, 'Really happy. I love you. Let's get married! I've just been told by my captain I'm on the winter tour.'

As it happened, at the end of the night I ended up getting a taxi with Nasser back to the hotel. By this stage, I was well and truly drunk, and in the back of the cab I started giving Nasser some friendly whacks on the arm and saying, 'All right, mate? . . . Fucking hell, all right? . . .' To me, I'd just got back so much in my life that it was unthinkable that the whole world would not share my happiness. I wasn't in a position to grasp that things might not look so rosy from Nasser's point of view. Suddenly, he turned round and grabbed me, ripping my shirt and pulling off a couple of buttons. 'Just get off me! . . .' he shouted.

'All right, mate, okay . . . Relax, relax . . .' I thought, '*Oh fuck, he's in one of his moods. Let him be.*' The next day, the team for Bangladesh and Sri Lanka was announced. I was in it and so was Nasser. But he was also handed a 12-month England contract, which I wasn't. No surprise there! The two of us didn't meet again until the team assembled at the airport a few weeks later. Nasser just came up to me, cool as anything and said, 'I think it's all right for us to talk now . . . It was bloody close, you know. They didn't want it to happen.'

I don't for a minute hold it against Nasser for the way he behaved. Things were just so different with me. While he cared desperately about his place in the England side, I didn't. I was just happy I'd got back and done well. For me, at that point, that was enough. So many shared experiences brought us together, but temperamentally we were different from our younger days. He remained incredibly passionate, while I was now so much more chilled out.

I'D GONE through another strange taxi-ride to get to the airport. I'd use the same man to take me to the airport, a Pakistani called Nor Khan, who loved cricket and took his commission very seriously. He'd come and pick me up smartly dressed in jacket and tie, his minicab gleaming.

I don't know whether he'd watched my century at the Oval but he chose this, our first meeting since then, to try and kidnap me. We'd only been in the car a couple of minutes when he asked if I'd mind meeting his family. 'Would you mind coming round and saying hello to my son? My family just live near the airport,' he said. Thinking that perhaps all he wanted me to do was sign a shirt or two, I unwisely agreed. 'Er, yes, okay . . . I'm a bit tight for time . . . We need to be at the airport in an hour. But okay, no problem . . .' He was such a nice bloke, I couldn't say no. I am not sure the old Graham Thorpe would have done the same thing. But now I saw things in a different light. I wanted to oblige him. So off we went, while our conversation about Pakistan was frequently interrupted by Mr Khan taking calls on his phone, which he conducted in hushed, urgent Urdu. He was probably saying, 'Yes, I've got him . . . Get everything ready . . .'

Eventually, we drew up in a residential street somewhere in Hounslow. We pulled up outside Nor's house, and out onto the steps to greet us came his wife, son and what looked like his entire family. In neighbouring houses, I could see a couple of curtains twitching. I was starting to have serious concerns when I was ushered inside, and saw everything, tea and cakes, the full service, the lot, laid out in the living-room. My mood switched to mild panic. I glanced at my watch. 'Hello, Graham, we've been expecting you,' Mrs Khan was saying. 'This is my daughter, and this is my son, and this . . .' I declined the food on the grounds that I'd just eaten lunch, but I could hardly turn down a cup of tea which proved to be scalding hot and difficult to bolt down. My hosts could not have been more charming, but this was hardly the time for pleasantries and small-talk.

Eventually, as I had feared, my phone went. It was Richard Nowell, the Vodafone representative who looked after the England players on tour. 'Graham, where are you? Are you on your way?', which was code for '*You're late*.' I could imagine the scene at the airport, the management looking at their watches, thinking, 'Oh, no, not again . . . He's not coming.' And there was I, having a nice cup of tea.

Mercifully, my Pakistani friends satisfied, we returned to the car and I ended up getting to the airport about half an hour late. Naturally, given my track record, I was treated to plenty of mickey-taking. 'We didn't know if you were going to show up or not,' said a smirking Ashley Giles. When we got on the coach, it was a case of, 'All right folks. Graham's here. *Now* we can leave.'

I FELT A REAL hunger for cricket. I wanted to go out and make the most of every day I had with England. I still had a lot to prove to myself and to others, although after the Oval I was confident I could deal with failure if it came. My first aim was to re-establish myself in the side and do enough to be selected for the spring tour of the West Indies. I didn't want to come back for six months and then disappear; I wanted to become a fixture in the side for a lengthy period. Given my age – I had just turned 34 – and the state of my back, I reckoned I might, if things went well, manage another two years at the most. In fact that's virtually what I managed, and

I'd say that to survive that long, and play as well as I did during that time, possibly rates as my greatest achievement as a player.

I had no concern about touring again. It was to be my first (uninterrupted) winter tour for some time – I'd missed Australia, and the tour of India had been disrupted by my return home – but many things had changed. For a start, I was now in a stable relationship. I had also retired from one-day cricket so that I, with other Test specialists such as Nasser and Butch, was able to return home for a couple of weeks between the series in Bangladesh and Sri Lanka. When you're away touring for several months, you have to get yourself into a particular state of mind, but that break made everything much easier.

I was excited at the prospect of what lay ahead. The last time we'd toured the subcontinent, in 2000–01, the team had won Test series in both Pakistan and Sri Lanka, an incredible achievement for England. When we'd left home, most people had given us little chance of avoiding two heavy defeats, and even we thought we'd do well to escape with a few draws. But that winter produced the first real signs that the team was progressing, and creating its own identity under Nasser and Duncan. We had a settled squad, game-plans and were well led. The greater professionalism Nasser and Duncan were bringing to the team was apparent. For many of us, including myself, it was perhaps our happiest tour. I think Duncan enjoyed it because there were a lot of thirtysomethings in the squad with whom he could share a few rugby scrum-downs on the lawns of the expat-clubs, after a few beers.

Winning those two series was Nasser's finest effort as captain, and under him I had my best ever winter, scoring more than 550 runs in the six Tests, more than half of them in the wins at Karachi, Kandy and Colombo. He was very thorough, tactically astute and always a pragmatist. Whereas Athers might have been reluctant to stick a 'sweeper' on the boundary to someone like Brian Lara early in his innings, fearing it was a sign of weakness, Nasser had no such qualms. On that tour, he was determined to make us as difficult to beat as possible, and even had to be talked out of holding back the likes of myself and Athers during a run-chase in Karachi because he feared that chasing 176 in 44 overs, we might get into trouble and lose.

He was all for putting the hitters at the top of the order and going for it, until we were perhaps three down. He feared that if they got too many early wickets they might go through us. But to me the pitch was not that bad. It was turning a bit, but no more. Nasser suggested Athers drop down the order, but Athers was having none of it. He insisted on opening and got a quick 20. I was another one Nasser wanted to hold back, but when Shahid Afridi starting bowling into the rough to the right-handers I said we needed a left-hander out there. Nasser agreed I should go in when the second wicket fell and, in the end, Hick and I shared the partnership that effectively won us the game.

We didn't have to take many risks and I didn't feel under much pressure, at least I didn't until Nasser, who'd dropped himself down to No 6, came in with 21 needed. He was fretting that we might run out of time, but umpire Steve Bucknor had already told me that he wouldn't take us off for bad light without offering it to us first. So as long as we could see it, we would stay out there. The Pakistanis slowed things down as much as they could, to about 12 overs an hour, and Waqar Younis, who I knew well from our time together at Surrey, seemed to take an age over every ball. Unsurprisingly, he seemed to be having problems keeping a shoelace tied. At one point I offered to help him, but he just smiled and said he could manage! Moin Khan, their captain and wicket-keeper, was chuntering away behind the stumps but the umpires were having none of it, and I told him a few times he might as well just get on with it because we were going to finish the match. Even though he was about to be the first Pakistan captain to lose a Test in Karachi, Moin could still smile.

Famously, of course, by the time the match finished with me edging the winning runs with less than three overs to spare, it was as near to darkness as most of us had ever experienced in an international match. When Nasser and I ran off, the best way to find our way back to the dressing-room was to head for the Pavilion lights in the gloom!

Now, returning to Asia, my renewed enthusiasm matched the mood of the squad on its first tour under Vaughan's captaincy. I think each England captain tries to make his mark on the side. Athers had to deal with things before central contracts came in, and wanted his players to be fresh for Test cricket and free from injury. Nasser wanted to toughen the side mentally, make us more honest about our games and harder to beat. And it became clear in Bangladesh that Mick wanted to turn his players into genuine athletes. Logically, it was the next step. There had been individual cases of players improving their fitness under Nasser – Flintoff steadily built up his strength and stamina over several years until he eventually became a totally different cricketer – but this was a case of raising the bar for all of us, and was very necessary given how sides like Australia were progressing in this way.

As a rule, youngsters can be a bit cynical about fitness training because they are often naturally fit, but I was keen to work on my fitness. Training had played a part in my picking myself up. In my early days I would train with a guy called Tim Laski, running sand hills and doing weights. It was also a good way of filling the time in Asia, where England teams tend to find less to do than in some countries. We trained exceptionally hard and it helped give the team an identity. Mick's plans fitted in with Duncan's aims, and I think the work we did on that tour laid the foundations for England's later revival; during our great Test run in 2004 against West Indies, New Zealand and South Africa, we regularly had everyone fit for selection. It even changed the culture of county cricket. Soon, everyone knew that if you wanted to play for England, you had to be incredibly fit.

Needless to say, I turned up to our first team session in the gym wearing the wrong kit! We'd been given official training clothes but I pitched up in the sort of gear I'd have worn to the gym at home. Afterwards, Mick came up to me and said, 'Duncan thinks you've done that deliberately . . . You've deliberately put on the wrong shirt.'

'Mick, you know me mate. I was just in a rush, slung anything on and charged out of the room . . .'

'The youngsters are going to be looking at someone like you to set them an example. I'm not going to give you a bollocking. But be aware of it.'

We didn't always train as a team. We were also expected to undertake our own sessions and were allocated partners, Nasser and I being put together. In fact, Nasser preferred to do his work in the morning, I might do mine in the evening, or we'd be in the gym at the same time but working on different things. We had different programmes and rarely did the same exercises, so in the end we pretty much worked on our own.

It was pretty clear that Nasser was on his last winter

of cricket and was going to do things his way. He was going to have his curries, and not do anything to jeopardize his body, particularly his shoulder problem. I could understand his attitude, and the management never went over the top about it. As ex-captain, and especially after the fuss over the tour squad, he tried hard not to get in Mick's way. He had been used to ordering people about in no uncertain terms, so it must have been difficult for him. You could tell some of the younger players thought he was a grumpy old so-and-so.

As for being fit, it was essential. We knew from previous visits to Asia that the conditions could be extremely tough. It could be very hot and seriously humid. Within five minutes of starting your innings, your shirt and gloves would be drenched in sweat, and it was hard to stop the perspiration pouring down your face. You needed a big supply of armbands, wristbands and headbands, and I used a lot of Vaseline to try and keep my eyes dry. These problems changed the whole nature of the game, and made everything that much harder. I reckon that given the extreme humidity and the tense match situation, the century I scored in Colombo in 2001 was my best knock for England at that stage, and probably remained second only to the comeback hundred at the Oval, just ahead of Barbados 2004. Although on purely technical grounds I rated highly the centuries against Australia in Perth in 1995 and at Edgbaston in 1997.

Predictably, we now won the two Tests against Bangladesh, despite the arduous conditions. I spent around four hours over 64 in the first Test in Dhaka in which we were given a bit of a fright. At one point, Bangladesh were effectively 127 for five in the second innings, and we urgently needed wickets to avoid being left something awkward in excess of 200. As it was, we needed more than 160 but knocked them off with few alarms. We went on to win the second Test easily.

Sri Lanka's bowling was obviously going to be far more testing. They possessed two world-class bowlers in Vaas and Murali. The off-spinner Murali was one of biggest challenges facing any Test batsman. Apart from anything else, he bowled so many of his side's overs that you had to come up with a way of dealing with him.

I always thoroughly enjoyed playing against him. He is a lovely bloke and we had some great contests. I would rate Warne as the greater bowler, though. Warne was always varying the degree he spun the ball, while Murali generally just tried to spin the ball as much as he could. Warne kept on developing during his career, changing his game-plans for each batsman, trying subtle new ways of getting you out. Murali was less sophisticated. There were fewer plans and fewer mind-games. He just kept on bowling, kept on spinning.

I first came up against Murali when he was an unknown teenager, bowling in a minor game on my second tour with England A in 1991. I just remember this bloke with this funny looking action, spinning the ball a mile. He got six wickets and only Darren Bicknell of the recognized batters got any runs.

He was less happy bowling to left-handers, and it was perhaps no coincidence that myself and Trescothick were our most successful batters in the 2001 series. To me, the fact that he spun the ball so much made things easier, isolating the areas where you could score. His stock ball turned away from me and created the chance to cut. He had a delivery that spun straight on, but to me it was easy to pick because it was quite obvious it was coming out of the front of his hand. I'd started that series quite negatively against him, before going onto the offensive in the second Test in Kandy where I went down the wicket to attack him quite successfully, during a big stand with Nasser. That was the game when I first started thinking about my children as a mental safety valve on finding myself getting too tense.

But now, two years on, Murali had a shock for us. He had developed a doosra, a ball that went the other way. To a left-hander like me, it spun back into my legs. At a stroke, it changed everything. Now, I needed to be sure which ball he was bowling: was it the one that spun away or back in? If it was spinning into me, I risked being lbw. The problem was that he seemed to be bowling his new delivery with a very similar action to his stock ball. I just couldn't tell them apart as they came out of his cobra-like hand. I had no choice but to play the ball off the wicket, which made the cut shot much riskier. A few of the right-handers in the team said they were able to pick him 75 per cent of the time, but I rarely picked him with certainty. Even so, I survived to face more balls from him than anyone else in the series.

I'd never been great at picking the 'other' deliveries of spinners. Mushtaq Ahmed had a very good googly, and Saqlain Mushtaq was one of the first to develop a doosra. I faced both during the 2000 tour of Pakistan and fortunately, by that stage, Duncan was on board and helped me develop the way I played spin. It was not until Duncan came along that I really improved my strategy. Before that Pakistan tour, I'm not sure I really knew what I was trying to achieve. Duncan made me face up to some key questions: if I was going to dominate a particular spinner, how was I going to do it? If I couldn't hit big shots, where was I going to get runs with limited risk? I wasn't big on hitting over the top, so I tried sweeping more. I used a heavier bat, too, to control my shots. With Duncan, I broke down the sweep into parts, thinking about where I should place my feet and how fine I should be hitting the ball. The plan involved manoeuvring fielders out of dangerous positions, and then working the ball into the gaps I'd created. You can tell the way I played from the fact I hit only one boundary in my hundred in Lahore.

In Sri Lanka in 2003, Duncan thought I should have

swept Murali more than I did, but I felt I was sweeping blind and Murali was not too proud to put a man out for the sweep to stop the boundaries. I shouted down the wicket to him a couple of times, calling him a coward, but he just shrugged and smiled. 'If that's your one shot for hitting me for four, I don't mind putting a man out,' he seemed to be saying. My average more than halved to 30, but it was still second-best in the side behind Vaughan, who saved the Kandy Test with a fine backs-to-the-wall hundred, his first as England captain. Murali got me out five times in the series, mainly with his new delivery.

I think it was a great team effort to hold out for draws in the first and second Tests, before we crashed to a massive defeat in the last game in Colombo. Batting last in Galle and Kandy, we not only survived but made Murali bowl almost 100 overs in the two fourth-innings combined. After I was out the second time in Colombo, stumped after being completely bamboozled by Murali's doosra, I went back to the dressing-room, threw my arms in the air, shouted 'Bollocks!', changed my clothes and went to the swimming pool behind the stand. I swam a few lengths, while the roar of the crowd greeted the fall of more English wickets. I needed to cool down in both senses!

A few months later, Murali's doosra was briefly banned by the International Cricket Council, before the authorities ordered a review of what constituted a throw and, under new rules, it became an acceptable delivery again. Many people I played with said Murali threw his standard delivery, let alone his doosra. Nasser was even accused (but cleared) of calling him a cheat during the Kandy Test.

While I was playing, my view was always that thinking a bowler might be chucking was never going to help you conquer anything. It was a negative thought; a bad thought. His action was extremely complicated, but he wasn't impossible to play. Frankly, I didn't think it mattered a jot what I thought about his action, provided the authorities ruled it legal.

That said, now that I know I won't have to face him in a Test match again, and have had the chance to study slow-motion replays of his doosra at length, I have serious doubts about its legitimacy. While Saqlain's doosra, for example, appears to come from his fingers, Murali's is apparently bowled with the arm. I certainly think the rules have been adjusted to accommodate him.

Towards the end of the Sri Lanka tour, I remember having a chat with Butch and Nasser and asking them how they thought the three of us had done. I thought we hadn't done too badly. Given the problems with Murali, a 1–0 defeat didn't seem too bad. But I got the impression that Nasser hadn't enjoyed the tour much, and wasn't sure how much longer he could carry on. He'd missed one match through illness and not made many runs in the others. And of course, it was no longer his team. It was changing fast and soon enough would learn to manage without Nasser, Butch or me. But fortunately, all three of us showed in the Caribbean that we were not quite finished yet.

THAT CHRISTMAS, I'd arranged with Nicky that she would have the children for Christmas Day and I would see them on Boxing Day. In fact, there was also a contact order by the court which stated that. On the one occasion I'd managed to speak to Henry on the phone from Sri Lanka I told him Daddy would be coming home with Father Christmas. Obviously, it would be the first time I'd seen Henry and Amelia in several weeks.

While I was in Sri Lanka, Nicky was having one of her 'turns' and, for some reason, would not take or respond to any of my calls asking to speak to the children. I arrived home on 23 December, and called Nicky to confirm the Boxing Day arrangements. She didn't answer, so I tried again the next day, leaving a message but still no answer. Then I called again on Christmas Day and left a message asking to speak to the children, to wish them happy Christmas.

I was getting really worried about Boxing Day and texted Nicky saying I hoped they were having a nice day, and that hopefully things would be better between us in the New Year. Finally, I got a text back from Nicky in the evening saying, 'No visit tomorrow'. No explanation, just 'No'. Exactly what I'd been frightened would happen.

I don't know whether it had anything to do with it, but on 19 December, during the Colombo Test, she'd sent me a text message saying something like, 'I love you so much it hurts, that's why I can't deal with you. I know you love somebody else and it may take me a lifetime to get over it . . .' Then, the next day I'd received another text message, telling me to ignore the previous message as she'd had a few drinks and was feeling emotional, and anyway she still thought I was a horrible, nasty so-and-so. I just felt sad because I'd moved on with my life, but it was clear Nicky had not. She seemed to be still in turmoil, perhaps regretting her decision to leave me. All I knew was it didn't bode well for my access to the children.

I was devastated but not very surprised when she unilaterally scrapped the Boxing Day meeting. This sort of thing had happened enough times for the pattern to now be clear. There would be an arrangement for me to see the children, then a last-minute change of plans. Often Nicky would just tell me that one of the children was ill, and that was it. I'd missed a couple of Henry's birthdays like that.

Amanda, Kitty (her two-year-old daughter), and I were going to my parents on Boxing Day anyway, and Nicky's house was virtually on the way, so we decided to drop by and leave the children's Christmas presents on the doorstep. After what Nicky had said, we'd assumed she'd made other plans and that they were going to be out for the day, and didn't expect anyone to be in. We even took bin-bags to put the presents in, to keep them dry against the rain.

It was around 10 or 11am when I parked the car in the street, leaving Amanda and Kitty inside, and walked up to the house. I immediately realized that Nicky, Kieron and the children were there, because there was a car in the drive and I could see Henry and Amelia upstairs at one of the bedroom windows. They saw me and started shouting, 'Daddy! . . . Daddy!' I knocked on the front door and Nicky answered.

'Just give me five minutes to see the children and give them their presents in the playroom,' I said.

She took one look at me and told me to get lost.

'Don't be ridiculous . . .' I started to say, but she slammed the door.

I started to walk away, thinking it best to leave her be, but then decided I'd leave the presents and turned back. As I came up to the door it opened and Kieron came out. I suspected he'd been sent by Nicky because he didn't look that keen. Seeing him standing there in front of the door, I found I couldn't leave.

'I want to see my children,' I said.

'No, you can't . . .' he said.

I was really starting to boil now, seeing this man who had helped break up my marriage blocking my way.

One of the most upsetting things about Nicky and I splitting up was that here was this other bloke bringing up my children. At the beginning it had driven me crazy.

'Wait a minute . . . ,' I said. 'Are you, of all people, telling me I can't see my own children at Christmas?' I asked him again. Was I hearing things right? He just stood there.

I can't remember exactly what happened next. I must have charged at him and then we were grappling on the driveway. Kieron is a bigger bloke than me and managed to get on top, but then Amanda came running up and started punching him on the back, shouting 'Get off!' Then I heard Nicky at the doorstep shouting to her mother inside to call the police.

Just as quickly as it had started, we suddenly stopped and got up. After no more than a minute the whole thing was over.

'Why don't you just let him see his children?' Amanda said to Nicky before leading me back to the car. 'Come on,' she said. 'The children know you love them.' And we left.

It hurt me so much to see the children at the window and then be unable to speak to them, but worse was to come. Later that day, Amanda and I both got calls from the *Daily Mail* asking what had happened. Incredibly, Nicky had phoned the paper and told them about the incident, or at least her version of it. Sure enough, a story appeared the next morning, although I don't think she came out of it looking that great because she said she had turned me away because it was 'inappropriate' for me to see the children. Not many people would agree that it was inappropriate for a father to see his children on Boxing Day!

Perhaps because that story did not come out quite as she wanted, a more lurid account appeared the next day in the *Sunday Mirror*, in which it was claimed Amanda had punched Nicky, and that I had tried to push past Kieron to gain entry to the house. Neither of these claims was true. What I found hardest to fathom was why on earth Nicky should think it necessary to involve the papers. To my mind, she was playing games with the children and had little thought for their feelings.

I knew Nicky wanted to hurt me, but couldn't believe she'd resort to hurting the children to do so. If she was prepared to go this far, in my heart I was frightened of what the future held. And I was right, the incident was to mark the beginning of a process where access to the children would become increasingly difficult and, over the next 18 months, I was to see them only three times.

FIFTEEN

Payback in the Caribbean

DESPITE THE setback in Sri Lanka, we went to the Caribbean believing we had a genuine chance of winning there for the first time in more than 30 years. For myself, Nasser Hussain and Mark Butcher, who had toured there before when Curtly Ambrose and Courtney Walsh were leading the West Indies attack, we sensed a real opportunity.

With those two great bowlers retired, there finally didn't seem much between our fast bowlers and theirs. We didn't want to underestimate the opposition – and we were right to be cautious because Tino Best, Fidel Edwards and Corey Collymore posed problems – but compared to earlier West Indies sides they lacked experience. They were likely to give us the chance to score that had rarely happened with Ambrose and Walsh.

Even if they dished out physical punishment, now we could give some back. In the past, we might have had guys who bowled line and length, but they didn't exactly give the batsmen a peppering. But Steve Harmison and Simon Jones had genuine pace. Neither had been in the side lately. Harmison had missed Sri Lanka because the management had told him to stay at home and get fitter, and Jones had been recovering from major knee surgery. But they had the potential to wreak havoc.

Before the team left home in February, Amanda and I had gone on holiday to the Maldives and then on to visit her father in Thailand. The more I thought about the tour ahead, the more confident I became that it might finally be pay-back time. Brian Lara had the genius to make any plans look stupid, but I felt that if we could nullify their middle order we had a genuine chance. We needed our attack to make its mark early and put them under pressure, because we knew from the series in England in 2000 that once the skids were under them the West Indies could collapse, big-time.

Even though we'd been beaten on our two previous tours there, I loved playing cricket in the Caribbean. The West Indies were my favourite team to play against, and the Caribbean was my favourite place to go. I liked the way they played their cricket, and the enthusiasm the people had for the game. It had a wonderful flavour. The crowds were full of people ringing bells, blowing conch-shells or laughing and treating Tests like one big party. They'd heckle you, always in good humour, about how Lara was going to give you 'big licks' and Ambrose and Walsh were going to 'clatter you on the head' or cut your throat, judging by the way they'd greet you with slicing motions across their necks. And often that's what happened. But I'd enjoyed some great battles with the West Indies, and learned a lot from playing them.

Now everything worked out better than we could have possibly imagined. As a unit, Harmison, Jones, Matthew Hoggard and Andrew Flintoff were a revelation. I'd been playing for England for 11 years and we'd never had such an effective and hostile attack. The striking thing was that here was a bunch of young guys for whom reputations meant little. They fancied themselves and thoroughly relished what they were doing, and we backed them up with good catching. I have to say that it was quite nice to see the West Indians hopping around on the back foot and taking some blows for a change. I'd been there plenty of times!

A big factor in the success of our bowlers was the presence of a specialist fast bowling coach in Troy Cooley, a former Australian state cricketer who had worked at the Australian and English academies. He knew all about the mechanics of the job, but what he really brought to our attack was realism. If you bowled a bad spell, how were you going to deal with it? Were you going to fold and disappear, or come back strongly? He made the bowlers accept that, in the end, it was up to them. Although we won the first three Tests, it was a closer series than that suggests. We had to win some crucial sessions. In the past, we might well have messed them up, but now we took them.

I remember facing Harmison in a championship match up at the Riverside in 2000, when he was 21 and still pretty raw, but it was obvious that he could play for England. He was tall and pushed you onto the back foot with his steep bounce, and just needed to improve his control, something that would obviously come. It was early season and the damp pitch provided perfect seaming conditions, which Durham exploited better than Surrey. Harmison didn't get many wickets but he dismissed me cheaply twice. As I recall, I top-scored in our first innings, but as no one reached 30 in either innings, that's not saying much.

Even though he was not the finished article, Harmison was included in three England Test squads that summer, though he wasn't chosen to play. He later suffered shin problems and, for a while, seemed to be treading water. He eventually made his debut against India in 2002, in the first Test after I dropped out of the side. He has played quite regularly since, but like Flintoff discovered he wasn't initially strong enough to handle the physical demands of international cricket. He was told to buck up his ideas and get fit, and we soon saw in the West Indies he had.

Although he bowled sharply in the nets in Jamaica, I wasn't sure about his control, but suddenly everything clicked for him on the fourth morning of the first Test.

The guys had bowled too short in the first innings. The West Indies batsmen don't move their feet much and love to cut and pull, and we fed their strengths. But the bowlers listened to Cooley's advice to find a fuller length. Once he had adjusted, Harmison was simply sensational. He made one small change, and all the work he had put in got him seven for 12 off 12 consecutive overs.

In fact the moment the West Indies were five down and still in arrears – we'd taken a first-innings lead of 28 – we knew we'd got them completely on the run. They were all out for 47, their lowest-ever score, but it might have been even smaller had I not dropped one of their tailenders, Adam Sanford, off Harmison in the gully first ball. The score was then 41 for seven. It was a straightforward chance and maybe I had too much time to think about it. But Sanford only scored one, and I had taken a good catch above my head at third slip to dismiss the dangerous Chris Gayle, so I wasn't too upset.

That performance did enormous things for Harmison. It got him into a great rhythm and he had his tail up for the rest of the series. He bowled beautifully on the first day of the next Test on a flat pitch in Trinidad. Everything was perfect. He seemed to glide to the wicket, which we came to recognize as a sign that he was on top of his game, and moved the ball away from the bat. He took six wickets, which did much to set up another win and put us two up with two to play. His 22 wickets in the series must rank as one of England's finest bowling efforts overseas.

Harmison has the potential to be one of our greatest fast bowlers. The biggest question-mark about his future surrounds his attitude to touring. He admits to homesickness, and from what he says it appears that nothing will change. Although I wouldn't say I ever felt homesick as such, I understood how he felt. I used to grumble about the time we were away because I felt some tours could have been shorter. In my early years, I wasn't that mature and was ready to complain about things anyway. To an extent I used it as a way of coping; it gave an extra edge to my game. But, with time, I came to accept touring as something you had to live with. Some of us harden to these things and some don't. It doesn't look like Harmison will. Homesickness appears to be a problem he'll carry around with him, and there will probably come a time when he'll have to decide how much cricket he really wants to play. Like me, he will have to find the right balance between his cricket and private life. Again, as he had with my personal problems, Duncan handled Steve with great sympathy and understanding on this issue.

The great thing about our attack was how each bowler brought something different. Whereas Harmison made the ball bounce awkwardly, Jones skidded it through, at over 90mph, and swung it too. He was also prepared to get into the batsmen's faces and was fined for giving Ramnaresh Sarwan a send-off in Trinidad. Flintoff, who also provided pace and aggression, had great control and made a personal breakthrough with his first five-wicket haul in Barbados.

These three allowed Matthew Hoggard to now play a different part. Before, he had often been cast as our spearhead but it hadn't suited him. He had felt under pressure to take wickets. But now he was able to concentrate on doing what he did best – getting the ball to swing.

One of the reasons we'd struggled to win Tests abroad was that we hadn't learned how to use the Kookaburra (the type of ball used overseas which gives plenty of swing, especially when new). Once it went soft, bowling was very hard work. What Hoggard was good at in the West Indies was swinging the new ball into their left-handers. There wasn't much they could leave.

Another big plus was the discovery of wicket-keeper Geraint Jones. Jones replaced Chris Read for the final Test in Antigua and, when we got back home, he kept his place for the Tests and also took over from Read in the one-dayers. There were reports that there had been a selection disagreement between Duncan Fletcher and Rod Marsh, who had worked with Read at the academy, and their decisions caused a lot of debate in the press. I don't know whether the reports of a 'rift' were true, but given what happened with me, I could imagine they were.

Jones had begun the winter as deputy to Read, who had been first-choice keeper since Alec Stewart retired. No one faulted Read's keeping, but he had made few runs and, between the second and third Tests, there was talk within the team about whether Jones should be given a chance to show what he could do. Some of us were asked who we thought provided the better overall package.

As it happened, a warm-up game was scheduled to take place against a West Indian representative side in Bridgetown before the third Test, and both Read and Jones played. Read failed again but Jones batted with real style and confidence for 66, an innings I watched at close quarters as we put on more than 100 together. Read still played in the Barbados Test but after another low score, and with the series won, the selectors decided to act.

I agreed with the change and thought it was the right time to make it. My view was that Read had been given a fair chance but there were a few areas of his game that needed improving. He wasn't going to give us the runs or stability we needed from a No 7 at that time. Although Jones wasn't as good with the gloves, he caught the majority of important catches and no one could argue about his batting. He had the potential to become an even better batsman and given time I felt his wicket-keeping would improve too. Ian Healy wasn't much of a batsman when he first played for Australia, but with time he became highly effective.

I think the whole debate showed how things had changed for England. With a winning side, much higher standards were being demanded and anyone falling short faced a hard time. I found this out myself a year later, when I went short of runs at the start of my last season. What we achieved in the Caribbean in 2004, and at home later the same year, moved the goalposts for all of us.

OUR VICTORY owed a lot to the new-look pace attack, but also to three old lags grinding out vital runs in the middle order. For all the talk there had been about the need for fresh batting blood, Butch, Nasser and myself, all veterans of previous West Indies tours, produced the goods in the three Tests we won.

Nasser called us the 100 Club because that was our combined age (Butcher 31, Thorpe 34, Hussain 35), but our experience was definitely an asset. We doused the fire of the West Indies attack, which usually claimed wickets with the new ball but never got completely through us.

In fact we were the only England players to have passed fifty by the time the series had settled. Butch and Nasser put on more than 100 together in Jamaica and Trinidad, while Nasser and I shared small but important stands in each of the first three games. I batted well with the tail in Trinidad and Barbados, where I scored one of the finest centuries of my life. God, how I have loved batting at the Kensington Oval!

It was often attritional stuff, but outside Antigua pitches in the Caribbean were rarely easy to bat on, and a first-innings score of 300 was usually enough to put you in the game. As matches went on, surfaces would crack and the bounce get lower. That was why Harmison's great performance in Jamaica was so important. We hadn't wanted to chase even 180 in the fourth innings, and thanks to him we didn't.

Although Ambrose and Walsh had retired, we knew the West Indies would still play the same type of game. The mentality of a West Indian fast bowler is always to challenge the batsman. He demands, can you hook? Can you take being hit? On my first Test tour of the West Indies, Nasser and I came up against a couple of opening bowlers for the Leeward Islands called 'Hungry' Walsh and John 'the Dentist' Maynard. They just tore in, bowled as fast as they could and tried their best to kill you. I reckoned they captured the essence of what bowling fast meant on those islands.

We'd not seen Tino Best or Fidel Edwards before, but we knew they were young, raw and fiery. We had no doubt what the equation would be: plenty of 'chin music' and body blows, concentration and courage. We weren't wrong. But I loved the challenge, and so did Butch and Nasser.

Aware that this was his final tour, Nasser was in more positive mood than he had been in Sri Lanka, and made runs in both warm-up games in Jamaica. Butch and I were slower out of the blocks. Butch sprained an ankle and hardly faced a ball before the first Test at Sabina Park. He was one of those guys who rarely performed well in practice matches, though it never affected how he played in the Tests. I suffered another bout of back spasms, and had to leave the field on the first day of the second match. I felt well enough to bat next day and scored fifty, but I was quite concerned for a while. It was another case of my back playing up once I returned after several weeks off.

I really struggled to get control of my thoughts before my first innings of that series. I'd seen Edwards bowl on TV, but never faced him. He had a slingy action not dissimilar to Jeff Thomson's, and one I'd not come up against that much. I found myself waking up at 5am on the second day of the game, when I was pretty sure I was going to bat (West Indies had batted first and were nine wickets down at the end of day one). I just couldn't get back to sleep and ended up pacing around my hotel room, thinking about how I was going to deal with him. I had taken a general decision that I was going to take a few risks to try and dominate the fast bowlers, but couldn't decide how best to tackle him.

As expected, when we came to bat, Edwards and Best really let rip. Edwards was slightly quicker, but Best also topped 90mph and was strong enough to come back well in later spells. Both charged in as though they'd never tire, and Edwards sent Trescothick's stump cart-

Hallelujah. Someone must have been guiding me when I scored a century on my England return, against South Africa at the Oval, in 2003.

LEFT: Henry and Amelia, aged six and four.

RIGHT: With Amanda, who made me happy again.

LEFT: Amanda and Kitty joined me when I was out in Durban during Christmas 2004. Amanda was pregnant with Emma.

RIGHT: Celebrating Amelia's 6th birthday in February 2005, two months early, on one of the few occasions I was allowed to see the children.

SUNDAY Mirror

MARCH 17 2002

65p

6 FREE PACKETS OF SEEDS PLUS A FREE GARDENS BOOK SEE PAGE 32

EXCLUSIVE: TRUTH ABOUT ENGLAND'S TEST-WINNER BY WIFE HE BETRAYED

He's no hero ..Graham is a two-faced serial cheat

WRONGED: Wife Nicky, who now has a new love, says: 'Graham humiliated me by sleeping around during our marriage – and now he disgusts me'

By DEBORAH SHERWOOD and MAGGIE O'RIORDAN

THE wife of cricket star Graham Thorpe broke her silence last night to say: "He's not a hero – he's a hypocrite."

Man of the Match Thorpe dedicated his triumphant double century in England's victory over New Zealand to his children. But Nicky, 32, says: "He's hardly ever been there for them."

Thorpe flew back from India in December saying he wanted to save his marriage. But today Nicky tells of his years of cheating - and her new love Kieron Vorster, Tim Henman's fitness trainer.

FULL STORY: PAGES 4, 5&6

SCORED: Thorpe after his double-century

REF ABANDONS TOP SOCCER GAME AS STARS BRAWL: SEE SPORT

LEFT AND BELOW: Nicky's ultimate betrayal – a six-page spread in the *Sunday Mirror* in March 2002. Over the next few years she sold several more stories on me to the tabloids, including this December 2003 piece.

ORPE NARKED

EX-WIFE ON THORPE

'He's a despicable human being with no morals.. let's lend him a Santa suit to see if he improves'

EXCLUSIVE

TEXT MATCH: Thorpe in action

BOXING DAY PUNCH-UP 2

to pull her off and got a smack in the left side of the head and she was thumping me."

Her mother Lynn Rayment called police but Thorpe and Amanda left before they arrived.

Nicky and Kieron, who have been together for two years, made statements to police.

Keiron, who was tennis star Tim Henman's fitness trainer, is pressing charges for forceable entry while Nicky is alleging common assault against Amanda. Nobody has yet been arrested but Surrey Police are looking into the allegations.

Nicky said: "I have had enough and I'm not taking any more. He arrives unexpectedly and doesn't make arrangements. I hope he gets done, although he'll probably just get fined."

She added: "I have never denied him access, but now I will insist on supervised access. He has a history of going on tour and not communicating...

morals. What is his problem, why can't we just talk about this? Let's lend him a Father Christmas suit and see if that changes...

ABOVE: Relaxing in Mauritius in October 2004.

RIGHT: Proud dad with new baby Emma, born August 2005.

LEFT: England score the winning run to take the sensational first Test in Jamaica in March 2004.

BELOW: Batting during my match-turning century in Barbados. I always loved playing in Bridgetown.

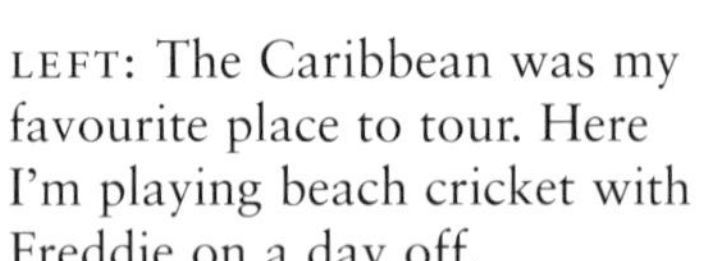

LEFT: The Caribbean was my favourite place to tour. Here I'm playing beach cricket with Freddie on a day off.

RIGHT: After years of losing in the Caribbean, we finally savoured victory in 2004.

RIGHT: I shared so many great moments on the field with Nasser Hussain.

ABOVE: My hundred in Durban in December 2004 – my last for England – helped save a Test that looked lost.

ABOVE: Celebrating England's historic seven Test wins in seven at home with Freddie in summer 2004.

RIGHT: One of England's best-ever results overseas was winning in South Africa in 2004-05.

LEFT: I played more Test matches alongside Nasser Hussain and Michael Atherton than anyone bar Alec Stewart.

BELOW: Golf was definitely only a recreational pursuit for me – I'm just drawing one in here!

ABOVE: Taking a breather – or possibly just resting my dodgy back!

RIGHT: Although some of their tactics are controversial, I support the Fathers 4 Justice campaign.

ABOVE: Duncan Fletcher was a great adviser, and a great coach, who helped save my career.

ABOVE: Michael Vaughan's talent as captain was encouraging us all to relax more and enjoy ourselves. It worked.

BELOW: Shane Warne was without doubt the best spinner I ever faced. He never stopped developing.

Walking out for my 100th Test at Durham in May 2005. Three years earlier, I would never have imagined such a landmark was possible.

Even at the time of my century of Tests, I suspected it might be my last game for England.

wheeling yards before he had Vaughan caught in the slips. I was next in and pretty pumped up watching this pair give it everything. Best hit Nasser twice on the head and Edwards struck Butch flush on his right forearm (fascinatingly for the rest of us, if not Butch, it later swelled to the size of a large marrow).

But because Butch and Nasser heroically stuck it out for almost three hours, and bad light and rain brought an early finish, I ended up facing just two balls from Edwards in the semi-dark that night. All those hours of anxiety for two balls! And I had to go through it all again the next night. Sure enough, I didn't play a big innings. I was out next morning for 19, hooking at Best who celebrated by charging the full length of the field like a Chelsea striker who'd just scored a last-minute winner. So much for an easy life without Ambrose and Walsh. Although Best and Edwards were nothing like as consistent as them, there were times when they were 10mph faster.

Edwards missed the second Test in Trinidad but Best, a confrontational, in-your-face character, made sure life was never dull. Pedro Collins, a left-arm seamer and Edwards's half-brother, came into the side and bowled well. With the fifth ball I faced, Best hit my left index finger with a beamer. Later, he smashed me on the right hand. My first thought was that it might be broken, but thankfully the glove did its job. I was also hit on the head and in the ribs.

After how I'd got out in Jamaica, they gave me plenty of short stuff, but I wasn't unduly worried. I'd decided I was going to take them on. I got off the mark with a pull that went straight over the keeper's head for four, and throughout the innings pulled and hooked well. The toughest period was losing Hussain, Flintoff and Read quickly to the second new ball, but Ashley Giles, who had little to do with the ball in a series dominated by pace, invaluably held up his end for an hour and a half.

In that time we added 85, a stand that swung the match our way. When we came together, we led by fewer than 30, and I kept telling myself that that was nowhere near enough given how difficult batting could be in Trinidad. I thought, *'Remember 1994 and 46 all out!'* Again, we didn't want to be chasing more than 180. In the end, we claimed a first-innings lead of 111 and, thanks to terrific bowling by Simon Jones, our target stayed under 100. My only regret was that I fell 10 short of a century.

We'd all but won the match by the fourth evening. We only needed another 28 and Butch and Nasser were batting. It was hard to resist starting the celebrations that night (victory would mean we couldn't lose the series), and it was a temptation we didn't resist. Butch, Nasser and myself went out for something to eat and found ourselves back at the hotel bar considering a nightcap. Butch and I tried to persuade Nasser to stay, but he wouldn't have it. He wanted to get off back to his room to have one last fiddle with his bat, and think about the morning. 'Don't go,' said Butch, in a last attempt to change his mind. 'You'll only nick your first ball if you do.'

What happened? Nasser, bright-eyed after his early night, nicked his second ball to the keeper! Having stayed up with Butch, I wasn't at my sharpest and had been hoping not to bat. Too bad. Out I went and off my second ball my heart was in my mouth when I also edged Adam Sanford to the keeper. Fortunately, Ridley Jacobs only got one hand to the ball and put it down. '*Thank you, Lord.*' In an instant the pressure was off. and Butch and I quickly finished the job with a flurry of fours. Nasser, you were warned!

I really looked forward to the Barbados Test. It was one of my favourite grounds in the world and I'd been lucky enough to have done well there on the two previous tours. I'd got 84 there when we became the first foreign team ever to win a Test in Bridgetown, a result made possible by Alec Stewart's two centuries, and four years later Mark Ramprakash and I scored centuries (Ramps's long-awaited first for England) in a game we might have won had heavy rain – a rare sight in Barbados – not washed out most of the last day. The atmosphere was always incredible because England supporters turned up in their thousands, and history oozed out of every corner of the ground. The stands were named after famous players such as Sobers, Worrell, Weekes,

Walcott and Malcolm Marshall, who tragically died of cancer in 1999. It was the West Indian equivalent of Lord's. To my mind, the only overseas grounds that can compare are Sydney, Calcutta and Cape Town.

Another reason I was looking forward to the game was that Amanda, having finished her law exams – she was studying to become a solicitor – was coming out on the first evening to join me for 10 days. After my runs in Trinidad, and the thought of seeing Amanda for the first time in five weeks, I felt very upbeat going into the game.

Vaughan won the toss and put West Indies in, as much to keep them under pressure as anything. We bowled really well on a good pitch to dismiss them for 224. Lara was out when he looked set, and once a long stand between Sarwan and Chanderpaul was broken another collapse was underway. But then we lost Trescothick early to Edwards before stumps. Even the thought of renewing Edwards's acquaintance couldn't spoil my evening. Amanda and I had a couple of glasses of wine before an early night, and I remained pretty relaxed about the game the next morning, even if I didn't have as much sleep as I would have liked!!

I wasn't expecting to bat as early as I did but Edwards, skiddy, fast and hard to pick up, proved a handful again and quickly removed Butcher and Vaughan. In no time, I was out to join Nasser, at 33 for three. Again, I got off the mark with a top-edged shot over the keeper for four, but I felt very focused from the start. Edwards was the most dangerous, but all the bowlers posed problems. They needed to win to get back in the series, and gave it everything. I had decided to think of Edwards as a Waqar Younis, who had an open-chested action and quite a low arm that helped him swing the ball. If anything, Edwards's arm was even lower, practically over the stumps at the point of release. The tactic worked. I took more runs off him than any of the others.

Although I managed to play myself in, wickets kept falling at the other end. Most of my partners got going but couldn't stay. Lara's tactics in the second half of our innings created enormous debate. He brought on Gayle, a part-time spinner, straight after lunch when we were struggling at 73 for four, and stuck with him for 11 overs while the quickies attacked from the other end. I think he feared that his quick bowlers, who certainly weren't as fit as our guys, would run out of steam. Perhaps he also feared we might start slogging Gayle, whereas in fact we just milked him for a couple of runs an over.

I had little stands of around 30 with Hussain, Flintoff, Read and Giles. Every little helped, but we really needed something bigger if we were to take a big lead. It didn't happen. When Hoggard went for nought just before tea, we were 155 for eight and in serious trouble. I'd got 66, but there was just Simon Jones and Harmison left.

I now batted with them rather like I did with Hoggard

in that Test against Sri Lanka at Edgbaston two years earlier. At first I wanted to protect them, but once they looked comfortable I gave them more of the strike and we took every run we could, on the basis that the closer we got to their score the twitchier Lara would get. Of course, every run was greeted with a big cheer from our supporters. The whole ground was packed with English faces.

Jones and I whittled 32 off the deficit before he fell to Best. In the next over, Harmy and I were unable to stop his being exposed to a whole over from Best. Harmy assured me he would be all right, and he was. He kept up his end superbly. I went down and punched his glove, and told him I was going to have a pop at Edwards. The second new ball was due and, apart from obviously wanting to reduce the deficit further, I was quite keen to get my hundred. I was on 92.

The first ball was a bouncer, which I top-edged to fine leg for four. I defended the next ball and then looked around; I wanted to hit another four but where was the best place? I noticed mid-off was halfway back to the boundary and decided I'd go down the pitch and try and flat-bat one wide of him. Fortunately, the next ball was of good length and I middled it sweetly: although mid-off dived, he couldn't get there and the ball ran to the boundary. What a great place to score a century! The roar that greeted me made it feel like I was in a football ground. A moment I'll never forget.

Harmy and I didn't throw the bat after that. We just kept on taking what runs we could, every one of them adding to the frustration of the West Indies. By the time Harmison was eventually out, we'd put on 39 giving us a lead of two runs. I can't say that that century was the best I ever scored, because the one at the Oval against South Africa must always take pride of place, but given the match situation and steady fall of wickets, this wasn't far behind. After my 119, the next biggest contribution came from Extras which totalled 20!

I was so exhilarated that I had another short night of sleep. I was hyperactive and up by 6am, going over what had happened, savouring every second. In the old days I wouldn't have felt like this. I would have concentrated on what was coming up next. But I learned how important it was to bask in the good days because I knew they couldn't last forever. I was less emotionally detached about things, and all the better for it.

Thinking that I wouldn't be batting for a while, and then that the innings would soon be over, Amanda had opted to stay at the beach on her first morning there, but she rushed down when she saw our fightback going from strength to strength. There was a VIP box set aside for players' relatives and she was in there, along with Harmy's family, in good time to see me reach my hundred.

The day at the ground ended controversially when I refused to allow one of the English journalists, Mike

Dickson of the *Daily Mail*, into my press conference. It was something I'd never done before but I was so upset about an article he'd written a while earlier and felt I didn't have a choice. I'd recently done a three-part series of cricket-based pieces with him but, for some reason, he'd inserted in the last piece a couple of comments about my private life which he hadn't cleared with me. Not only were they factually incorrect, he knew them to be incorrect. He said that Nicky had met Kieron after separating from me, whereas in fact her relationship with Kieron caused our split. He also wrote that I had had problems over getting access to my children, 'although Nicky's supporters would say she has been the more reasonable'. I was incensed, and the press conference gave me an opportunity to vent my anger.

The incident caused a bit of concern among the England management, who thought I might continue banning Dickson from press conferences. Duncan asked me to let the matter lie, but I reminded him how upset he had been the previous year when Geoff Boycott wrote a piece in the *Daily Telegraph* criticizing Duncan's attitude towards county cricket. Duncan had insisted on being allowed to respond with an article of his own in the same paper, putting across his case. I didn't think Duncan had yet made his peace with Boycott. When I said this, Duncan was sympathetic to my position but suggested I met Dickson and talked things through, which we did in Antigua. I asked him to explain why he wrote what he did. First he said his editor had asked him to insert the comments, then he admitted that he had bumped into Kieron at a party, and he had persuaded him to. To this day, I don't know why he did it.

We'd only taken a small lead in the Test, but the psychological boost from our comeback was huge. Harmison got Gayle cheaply on the second evening and, although we expected a hard fight, the next day the weather now gave us a helping hand. Barbados is normally guaranteed blue skies but the day was overcast, perfect conditions for Hoggard to swing the ball. With Lara fighting tooth and nail, Hoggard took only one wicket in the first hour – Daren Ganga taken at third slip, where I somehow got my stiff limbs down low to complete the catch – but in the first over after the drinks interval Hoggard achieved a high-class hat-trick taking Sarwan, Chanderpaul and Ryan Hinds. When Jacobs fell a few moments later, the West Indies were 48 for six and the game was up. They were eventually all out for 94, and we knocked off the runs needed for the loss of just Trescothick and Vaughan.

Winning any series felt great, but this one was especially sweet given that I had contributed in such a big way, and given all the batterings we'd taken from West Indies down the years. Now we'd had our revenge in their back yard – and where better to complete the job than at the Kensington Oval?

GETTING OUT Brian Lara for low scores played a huge part in our overall victory. He was always a key wicket. The likes of myself and Nasser had seen him score so many runs over the years that we knew he was capable of anything, and to hear the ball nick his bat the way it did in the first three Tests of that series was astonishing.

Flintoff in particular caused him real problems. For the first time I could recall, Lara's footwork became unsure and he was hopping around in discomfort. He was forced to take risks. In three matches he barely got a run and, on that last day in Barbados, he really took a physical pummelling. It was a rare sight for England supporters.

That night, after we'd clinched the series and our celebrations began, he and his team came into our dressing-room for a drink. We had a good chat and he opened up a fair bit, admitting he'd had difficulties in the series. He bemoaned how much more intimidating our pace attack had become. 'What's happened?' he said. 'Where have all those people like Angus Fraser and Dean Headley gone?'

As the series went on, and it became evident that England were in with a great chance of winning their first series in the Caribbean for more than 35 years, we could see the pressure building on him. He got rattled a few times. In Jamaica he dislocated a finger dropping Butcher in the slips, and in Trinidad was fined for having a set-to with the umpires about the light. He didn't want England winning in the Caribbean on his watch, and seemed to feel he had to be aggressive towards us on the field, although off it he remained easy to deal with. For me, he was always a decent guy.

For such a great player, it must have been desperately frustrating to have played in a great team and then seen it brought down so low. As captain, he had an impossible job, and inevitably he took a lot of flak for the failings of his players.

Few cricketers lived under such an unforgiving spotlight as he did. Obviously, I held him in special regard because I'd learned so much from watching him. I sometimes wondered to myself whether I would still be playing if I hadn't had his example to follow. And so, after all he'd been through that series, how could I begrudge him reclaiming his world Test record in the final Test in Antigua?

It was an amazing feat of concentration and skill but, as I said, he was capable of anything. We thought Harmison had had him caught behind before he had scored. We thought we heard a nick but the TV snickometer was unclear. After that he played himself in with the ominous care we feared. He wasn't just batting to make up for all his failures earlier in the series, but to make sure the West Indies didn't lose the game and suffer a whitewash on home soil. Had that happened, he might well have had to resign the captaincy. But on an absolute beauty of a pitch, it soon became clear we weren't going to witness a whitewash but another piece of batting history.

I was the only survivor from the England side against whom he'd scored 375, 10 years earlier, although Nasser was also on that tour but didn't play in the game. The only man who had a better view of both innings, I suppose, was umpire Darrell Hair, who stood in each game. But when I think back on all the brilliant innings I saw Lara play, I don't just think of his 375 and his 400. He scored seven centuries in Tests in which I played.

He was, quite simply, the best batsman I played with or against, ahead of Sachin Tendulkar, Steve Waugh and Ricky Ponting, in that order. And amazingly, Lara told me afterwards that he had had trouble sleeping during that game, and slept only a few hours on the first couple of nights. He broke the record on the third day, passing Matthew Hayden's 380. Again, he was under so much pressure; and it was all the more remarkable that he could bat for so long making so few mistakes. Yet he certainly didn't look under that much pressure when he was at the crease. It was just very obvious he wanted to keep on batting and batting.

I was really pleased for him. I was also pleased for myself, because as it happened I had asked him after Barbados if he could sign one of his shirts for me after the series was over. When he moved to 313 on the second evening, and it was quite clear he had 380 in his sights, I remembered my request and thought I'd better remind him of it sooner rather than later. Once the record was his again (and I had no doubt he'd get there), everyone would be wanting him to sign things. When I saw him at breakfast in the hotel the next morning, I tapped him on the shoulder as casually as I could and said, 'You'll remember to do that shirt, Brian, won't you?'

He said he would and, after the game – which we drew thanks to centuries from Flintoff and Vaughan – he was as good as his word. He signed it, 'Thanks for fielding through two world records. Best wishes, Brian Lara.' What a souvenir!

I have to admit that perhaps I didn't try as hard as I might to cut off the sweep shot from Gareth Batty that took him clear of Hayden. I was fielding on the backward square boundary, and the ball came racing down a few yards to my right, but I'd been in the field quite a few hours and my back was feeling a bit stiff and, hey, who cares? He'd have probably got the record a few minutes later anyway!

SIXTEEN

The Magnificent Seven

A LOT OF THINGS fell into place in the Caribbean. The team gelled into a really strong and forceful outfit. The batting gained depth and experience, and after a year of chopping and changing – often because of an unfortunate spate of injuries – the bowling attack was stable and at times quite ferocious.

The way we won sent our confidence soaring. The side was quite a bit younger than the one I'd been used to playing in pre-2002 – Atherton, Caddick, Gough and Stewart had all gone – and all of a sudden this felt like a team with a future. There was a real sense of excitement.

How fast things change. Only a few months earlier we'd had to scrap to get a draw in a home series against South Africa and, despite showing guts in Sri Lanka, had deservedly come off second best. I wasn't in the side and didn't know if I'd got a future with England. Now

I'd scored two centuries and a ninety, all in games we'd won.

I returned home from Antigua with the other Test specialists, leaving the rest of the boys to battle out a 2–2 draw in the one-dayers that perhaps showed that winning the Tests was not as easy as some thought. The domestic season had already begun by the time we got home, but we were all instructed by the ECB to rest for a couple of weeks before returning to our counties. I had been handed an England contract for the summer, along with Harmison, Hoggard and Simon Jones.

Coming back from a series in the Caribbean is always hard as it runs straight into our season, but this time our return was especially tough for the likes of Vaughan, Trescothick and Flintoff who had played in the Tests and one-dayers. And the season was going to be the longest ever, thanks to the addition of the one-day ICC Champions Trophy in September. If England reached the final, some of the team were looking at nearly 50 days of international cricket. Fortunately, I could just concentrate on three Tests against New Zealand and four against the West Indies.

I warmed up with two championship appearances for Surrey. After several highly successful years, Keith Medlycott and Adam Hollioake had both stepped down. The club had gone back to another Australian coach in Steve Rixon, who'd had a successful stint with New

Zealand, but more controversially the captaincy went to Jonathan Batty.

Jon was in a difficult position. In others circumstances the job might have gone to Ian Ward, but he had fallen out of favour with some powerful people at the club. He hadn't liked the relaxed culture towards the end of Adam's time, and had been allowed to leave for Sussex. We shouldn't have lost him. After Stephen Fleming, the New Zealand captain, had turned down the captaincy, the job was offered to Jon who was already opening the batting and keeping wicket. He was a fighter and hard worker, but struggled to stamp his personality on a dressing-room in transition. I wasn't around much, but in the few games I played I could see the problems. It wasn't really about people falling out with each other, but about the direction we should now take.

We started shakily. Helped by 82 from Ward, Sussex outplayed us and we then lost to Middlesex, who made light of scoring over 400. My first game, against Northants, was ruined by rain but in the second we lost again, this time to Warwickshire. At least I scored runs in both innings. I played only once more in the championship season. Things didn't improve for the team until late on, when four wins in the last five matches hauled us into third place. Unsurprisingly, Jon was replaced as captain during the winter, with Butcher taking over.

Our recent series with New Zealand had been close.

They'd held us to a draw in New Zealand three years earlier, and beaten us the last time they'd come to England, so we were definitely not underestimating them. But they arrived with injury problems, and the absence of fast bowler Shane Bond was a big blow for them. He was quick and a proven wicket-taker. Even without him, though, they were a disciplined side that didn't give up. They had a long tail, and Fleming always had plans to try and keep them in the game. Whatever the eventual 3–0 outcome suggested, there wasn't a huge amount between us. Twice we had to knock off over 250 in the last innings.

We were all reminded how fast things can change during the first Test at Lord's. On the first day of practice, I saw Vaughan, who was batting in the nets, go for a sweep against a net bowler and fall over in a heap. As soon as he began hobbling away, I knew we'd have to change our plans. Vaughan was then still opening the innings, so who would take his place? Butch didn't want to give up the No 3 position, so Andrew Strauss was called up again, as happened the previous year and for the opening Test in the Caribbean when Butcher sprained his ankle. This time, though, he played.

Strauss wasn't just familiar with Lord's, his home ground, but looked very composed and totally settled in the dressing-room. There were not too many frills about him, he just went quietly about his job. It probably helped that he'd been around the side a bit and played some one-dayers. It's rare to see someone look so much at ease so soon. I remember Nasser once telling me that Duncan thought Strauss could play and had a good work ethic and, not for the first time, Duncan was spot-on. I found Strauss good natured and determined.

This was my first Test at Lord's since my nightmare game two years earlier. Bizarrely, I found the same group of New Zealand supporters who had taken the mickey out of me in the past back in the stands. When I was fielding on the Nursery End boundary, I could hear them in full cry above me. All the old tennis jokes came out. I thought, '*Christ, these guys have good memories.*' But where before I'd turned my back on them and hated every second, now I turned around and mimed a few tennis shots back at them, which they loved.

The surprises didn't stop there. When we batted, Strauss scored a century, the first England batsman since myself 11 years earlier to do this in his first Test. For a newcomer to perform straightaway like that was a huge boost to the side. It can often take someone time to settle which puts him under pressure, and also adds to the responsibilities of the rest of the team. But Strauss looked completely at ease, and during an opening stand of almost 200 with Tres – the acting captain in Vaughan's absence – kept us right in the game. In some respects, when someone came into the side knowing they had a one-off chance – as with Strauss because everyone expected Vaughan to be fit for the second Test – they had little to lose and plenty to gain. Strauss didn't hang around.

Despite our good start, we were in a scrap to win the game. Butch and Nasser got some runs but were unable to make big scores. I fell cheaply to Chris Cairns. With New Zealand having made 386, it took a century stand between Flintoff and Geraint Jones on the Saturday afternoon to lift us into the lead.

While these two were batting, I remember sitting out the back of the dressing-room with Nasser, in the TV area, where we often went to listen to the commentary and chuckle at some of the things the pundits were saying. Within the space of a few days, the look of the England batting had changed. Jones was playing with real panache and making the debate about himself and Chris Read look redundant, while Strauss's performance had made everyone start thinking, especially Nasser, the oldest batsman in the side and therefore perhaps the most vulnerable.

I think he'd got one ear on the commentary to try and get a feel for what people were saying. Nasser had always cared more than me what the TV guys were saying. At one point he asked me what I thought he should do. I knew that he'd set his heart on playing another four games to get to his 100 Tests, but could sense he was rethinking his position fast. He must have feared the media might turn on him if he was seen trying to hang onto his place, and wouldn't have forgotten that the previous summer Mike Gatting had criticized him for saying that he intended to play on for his hundredth cap. Nasser must have seen his plans disintegrating in front of his eyes.

I said, 'Why worry about it now? We're going to Headingley next. They might want seven batsmen. We might all play.'

He seemed unconvinced, 'I don't want to stand in the way of others.'

My impression was that he didn't want to drag things out. He knew the end was not far away – he planned to go at the end of the season anyway – and wanted to beat people to the call. But I didn't think much more about it during the rest of the game. Like I've already said, I'd got beyond worrying what England selectors might do, and whether Hussain, Strauss or anyone else played in the next game was a matter for them.

Fate now intervened. Two days later, we found ourselves chasing 282 to win, a challenging target but we felt we could get it and the pitch was good. With Tres and Butch falling early, Nasser found himself going out to join Strauss and the two of them put on more than 100 together before Nasser – never the best judge of a run! – managed to run out his partner by calling for a risky single to point. Oh dear. Not a clever thing given the match situation and Strauss's position (he was in sight of a second century in his debut match). Cynics might have thought Nasser was deliberately running out the man who'd just emerged as the main rival to take his place! It was such an awful mistake that I'd have had a good laugh about it, but I was next man in and too busy going down the stairs and through the Long Room. As I walked out, I knew my first task was going to be calming Nasser down. We'd lost three wickets and were only about halfway to the target; there was plenty to be done. Lose one wicket and you can easily lose two or three.

The first thing Nasser did was walk down the pitch towards me and shout, 'Make sure you call loudly!'

I thought to myself, 'Yeah, good one. You've just run Strauss out and you're telling *me* it's too noisy to hear each other. I know what you're thinking – "I've just made a huge fuck up."'

'Look mate, just fucking calm down,' I said, walking up to him. 'Forget it. Little Jacob [his son] could snap his hand off in the door tonight . . . It's just a game of cricket . . . Okay?'

I could see he was seriously pumped up, but he quickly calmed down and batted really well. I did my usual thing of trying to get us thinking about our partnership, and putting on 100, which we did, and reducing the target by setting mini targets of 10 runs. As we got closer, I realized we were on course for one of our best wins. I also realized there was a chance for Nasser to get a hundred. He was very focused and hitting better shots than me. I remember him hitting three boundaries in the first two overs with the second new ball, taking him to 87. We now needed 22 more. It ought not to take much, I thought, to make sure he gets there before we win.

This was a situation I'd been in before, and controversially. On New Zealand's previous tour in 1999, when we were chasing slightly more than 200 to win the first Test at Edgbaston, Alex Tudor, a Surrey teammate and then one of England's most exciting prospects, had been sent in at No 3 as nightwatchman and stayed to play the decisive innings. When I joined him, he was on 84 and we needed another 34 to win.

As with Nasser at Lord's, time was not an issue and I accept now that I should have helped Alex more than I did, in what would be probably his only chance to score a Test century. All I can say is that it wasn't my main consideration. For a start, a hundred for him had only become realistic moments before I walked out to bat: in the previous over, he'd hit Simon Doull for four fours, two of them from miscues. It had not been a batsman's game. Wickets had regularly tumbled to the seamers, and the attitude in the dressing-room was that we should get on and win it as quickly as possible. And don't forget, we'd just failed badly at the World Cup and it was Nasser's first game as captain. As for me, 1999 was my bad year and I was struggling with everything: my relations with the management, my form, even my appetite for playing the game.

When I got to the middle, I asked Alex whether he wanted to get a hundred and he told me not to worry about it, but I shouldn't have listened. Instinct took over and I played quite aggressively and by the time the scores were level Alex needed to hit a six to reach his century. He could only manage four, leaving him stranded on 99. As we walked off, I got a bit of stick from the crowd.

Sadly, Alex's international career failed to take off. He had a lot of talent. I never like to criticize bowlers because what they do is very hard work, and Alex's action obviously put a lot of stress on his body, but there were times when he perhaps needed to modify his training to concentrate more on strengthening other parts of his body to get through the rigours of daily bowling. I've always liked Alex and was really happy to see him have a good start to the 2005 season after moving to Essex.

I think it showed how much I had changed, and how much more positive and confident the England team had become in the intervening five years, that I behaved differently at Lord's in 2004. I took account of the bigger picture. It certainly felt strange to block balls so that Nasser would get back on strike. I'd never done that before. I played out dot balls at the end of four overs in a row, and after the fifth ball of the last one Nasser – now on 94 – shouted down from the non-striker's end, 'Play fucking properly! . . . Don't worry about me!' But I ignored him and played out the sixth ball as well, then went up to tell him, 'Right, mate, you'll get your hundred here . . .'

And he did, with two lovely fours off Chris Martin, the first through mid-on, the second through cover, before we ran the single to win the match. When he got his hundred, he went down on one knee and punched the air. As always with Nasser, there was a lot of passion. It still hadn't clicked with me that there might have been more to his behaviour than delight at scoring a century and winning the game.

We ran off back to the pavilion, me following behind through a packed and cheering Long Room thinking how much better this was than my last Test here, and it wasn't until we got upstairs, and got through the jumping around in the dressing-room to snap open a beer in the back room, that I realized what Nasser might be thinking. He'd pretty quickly switched on the TV commentary and then turned round to me and said, 'What do you think? . . . I'm not going to top that . . . What do you think about me calling it a day?'

'Christ, really? . . . Do you think so?'

'Yeah . . . I don't think I can do any better than that . . . That's pretty much it . . .'

Then someone came into the room and so we went quiet, and we were quickly taken off to do some press interviews where Nasser dropped some pretty plain hints that he was retiring with immediate effect, which he made official a few days later. As always, instinct had played a big part in his decision. A week earlier, his place had looked secure. Now he'd gone, I was at 34 the oldest man in the team.

IT TURNED into the most incredible summer. Maintaining the momentum we'd acquired from the Caribbean and Lord's, we won the two remaining Tests against New Zealand and all four against the West Indies. Amazingly, these were our first whitewashes in series of more than two matches since 1978, when I was still at school. As for winning seven Tests out of seven in a season, that was unique. And it made English cricket very big news again, to an extent I'd not experienced.

There were times at Headingley and Trent Bridge when New Zealand were well ahead, and the West Indies made a lot of the running at Old Trafford where we weren't quite on top of our game, but we kept turning things round. We dug deep and played some really good cricket. And our self-belief just grew and grew. I remember a team meeting at which we discussed our goals before the West Indies series. This was not the sort of thing we'd often done before, and maybe if we had we would have been more consistent. In the bad old days, we'd been too good at winning one match and losing the next ('the great-shit era,' we called it). Now, we'd realized how writing down our aims helped us focus.

At one point I said, 'Look, why can't we win all seven

this summer?' And the idea had gone up on the board at the front of the room. We talked about it and decided it was something that, without being presumptuous, we could achieve. We were winning, had beaten the West Indies decisively in the Caribbean, and saw no reason why we couldn't carry on winning. So, chasing 4–0 became one of our targets and set us thinking how we might do it. It typified the new purposeful attitude in the dressing-room.

We were feeling the benefits of the team's strong work ethic and willingness to face up to things honestly. For example, we never treated the West Indies batting line-up with anything but respect. Gayle, Chanderpaul and Sarwan were no pushovers, let alone Lara. But we were also ruthless, and I could tell our attack had a hold over them. As in the Caribbean, the big thing was stopping Lara. Now, thanks to careful planning and intelligent bowling, we didn't let him get one century.

And Vaughan encouraged us to relax and enjoy our cricket. His attitude was that we were always all under pressure. You might be short of runs, or short of wickets, or your family had come to watch that day, but the pressure never let up. So he felt it was important not to do anything that might add to the burden. He believed that people played best when they were relaxed, and I'm sure in most cases that's right. His outlook was quite different from Nasser's, but very similar to Adam Hollioake's.

Whereas Nasser was always the one to speak in the team huddle at the start of a day, Vaughan liked to share the job around. He'd tap you on the shoulder after practice and ask you to say a few words of encouragement, and you'd nervously go away and think of something. (When asked to speak, Butch once said, 'When it rains on one man's house, it rains on all our houses.' It sounded profound, but I'm not sure any of us knew what he really meant. It got a good giggle anyway.)

It was a good idea and brought the team together. I tried not to make mine long or serious. I'd say something like, 'Whatever it is that's going to motivate you today, whether you are doing it for your family, your kids, or the new BMW you want to buy at the end of the season, find your motivation and enjoy it. Something far worse could happen than a bad day at the cricket.'

Hardly great oratory, but Mick didn't seem to mind me doing it. He asked me to do it a few times and I was happy to oblige. Whereas in years past I was a guy who tended to sit at the back of the dressing-room and concentrate on my own game, now – older and wiser – I realized that there were things I could pass on that might benefit other players.

The thing I remember most about the summer of 2004 was how happy we'd all be for each other when somebody else was successful. In my early days, I sometimes felt there were people who were a little envious of me having a good day. Now, someone would look you in the eye and say well done and you knew he meant it. I think we all knew how hard everyone else was working, and how hard these highs were to achieve at Test level. There was genuine warmth, and we all had a taste of the good days.

Everyone was especially pleased for Ashley Giles who, after a slow start, picked up nearly 30 wickets in the previous five Tests. In my time, England never had a magical mystery spinner of the sort we came up against in Asia and Australia, but in Ashley we had a popular and honest, hardworking finger spinner. He had been through some tough times on the pitch, but shown himself strong enough to deal with them. He hadn't been asked to bowl much in the West Indies, and had taken some stick from spectators and media, and he had started to question what he was doing in the team.

What Ashley had gone through was something we all went through at some stage. Nasser even used to say to me sometimes during big matches, 'In a year's time, is anybody really going to care about what's happening here?' In fact that was just the sort of attitude you needed to cope, although at times it was obvious Nasser cared very much about what was happening. There wouldn't have been much point telling him that in a year's time not many people would give a damn!

The fact was, we operated in a harsh environment and unless you were strong it could badly affect you. Around the time of the final Test against New Zealand,

Ashley spoke to our psychologist Steve Bull, and I'm sure Steve would have given him a few helpful pointers, but ultimately it came down to Ashley to sort his own problems out, and that's what he did. Trent Bridge was the start of his revival. He had an excellent match with bat and ball. He and I knocked off the last 70 runs together to win the match, and I think that from then on he began to see himself as an essential member of the team, and that helped his confidence grow further.

And there was now great confidence in the England team. Giles could bowl over the wicket into the rough and it was not deemed a negative tactic. When Phil Tufnell used to do it he took so much criticism that it freaked him out. 'I can't bowl over the wicket or I'll get slaughtered,' he'd say. The difference now was that we were winning; when Tuffers was doing it, we weren't.

We were ruthless. The batsmen made sure that when it was their day, they cashed in. Between us we scored 13 centuries in the season, another record. (Back in 1999, we couldn't even manage one hundred between us in four matches against New Zealand.) It was a healthy culture of success that I'm sure helped the new guys who came into the team. Strauss, Geraint Jones, Robert Key and Ian Bell were not in the side at the start of the year, but all scored runs when they got their chance. And that hadn't always happened in the past.

The lower middle order scored many crucial runs, and did their share of digging us out of trouble. Flintoff's batting went up a notch. He was one of those who had really benefited from working on his fitness. He always batted best when he was positive about what he was doing, even if that meant pulling in the reins. Once I had to give him a little shake and tell him to get his head down, but the crucial thing was, he listened. That happened when I partnered him in the early stages of his big century against the West Indies at Edgbaston. It was a slow pitch and Dwayne Bravo and Corey Collymore were bowling outside off stump, and he started playing loosely. I could tell he was not concentrating, and told him that unless he got behind a few deliveries and played himself in properly, he was soon going to chip a catch to extra cover. 'Then soon you'll be hitting it where you like,' I said. And he was.

Although he'd done some eye-catching things for England before, Fred was now showing the consistency of a genuine, world-class all-rounder. Rarely would a match go by without him making his mark with bat or ball. He became English cricket's biggest star, and things started to change hugely for him. He was being asked to put up with a lot more than the rest of us, but he handled it well. All the attention wasn't exactly new to him, I suppose, because in the past he'd handled a lot of expectation and taken a fair bit of abuse over his weight. Even though he was now getting praised, he still had to cope with it, and that's as hard as handling the criticism. Whether he was at that stage a genuine Test

No 6 batsman, though, I wasn't sure. Maybe against some attacks he was; against others he wasn't.

Geraint Jones's batting at No 7 was very important to our success. After I was out at Edgbaston, Jones and Fred pulverized the West Indies bowling in a way we'd got used to seeing Australia's lower order doing, but rarely our own. The two of them shared three century stands during the summer. Jones showed the value of someone coming it at No 7 who could take advantage of tired bowling, and he scored a really skilful hundred against New Zealand at Leeds, as did Marcus Trescothick. Although New Zealand scored over 409 and we made 526, batting was difficult when the skies clouded over. There were cracks all over the pitch and some deliveries threatened serious damage. I was hit in the ribs and Fred also got hit.

I had my share of success too. I scored centuries against New Zealand at Trent Bridge and the West Indies at Old Trafford, finishing as Man of the Match in both games, and also hit three other half-centuries, one when I was batting with Nasser at Lord's, and two in the game at Edgbaston. Overall, I scored over 500 runs and topped our averages for the two series with 523 runs at 65.4. There were times – I remember Trent Bridge was one – when I felt really relaxed and extremely content with most things in my life. I was thoroughly enjoying being back in the team and savoured every game.

To see the side home at Trent Bridge was highly satisfying. When I went out to bat on the fourth day we were in a bit of difficulty at 46 for three, chasing a big target of 284, but I was confident we could win. The Kiwis bowling was depleted – they were without a frontline spinner because Daniel Vettori had pulled a hamstring at Leeds and wasn't playing – and the pitch was slow. The match wasn't going to end in a draw, and I thought if I could build a couple of partnerships we could still make it, and that's basically what happened.

Everything went well for me, despite various distractions. For a start, I was having problems with my bat and towards the end it started to break towards the 'toe' – strange because it was a brand new bat – and I had to patch it up with tape. I was also moving into a new house in Putney that day, or rather Amanda was having to do the move by herself, so I was keen to get the game over and get back to London. We'd been living together for several months by then, and had decided to buy a place together. But everything worked out perfectly – just. I hit the ball well through the off-side, Jones and Giles seemed to share my eagerness to get the job done, and by claiming the extra half hour we won on the Sunday evening with four overs to spare. I got to my hundred two overs before the end.

I also remember that day because I shared perhaps the most crucial partnership with Mark Butcher. I went out to join him, and we put on 80-odd. Funnily enough, it was one of the few stands I can recall having with Butch playing for England. We obviously batted together quite a lot at Surrey, but for some reason we seemed to miss each other in Tests, even though we played around 40 times together. We put on a few runs in Brisbane and in Galle, but I can't recollect any other occasions; strange when I think how often Nasser put on big runs with Butch or me.

Butch played a good innings of 59. He was really positive too, despite nursing a broken finger. He'd had to battle with a few injuries in his time, but his luck was about to run out. Shortly before the start of the West Indies series, he tore a quad muscle in a Twenty20 match and then when he was on his way to see the physio some guy shunted into the back of his car, giving him whiplash. He was very proud of having appeared in more than 40 consecutive Tests for England, but he was now forced to sit out the whole of the West Indies series. He'd have scored lots of runs had he played.

Instead, he had to watch Rob Key fill his boots. Rob had been on the fringe of the side for a couple of years. He had gone to Australia in my place when I pulled out, and would probably have been selected had Michael Vaughan decided he didn't want myself and Nasser in the same side the previous winter. In the end, he'd not made the tour party.

I liked Rob. He had a dry sense of humour, and was a good bloke to have in the dressing-room. I felt he had the right technique and attitude to be successful in Test cricket. Even though there was intense competition for batting places, and he was obviously keen to do well, he didn't get too uptight about things. Like Vaughan, he could quickly get over being out cheaply, and would then go out and score runs in his next innings. He didn't worry for too long, like I did early in my career. He and Butch had the ideal temperaments for a No 3. I'd have been hopeless. I'd never have been ready in time!

My other hundred at Old Trafford was far harder going. As at Trent Bridge, I found myself walking out to a mini-crisis; we were 40 for three, replying to 395. Despite being 2–0 down, the West Indies had picked themselves up and even when they couldn't get me and Andrew Strauss out, they kept things pretty tight. I had one huge slice of luck on 58, when Sarwan put me down at point off the left-arm leggie Dave Mohammed. Bravo in particular bowled well at us from round the wicket, and in the end got us both out, but we stayed together for more than three hours and put on 177.

I had not batted with Strauss before. What struck me watching from close quarters was how similar his set-up was to mine. He also confirmed my early impressions of someone who was not easily ruffled. If he played and missed, he simply shrugged his shoulders. Left-handers can be good at that for some reason. Strauss and Flintoff were both out late on the Saturday but I survived to stumps, a dubious privilege as the next morning my old friend Fidel Edwards bowled one of the fastest and most torrid spells I've ever faced. Old Trafford could be our quickest pitch at times; often it would start slow and get livelier as it dried out.

Edwards hit me on my right hand – I looked up to see 95.7mph on the screen – and I was sure my little finger was broken from the moment it happened. I didn't want to go off though, as I knew it would stiffen up straight away. Also, I was on 91 at the time and wanted to reach my hundred, but the match was still also in the balance. The next ball hit me on the head, and I was pleased to see he'd saved the fastest ball of the match for that – 97.1mph!

I could barely grip the bat though, and my scoring slowed to a trickle. I managed to battle through to my hundred but only added 20 runs in the session. I was finally out soon after, after batting six and a half hours for 114, and although we were 60 behind we were still in the game. Then Harmison, Flintoff and Giles gave us a great chance by dismissing West Indies for 165 second time around.

I had an X-ray which confirmed the break, but Duncan was keen for me to bat if required on the final day. I faced some throw-downs that morning but the finger was very sore, and I went to hospital for what was supposed to be a flying visit for a pain-killing injection. But I was kept waiting before a doctor saw me, and when he injected the needle in my hand he seemed keen to wiggle it around in the joint. Before I knew it, my long-standing aversion to needles had jeopardized England's pursuit of a sixth successive win.

Not only did I pass out, but when I came round, my blood pressure stubbornly refused to return to its normal level. Every time I stood up I felt faint, and I was told I had to stay under observation with suspected concussion and couldn't return to the ground. In fact I'd suffered problems with low blood pressure before, and passed out a couple of times after being hit in the nets at the Oval.

It wasn't long before Duncan was on the phone, finding out what was happening, and telling me we were 40 for two. Fortunately, Key and Vaughan stopped the West Indies in their tracks and, by the time I finally got back to the ground at around 4pm, Key and Flintoff had things under control. They took us home about an hour later. I'm glad I wasn't needed because I hadn't been looking forward to batting, and was worried that if I was hit in the same place it might do long-term damage.

The injury meant I missed the final Test at the Oval three days later. I was named in the squad but couldn't catch the ball or grip the bat properly, and the day before the game ruled myself out. Bell came into the side and scored a cool-headed 70 that suggested he could live up to all the expectations people had had of him since he played in the 'junior' England sides. He looked a highly organized player.

I didn't stay and watch but, when it was clear on the third day that we were going to win after tea, Phil Neale, the England manager, phoned me and said Duncan wanted us all together for the post-match celebrations. So I drove up to the Oval, put on my whites and did a lap of honour with the rest of the lads. It felt funny, not having contributed to the game, but Duncan was very keen that we'd all be included.

And what Duncan said to us in the dressing-room afterwards was high praise. He told us we could be proud of what we'd done. The management might have put the structure in place for a strong England team, but we'd had to do the job on the field. People could tell us to train, but we knew what had to be done and we did it. He said we'd got out of the summer what we'd put in. But, being Duncan, there were words of caution too. He warned us not to be complacent.

It was a truly amazing time. Being easily the longest-serving member of the side, I had a unique perspective on just how far the England team had travelled. I had witnessed an incredible journey. Of course, each player still had to find his own motivation, but the environment in which we were playing was so much better than it had been 10 years earlier. The key thing was that if things went wrong we accepted it so much better, and easily recovered.

SEVENTEEN

Fathers 4 Justice

MY FEARS that my relationship with Nicky had reached a new low after what happened on Boxing Day were soon realized. I managed to see the children in the February before I went to the West Indies, and one of the first things my five-year-old daughter said to Amanda was, 'Why did you hit my mummy?'

Even though I had met Amanda some 14 months after splitting with Nicky, and after Nicky had moved in and settled down with Kieron, she absolutely hated Amanda. I'm sure it's a classic divorce situation – the ex-wife and mother sets about turning the children against the father's new partner. Some, though, take it to another extreme. I've had it all: texts after a visit claiming that Amanda had hit one of the children, Nicky claiming that Amanda had made silent calls to her home and, worst of all, her insistence that Amanda was unstable and could not be present when the children saw me.

After that February visit, Nicky was in a rage about something as usual – I can't even remember what it was – and we exchanged a few heated text messages. Nothing new about that, but when Kieron then sent me a text message saying that he had discovered our home telephone number, and that he'd keep Amanda company by calling her while I was away on tour in the West Indies, I decided he'd gone too far and complained to the police.

Things were so bad after that that I grew desperate, and did the only thing left to make Nicky see sense. I stopped paying her maintenance. Now you might think that while Nicky has the power to stop me seeing the children, she relies on me to support her financially, so that must give me some power. Well, you're wrong. It turned out to be a huge mistake. Not only did Nicky immediately sell a story to the *Sunday Mirror* ('He doesn't even pay for his children . . .'), but her solicitors were gleefully all over me like a rash. Even after I reinstated the payments two months later, the legal wrangling took over a year to sort out and cost me well over £15,000.

Henry's eighth birthday was in November 2004, and I was desperate to give him a birthday party before I left for the tour of South Africa, especially after what had happened the previous year. Then I'd arranged the party, and bought the cake and presents, but Henry phoned in the morning saying he had a cold and couldn't come. I was really beginning to see that the advice I'd had early on, from a friend of a friend who was a judge, was spot on. He'd told me that if the mother doesn't want contact, you're in trouble.

This year Nicky said I could give Henry a party so long as Amanda wasn't there, insisting that I get a solicitor's letter to say that Amanda wasn't going to be present. Nicky knew that Amanda and I had recently bought a house together, so her demands were pretty outrageous. Still, I knew better than to tell Nicky what I really thought.

I had really struggled at the beginning to see Kieron living with my children, but I'd had to accept it. I realized, too, that it wouldn't do the children any good if I told them what I really thought of the man they were living with, so I always made a concerted effort to act normally when his name was mentioned. Obviously this became a lot easier after I met Amanda and wasn't so desperately unhappy, and Amanda really encouraged me to see how important it was to hold my tongue. It just seemed so unfair that Nicky wouldn't do the same.

I gave Nicky all the assurances I could that Amanda wouldn't be there, but at the last minute she left a message on my mobile saying she didn't believe me, and that the date was cancelled. Yes, I was devastated, but I also felt something new this time – acceptance. I'd had a feeling that something like this would happen, and was prepared for the disappointment. But I was still determined to see Henry and called his headmaster to arrange to see him at school one lunchtime, and give him his presents. The headmaster asked me if I had any proof that I was not barred from seeing Henry; I told him I did and that I'd send him a copy.

I had applied to the court for a contact order to see the children when I first started experiencing difficulties seeing them in the summer of 2003. Usually, contact orders give the father the right to see the children every other weekend, and possibly also on Wednesday afternoons. Due to the nature of my job, my contact order involved my giving Nicky possible dates as soon as I could, for her to agree. This obviously involved a little co-operation and flexibility on her side, but what happened? My solicitor would give her a list of dates for the summer, and Nicky would say she couldn't do those dates and proceed to give a new list of days when she knew I'd be playing cricket. She kept saying I wasn't going to dictate the dates of my visits. The order also said I was to have contact with the children on Boxing Day 2003, and much good that did me.

But back to that morning when I'd agreed with the headmaster that I'd visit Henry. Amanda and I went to the gym as usual. We took two cars because afterwards I'd drive straight to the school. Amanda stayed at the gym and had coffee with friends. When she got back to her car, she was surprised to see that my car was still in front of hers, and that I was in it. When I looked up, she could see that I'd been crying.

Just as I was about to leave for Henry's school, the headmaster had called. He'd been apologetic, but basically said that he'd had to tell Nicky that I was going to see Henry, and she'd said she didn't want me to see Henry or be anywhere on the school premises. It was a case of, 'I'm sorry but it's more than my job's worth.' I ended up driving to the school anyway that afternoon to leave Henry's presents, but I didn't get to see him. I left for a two-month tour of South Africa a few days later.

I only saw the children twice in 2004, and have seen them just once in 2005 at the time of writing. The last few visits were so fraught with problems that the situation became worse than ever. On one visit, the first thing Amelia said to me when she got in the car was, 'Daddy, why don't you want to see us any more?' It absolutely broke my heart. I knew Nicky was bitter and angry with me, but how could she hurt the children like that? It was clear to me she had lost sight of what really mattered – the children – and I could see that they were suffering because of it. It was even worse for Henry because he was that much older and capable of understanding more. When I saw him after returning from South Africa, he told me he supported the South African team. Kieron is South African, so it didn't take a genius to work out what was going on there. It was sad for Henry though, and he missed out. He had reached an age when he could go to watch a Test match and enjoy it, but Nicky just wouldn't allow it. There were times, though – like when we were all having fun in the swimming pool together – when he was like any happy, normal eight-year-old child with his father, but at other times I could see he was wary, and asking himself if his dad really loved him.

And just when I thought we'd reached rock bottom, there was more. When Nicky first started to make access difficult, about the time I met Amanda, she had my mobile telephone number barred from calling her home number. It made me very angry because there I was paying hefty maintenance every month, and she would not even let me call the children at home. In reality, it just meant that I started contacting her via her mobile phone, often by text message. Unbeknown to me, Nicky saved all the text messages I sent her in a six-month period, and decided to complain to the police that I was harassing her. This was a ridiculous suggestion, not least since she'd sent me the same number of messages, or more. I told the police all this when they came to see me at home, but they said that to save police time when investigating such matters, the procedure was simply to issue a warning whenever such a complaint was made.

This was just after Nicky had refused to let Henry visit me for his eighth birthday, but luckily I had recorded some of Nicky's phone messages that she'd been leaving me. I'm not sure why I did it. Maybe I was feeling vulnerable that the children were being turned against me, and wanted to be able to prove to them when they were grown up that I *had* wanted to see them. It was a good move. When the policeman heard Nicky on the message clearly stopping me from seeing the children, even saying that I had to do what she told me because she held the trump card (i.e. the children), and calling Amanda and I all the names under the sun, he said he would pay Nicky a visit and warn her about harassment too! It seemed like a small triumph on the day, but really it was just a waste of police time and Nicky ended up getting even angrier with me.

I soon realized that I had to speak to the children about my problems in seeing them. It was a difficult decision, and I thought long and hard about it. Although I didn't want to trouble them with my problems, I had to take the view that it was probably worse for them to be left thinking that I didn't want to see them. And so, when they visited me early in February 2005, I sat them down and explained that sometimes when mummy was angry with daddy, she didn't let daddy see them. I told them how much daddy loved them, and that I always wanted to see them. I don't know if it was the right thing to do, but as a parent you have to follow your instinct and do your best, and that's what I did.

Nicky went into a rage when she heard, and all hell broke loose. After a series of phone calls in which she screamed abuse before hanging up, the phone rang again. This time it was Henry. He said, 'Who's speaking?'

'Hi Henry, it's daddy . . .'

Before I could ask how he was, he shouted down the phone, 'Leave me alone!' and hung up.

There was a moment of stunned silence. I could hear his words ringing in my ears. That was it. Game over. How, how, *how* Nicky could do that to Henry I will never understand. But I knew then that things had to change. I just couldn't allow my son to be caught up in the middle of this fighting any more. Something had to give, and it would have to be me.

I told Nicky that I wanted the children to visit whenever they could, but that I would wait for her to tell me when she felt ready. There was to be no more of me chasing and fighting for access. I would send the children cards regularly to say that I loved them, but apart from that I would let them get on with their lives. Perhaps it would help, too, if both of us had time to reflect on what we wanted for the children. I had not entirely given up hope that, at some time in the future, I could have a good relationship with the children, and maybe even with Nicky.

I remember getting into a taxi around the time Nicky and I split up in 2001, and the cabbie and I got talking about divorce. He told me he no longer saw his children from his first marriage, and that he'd remarried and had another child. I remember wondering how he could do that. That I'd never be able to not see my kids and walk away from them. I privately thought he was a bit of a useless father. But I've since learnt how complicated things can get, and I can understand how some fathers are pushed to that point.

In Britain, according to a shocking statistic more than 50 per cent of fathers lose contact with their children within *two years* of divorce. Maybe there are some selfish and uncaring fathers who walk away from their families, and who don't financially provide for their children. But then there are plenty of dads out there who do care desperately and want to see their children, but who are not allowed to for one reason or another, often because of acrimony with the mother.

In the last couple of years, the fathers' rights protest group – Fathers 4 Justice – has pulled off some spectacular stunts, usually with someone dressed as a children's hero (e.g. Batman) to draw attention to the fathers' plight. Some of the stunts have been controversial, but they have rightly brought the matter to the attention of the government and public. The message is, yes, children do need their mothers, but they need their dads too, and fathers have an enormous amount to offer. There are plenty of statistics which show that a child who has the input of a father will do better socially and academically.

I have been asked why I don't go back to court. In

theory, a father can go back to court to try and enforce contact, but it costs about £2,000 a time and you may be forced to go back to court as many times as the mother comes up with excuses, without achieving anything. In my case, I'd already spent over £120,000 in legal fees for the divorce, so besides not wanting to face any more court hearings, I simply couldn't and can't afford it.

Amanda is studying to be a solicitor, and tells me that family lawyers are supposed to abide by a code of practice which says that they should take a conciliatory approach to family matters, especially concerning children. Well I don't know about that, but I do know that the approach of Nicky's solicitors has been anything but conciliatory. Amanda has been shocked at how long, acrimonious and expensive my divorce process has been, and that's why she has decided to practice family law because she thinks it should be done differently.

One of the things that I'd most like to see is compulsory mediation at the beginning of divorce proceedings for all couples with children. When we first split up, I'm sure neither Nicky nor myself could have envisaged how things would end up as regards the children. Separating couples ought to sit down around a table and talk before bitterness and acrimony sets in and positions become entrenched. Part of the process should involve teaching the parents how damaging and harmful fighting over, and using, children can be. Perhaps getting teenagers and young adults to attend and describe how much the experience hurt them, would help get the message across.

Yet the bottom line is, no matter how many times you go to court, you need the co-operation of the mother in order to make access work. Both Mark Butcher and Darren Gough split from their wives, though, as far as I know, their ex-wives never created problems about them seeing their children. And Amanda was not difficult about her ex-husband seeing their daughter Kitty, despite how he behaved.

But for many fathers it's not that easy. I have received many letters from fathers in similar positions to mine who think that the law gives the mothers freedom to be unreasonable, if that's how they want to play it. Some of the letters brought tears to my eyes, from dads who had not seen their children for years and were now suffering from depression. And that's why I support Fathers 4 Justice, trying to give dads more rights to see their kids. There were times when I seriously thought about putting an F4J logo on the back of my bat. Looking back, I wish I had.

While F4J advocates a 50–50 residence split, I wouldn't go that far. I don't think that's beneficial for the children because they need a place to call home. If they are living with the mother, she must be positive about the children seeing their father and, in some instances, meeting his new partner. Of course it's not always that easy. Divorce is never a nice experience, and people can cause each other a lot of pain. But I do think parents have a responsibility to work together for the good of their children.

I'm sure Nicky and I both hurt each other enormously in different ways through our divorce. But whatever has happened, I don't wish Nicky any ill. She is the mother of my children, and I wish them all only happiness in their lives. I just wish I could be a part of it too.

EIGHTEEN

Grit and Glory

WHEN IT CAME to my cricket, I didn't really believe in luck. I reckoned it was down to yourself to make the best of things. Talking about good or bad luck meant making excuses. But, at the same time, there were things beyond your control that could have a massive bearing on your career. You needed slices of good fortune in your journey as a professional sportsman.

Ultimately, injuries are the killer for all sportsmen. Personally, I went through a large part of my career fearing that my back might pack up at any moment. If I was starting out in the game today, I could probably avoid trouble by working hard to build up the strength in my lower back, but ten years ago we didn't know what we do now about the importance of developing what is known as 'core stability'. I missed a large part of an Australia tour because my recovery from back surgery was misjudged. Lots of players have had problems in this region of the body, Michael Atherton and Andrew Flintoff among them.

After my back operation in 1998, I got through around 50 Tests on a diet of painkillers without which I would have never made it onto the field many times. The area around the repaired joint and scar got stiff and needed mobilizing and the best way to do that was with the help of painkillers. I didn't take them when I wasn't playing, but I couldn't have managed without them on days when I was spending so much time bending over a bat or standing in the field.

I can't recall the last Test I played without painkillers; it may have been on the Pakistan tour of 2000. I often feared that I would wake up with my back so stiff that I would be unable to get out of bed and crank my body into action. My lack of mobility towards the end of my career certainly affected the way I played. I wasn't flexible enough to duck and dive out of the way of the short ball, so I had little choice but to take it on, which was fine because I was temperamentally happier doing that anyway.

I underwent as many exercises as I could in an effort to keep my back loose, but as I approached my last tour with England I knew I was living on borrowed time. I was on three Ibufren tablets a day. I knew such heavy doses were not good for me but without them I wouldn't have got through the Test series.

I also feared that if I was forced to sit out a game,

I might never get back in the side. In professional sport, careers can hang by the finest of threads. One day things are going swimmingly, the next day something occurs that changes everything.

I had watched what happened to Mark Butcher. He hadn't missed a Test match for three years when he suffered a relatively minor injury playing a one-day match for Surrey and then, on his way for treatment, was involved in a car accident. Then, in South Africa, he damaged a wrist in the gym and was unable to pick up a bat in earnest over the course of the next six months. It was a horrifying run of misfortune.

In the space of a year, he played just twice for England and, to make matters worse, saw Rob Key and Ian Bell, the two guys who filled his place, score mountains of runs. Butch was desperate to return but had to resist the temptation to rush back or he might have made things considerably worse. I felt so sorry for him. I hoped he would hang in there and eventually get another chance. There was still time.

The sheer fragility of our careers was one reason the Zimbabwe issue made me so angry. There were those – mostly people outside the game – who seemed to expect a bunch of sportsmen to take a moral stand against the regime in that country. Now, I make no defence of Robert Mugabe. What has gone on in Zimbabwe is despicable. But, as an England cricketer, if the British government was not telling you directly not to go there, and our cricket board was not telling us specifically not to go there, then that put you in a very difficult position. It was a big decision for a player to make alone and it should never have come down to that. A professional cricketer has a living to earn and knows that if he gives up his place then someone else will take it and if that person does well he might never get back in. He will have taken a moral stand, but at huge personal cost – and for what? I honestly don't believe that those people who passed judgement would have dreamed of taking such a gamble with their own futures.

In 2004, England were originally scheduled to play two Tests in Zimbabwe. In the end, the matches were cancelled because the Zimbabwe team withdrew from Test cricket for six months because of a players' strike, although the one-day series, in which I was obviously not involved, went ahead. Had the Tests been played, I would have faced a very difficult decision. I had only just battled my way back into the side 12 months earlier and I am not sure that I could have afforded to give up my place. I think I would have had to make myself available. But I would have done so with a very heavy heart.

Anyone who dismisses sportsmen as politically naive for thinking like that are being totally naive themselves about the nature of our work.

Maybe it is because we know our careers hang by threads that so many sportsmen like to gamble, whether it is dressing-room card schools, a flutter on the horses or a trip down the casino. I got into gambling in Sri Lanka in 2001 at a time when I was making a conscious effort to take a more relaxed approach to my cricket. On quite a few of the nights we were in Colombo, myself, Athers, Nasser, Alec Stewart and Michael Vaughan would take a couple of rickshaws to the local casino for an hour or so. We found it a good release after the tensions of the day.

It was something I carried on with on later tours. I went out to the casino with Steve Harmison and Robert Key the night before the series began in South Africa in 2004 just to stop us thinking about the next day.

There was a certain adrenalin rush to placing a bet but I tried to keep things in check by limiting myself to £150 a night. I fully expected to lose it all but I was happy to do so. It was a good night out and helped me clear my mind ahead of a big innings. The really dangerous time to hit the tables was after a Test had finished. Then, your mind could be so frazzled it was easy to lose track of your losses.

There was also something liberating about abandoning yourself to chance. It made such a change from burning up so much energy preparing for what might next happen out on the pitch.

AS FOR MY PERSONAL LIFE at this time, I felt happier than ever. Amanda, Kitty and I had settled into our new house in Putney, and I found I really enjoyed living amongst the hustle and bustle of London. I love the fact that there is so much on my doorstep – that I can pop out to my favourite Thai restaurant which is just around the corner or meet up with friends for a drink in a pub by the river.

When Amanda and I first met, her daughter Kitty was a chubby 11-month-old baby. I really enjoyed having a child around again, and found it helped me cope with not being around my two children a bit better.

But early on in our relationship, I had told Amanda that I was worried about whether I could love Kitty as if she were my own child. I suppose it's a situation many men will be familiar with when becoming a stepfather. Amanda was understandably upset, but understood my point of view and knew I was just being honest. At that time, I couldn't have envisaged how well things would turn out.

Now I couldn't imagine being without Kitty and I love her as if she were my own. She is three and a half and such a beautiful, sweet and loving child. I was lucky that she was so young when Amanda and I first met, so that she can't remember me not being around. She calls me Daddy, and as far as she's concerned I am her dad. For my part, I do all the things a dad would do for her – from taking her to nursery, to swimming, to giving her a bath. It all feels very natural and I feel lucky to be given a second chance and to be part of a family again.

Just when I thought things couldn't get any better, they did. The evening before I left for South Africa, I came home to find Amanda rushing to the door to greet me saying, 'Guess what?' I could tell from her face it was good news. She was pregnant. I was absolutely thrilled – it was something we both wanted and the icing on the cake for us. And it certainly helped me, in the months away in South Africa when things got tough, to reflect that we were having a baby. It was early days so we didn't tell anyone. It was our secret.

But there was one cloud on the horizon. Amanda's ex-husband was insisting that she stayed in London over Christmas so he could see Kitty. Of course, I wanted Amanda and Kitty to visit me in South Africa over Christmas and New Year, as most of the other players' wives and girlfriends were doing. Once again it seemed that solicitors had intervened, and Amanda's ex-husband was advised to take her to court over the issue in early December. By that time I was already in South Africa and hated not being able to be there to support her. I was very worried about her as it was all so stressful and she was newly pregnant.

At times like that it really did seem that we were getting it from both sides. On the one hand I had enormous problems getting any contact at all with my children, and on the other there was Amanda who never did anything to hinder access but still found herself on the receiving end of endless legal wrangling. I couldn't help feeling angry at Amanda's ex – he got all that contact and still made problems. I just don't think he realized how lucky he was. Once again I was left thinking that if Nicky was half as accommodating as Amanda over access, I'd be seeing my children an awful lot more.

Amanda decided to represent herself in order to save money, and took along her best friend Andrea for support. In the end the hearing was straightforward and the judge ruled that she should be allowed to travel to South Africa over Christmas, much to our relief.

BY THE time I left for South Africa in late November 2004, I knew that in terms of my cricket career only a few cards were left to be dealt me.

Since my comeback, I had never envisaged playing for England beyond the summer of 2005, when I would turn 36. It was not that I wanted to give up, but I knew that physically I probably would be unable to withstand the punishment any longer. If only I'd had the body of Graham Gooch, maybe I too could have gone on beyond the age of 40!

The prospect of giving up did not particularly concern me. Having had time out, I had experienced what it was like, so I now felt well prepared, whereas in my early days the thought of not playing any more cricket would have filled me with alarm. But I was concerned about how the final months of my international career might pan out. I had to be still worth my place and that meant maintaining a high standard of performance. South Africa were a very tough side on their own patch and then we faced the Australians at home.

There was nothing bigger than an Ashes series and I was desperate to play in it. But with England playing so well, and harbouring real hopes of getting something out of both series, I was very conscious of not doing anything to let them down. I didn't want to be seen hanging on just so I could go out at a time that suited me. I had to do the right thing by the captain and coach. I owed it to them. But I didn't want to discard myself too quickly either: I knew that if I played well I had something to offer the team and still backed myself to score runs against any side.

I arrived in South Africa genuinely unsure of what the next few weeks held. I knew that if the tour didn't go well for me, I would be in a vulnerable position as the oldest man in the team. Could I do enough to put myself in the mix for the Ashes? The nearer you get to the bottom of the deck, the more you worry about what's left in the pack.

It was clear the tour was going to be a gruelling test of our physical and mental strength. The schedule was not ideal: the five Tests were shoe-horned into 40 days and there was only one serious warm-up match, a three-day game in Potchefstroom against South Africa A. This was how modern tours were, and as players we were happy to be away from home less, but we would certainly have preferred an extra warm-up match.

Generally, once a series was underway I was happy to keep going with the Tests rather than break off for more warm-up games. Such matches had come to seem irrelevant. Unless someone was having a shocking run of form, the management was unlikely to change heart about the make-up of the side. They might want a fresh pair of legs among the pace bowling at some point, but as far as the batsmen were concerned they would probably prefer to stick by the guys in the team rather than bring in someone who'd had little cricket for a few weeks.

Typically, Duncan refused to allow us to complain, even when we were well beaten by South Africa A. He just told us that we would have to practise more and draw on our mental resources. He told us that we would simply have to move up a gear for the Tests, something we had got better at doing in recent times. One of the things he had drummed into us was accepting the difficult things that were sometimes thrown at us. When that happened, there was simply nothing to be gained from making excuses. That had been one of his messages when I first toured under him in 2000–01 to the subcontinent, where things often happened that you could grumble about if you had a mind to. Although he publicly said he was happy with the South Africa schedule, I'm sure Duncan would have taken another match before the Tests had he been given the choice.

There was no doubt we hadn't played enough cricket going into the first Test in Port Elizabeth, although I suppose that if you had got runs or wickets in Potchefstroom probably you would have been keen to get on with the real business. Anyone watching that game must have been able to tell who were the guys who had just joined the tour and who had been playing the one-dayers in Zimbabwe. Michael Vaughan, Andrew Strauss and Geraint Jones, for example, hit the ball much better than many of the rest of us. They had the quickness of eye, the sureness of foot movement, the confidence in their techniques, that new arrivals like myself lacked. We struggled against some decent swing and seam bowling from Charl Langeveldt and the left-armer, Charl Willoughby. I was leg-before for nought in the first innings and played on for 11 in the second.

After the game, Duncan left the dressing-room and Michael spoke to us alone, telling us that he thought our attitude had been poor. It was a good thing to say: it gave us a sharp reminder that we would need to improve dramatically if we were to have any chance in the first Test. There are times when every captain has to put his foot down and this was one of them and it was right that he handed out the bollocking rather than Duncan. After all, it was Michael who was on the pitch with us. He was the man we had to follow.

I was concerned about my mobility. I'd done a lot of training before the tour but didn't feel cricket fit – the sort of fitness that only comes from standing around in the field all day, or batting for long periods. I'd had the best part of three months off since the English season and was aware that whenever I resumed playing after a lay-off it usually took me a couple of weeks for my back to feel really loose. Still, as Duncan said, there was nothing to do except move on to Port Elizabeth, get in the nets and draw on my experience.

That we won a hard-fought series of many twists and turns owed a lot to our planning (off the field, if not on it) and confidence. We won the first Test, and lost the third, before winning the fourth. There were times when both teams threw away chances to put games beyond reach but overall I believe we clearly showed we were the better side. We might well have won 3–1 because the weather cut short the second Test in Durban with us needing just two wickets for victory. I reckon that in a five-match series the best side normally comes out on top and we did on this occasion. We didn't play as consistently well as we had at home the previous summer but we deserved our victory.

For all the unease about the shortage of preparation, we had arrived in South Africa genuinely believing we could win, even though South Africa could be such a difficult place to triumph. That self-belief proved crucial and was perhaps the difference between the teams. The bottom line was that we thought we could win, and perhaps they thought they couldn't.

By the time the first Test in Port Elizabeth arrived, we were very focused. We'd had a lot of team meetings and gone through our plans with great care. Sometimes these came off, sometimes they didn't. This time a lot of them did, right from the moment that Matthew Hoggard had Graeme Smith, the South Africa captain, caught edging an outswinger off the second ball of the game.

The bowlers hit good areas and kept up the pressure, and that's generally what makes batsmen make mistakes. We dismissed them for 337 and 229 and thanks to Strauss continuing his good form and underpinning both our innings with 126 and 94 not out, we won by seven wickets.

Well though we played in parts, South Africa seemed off the pace, especially for a side that had just come off some hard cricket in India. They had a new coach in Ray Jennings, who was reportedly not short of new ideas, and there was also talk of wrangles within their team about racial quotas hampering selection. It was a strange experience. On our first tour of South Africa after the collapse of apartheid, in 1995–96, I felt they were a nation united in sending the England cricket team packing; now, we met some of their followers who wanted us to give their team a thrashing because they were disillusioned with the way the game was being run in their country. I had always thought of South African cricketers as disciplined, hard-working and hard to beat. Those characteristics came out as the series progressed, but in the early stages of the series, we certainly looked the more organized team. How things had changed!

I helped Strauss knock off the last 95 runs needed for victory, my share being 31. It was a very special moment when he hit the winning runs as it was our eighth Test victory in a row, something no England side had achieved before. I felt especially privileged as this was the third time I'd been batting when one of the wins was sealed (the other times were against New Zealand at Lord's and Trent Bridge). I had also been at the crease when we got home in Trinidad earlier in the year.

On a personal level, my concerns over the schedule proved justified. I never felt entirely happy with my game and it became a case of trying to iron out flaws as I went along, which was hardly ideal. That was the downside to playing one Test after another. It was noticeable that, broadly speaking, the players who were in form at the start of the series (Trescothick and Strauss, for example) were still in form at the end, while those of us who struggled for touch never really found it. It frustrated me that I couldn't find form and that frustration was a distraction in itself.

I did play two really important innings, though, to help us draw the second and fifth Tests. Had I failed, we might conceivably have lost both games, so I certainly felt

I played my part in the overall result. But they were gritty rather than stylish knocks and I couldn't kid anyone that I was playing at my most fluent.

They do say, though, that a good batsman makes runs even when he's not playing well and I reckon I did that by scoring 118 in Durban and 86 in Centurion. I'm not quite sure how I managed it but I guess it just proved, again, the value of experience. My body wasn't moving as well as it had ten years earlier, and my reflexes weren't perhaps as sharp, but I chiselled out runs in a way I would have died for when I was 25 years old and kept on failing to turn fifties into centuries. The great thing about experience was that it helped you recognize situations when the team really needed you to perform.

My problems began in an unexpected quarter. South Africa decided to go into the first Test without a specialist spinner and this left them reliant on Graeme Smith's occasional off-spin to bring some variety to the attack.

Smith had had little success in international cricket but for some reason I had real problems with him. To my embarrassment, he bowled me round my legs for four in the first innings. I would have much preferred to face Nicky Boje, because I'd have had a better idea of what he was going to do, but he was unfit. Normally in Tests, bowlers put the ball in predictable areas and it was Smith's inconsistency that I found hardest to deal with. He was not a joke bowler but would sometimes drag a ball halfway down the pitch and at other times give you one that was a yard wide. Then there might be a full toss. I was genuinely unsure how best to play him. I was reluctant to go down the track in case he threw in a wide ball. He needed putting in his place with a couple of early fours and that was certainly what someone like Alistair Brown would have looked to do. But my game wasn't equipped for that sort of thing and I ended up playing him badly. He made me very uncomfortable.

Another, slightly more illustrious bowler dominated my thoughts during the second Test in Durban over Christmas. As I've said before, Shaun Pollock gave me more trouble than any other fast bowler. I worried about him more than, say, Curtly Ambrose and Courtney Walsh, who both got me out more often. Ambrose was a handful because he projected the ball from such a great height but he didn't swing the ball and his deliveries generally went across me and, being a short man, I was usually able to get under his bouncer. He didn't like conceding runs and bowled just short of a full length that made it almost impossible to drive down the ground (I can only remember ever doing it once) and left you working very hard for runs. I looked to score off him with back-foot pulls, nudges off the hip and quick singles. Walsh was very different. He varied things a lot, bowled a fuller length and could swing the ball. He had a good bouncer too and, as I've recounted, towards the end of his career had a very good slower ball that made him an absolute nightmare to face.

But Pollock had the knack of getting me into bad positions. He would get close to the stumps, bowl a fullish length and swing the ball back in a shade. He would draw me into trying to drive him through mid-on. He'd bowl three balls slightly across me, trying to drag my right foot and my head outside the line of off stump, before giving me the inswinger which he'd be hoping I'd play across and miss because I was off balance. I knew exactly what he was trying to do, but that's not the same thing as stopping yourself doing it! He was a subtle and intelligent bowler.

It didn't help either that while Pollock bowled straight, his new-ball partner Makhaya Ntini came in from wide of the crease and slanted the ball across you. It was short-pitched, aggressive stuff and again you had to work out which balls you could safely leave and which ones might shape back into you. Pollock and Ntini were individually difficult, but as a pair the problems multiplied.

Pollock's plan worked to perfection on the first morning in Durban, when he led an excellent South Africa bowling performance in typically humid, seamer-friendly conditions for Kingsmead. I was one of his four wickets as we were dismissed by tea for just 139. When we trailed on first innings by 193 we were in serious danger of losing our unbeaten record in Tests in 2004 at the last hurdle.

Strauss and Trescothick led a great fightback with an

opening partnership of 273 but the match was still in the balance going into the fourth day. By that stage I was feeling pretty desperate about how I was playing. That morning, Butch gave me some throw-downs and I hit the ball terribly. I left the nets feeling even worse than I had when I entered them, which was saying something. As we walked away, I said to him: 'I just don't think I know how to bat at the moment.' I tried to stifle the thought that my game might be entering some sort of terminal decline.

Fortunately, although I wasn't sure what to do about the way I was hitting the ball, I realized that this was another of those occasions when I was getting too tense about the whole situation. Yes, I was in bad touch, but if I kept fretting I would give myself next to no chance of succeeding. I needed to relax.

At least Amanda, her sister Caroline and Kitty had arrived for Christmas a few days before the Test which picked me up a bit. But I was still worried about my cricket, and would moan to Amanda about my batting and not liking my bats. But poor Amanda was suffering from morning sickness and just told me she didn't want to know!

During the game, I spoke to Caroline about how unsure I was feeling. She suggested that before I batted I should read the copy of the Bible she had given me before I left home and when I walked out to the middle offer up a prayer. 'You may think I'm talking a load of rubbish,' she said, 'but it can't do any harm. So why not give it a try?' And that's exactly what I did. I read the passage about the two men on the road to Damascus and, as I walked out to bat on the fourth morning of the game, said a short prayer. It was the first time I'd ever done such a thing in a game and although I was well aware that doing well in sport was not simply a matter of going round praying for God's help, I think the process did help my approach to that innings.

Soon after I went in, Butch was out, leaving us 314 for four, only 121 ahead. The South African bowlers had looked out of sorts the previous day during the big stand between Trescothick and Strauss, but now they put much more into it in search of a decisive break-through. Our progress was painfully slow. It was a matter of trying to survive and waiting for them to tire.

Jacques Kallis bowled a really good spell and had a close lbw shout against me turned down. I tried to be positive and relaxed but it wasn't easy when I was struggling to middle the ball. I remember taking on a short ball early on and hooking it for four, and slog-sweeping Boje, and by the time I'd reached 20 things began to fall into place. Maybe I could still play, after all.

Bit by bit my confidence returned on what proved to be an extremely satisfying day. I shared in two century stands – the first with Fred, who played very solidly for 60, to dig us out of trouble and the other with Geraint Jones, who really drove home our advantage with an aggressive 73, to put us into a position from which we could not lose. We declared at 570 for nine, with me 118 not out. South Africa lost Smith that evening and were four down by lunch on the final day. Arguably we should have won even before bad light forced an early end to the game but for two hours we couldn't get past Pollock and AB de Villiers.

I reckon that, given how I had felt beforehand, the match situation and the heat and humidity, that innings was among the best I ever played for England. I simply fought so hard. I certainly left the ground that night wondering quite how I'd managed to summon up such a performance. There were probably a few other people who wondered the same thing. I know Butch did!

Although our winning streak had ended, Duncan told us how proud we should be that we had gone through 2004 unbeaten. We had won 11 of our 13 Tests and been denied only by Brian Lara's genius in Antigua and the weather in Durban. Apparently, no other Test side had ever gone through more matches in a year without defeat. It was an incredible achievement and seemed all the more amazing to me as I could remember when England Test defeats were routine occurrences.

Our unbeaten run, and my new-found confidence, didn't survive the New Year Test in Cape Town. Having bowled last in Durban, and with only two days off between games, we would have preferred not to bowl first, but we lost the toss and South Africa put themselves in the driving seat by scoring 441 on a good pitch. We batted poorly throughout, with no one reaching fifty in either innings, a damning fact given the conditions. I was out cheaply to Langeveldt, called up for his first Test appearance, in the first innings and battled away for around 30 overs for 26 in the second before Pollock had me caught behind off another of his nip-backers. It was a good delivery.

With six days off before the fourth Test, some of us relaxed with wine-tasting trips around the Cape. My group included Ian Botham, an infamous drinker and a man whose company it would be dangerous to keep on a regular basis – I think you'd be constantly nursing a hangover. You have to carefully choose the times you socialize with him. Beefy was always interesting company. I'm not sure I agreed with all his views on cricket but I'd always listen to what he had to say. For me, there was no bigger hero in the game – he and Viv Richards were gods to me.

Having not got many runs in Cape Town, I was perhaps overly anxious to do well in Johannesburg. I watched a lot of cricket during that match before I batted and I'm not sure it did me any good. On the first day, we lost an early wicket but then only one more in the next five hours. By the time I got to the crease it was late in the day and South Africa had the second new ball in their hands. In the second innings, I sat through a stand of 124 between Trescothick and Vaughan before going out to bat. I don't know if it had anything to do with me getting out for nought and one, but looking back I think I used up too much mental energy beforehand.

Our victory at the Wanderers was one of our very best. On the final morning, most people would have thought the best we could have hoped for was a draw. But Vaughan, who was improving as a captain with every series, remained really positive and the aggressive way we played set South Africa back on their heels and played a big part in us dismissing them in the last two sessions of the game. He had declared our first innings at 411 for eight when some of us, myself included, thought he should have batted on, and there were times in the game when it looked as though he had got this wrong. But in the end, you could only say that his boldness had paid off. Once Hoggard claimed three early second-innings wickets, you could easily imagine the panic sweeping through the South African dressing-room. There was nothing to lose for us, and everything for them, and it showed.

I'd done nothing with the bat but couldn't have cared less as I crouched under the helmet at short leg and we worked our way through their lower-order batting. The light threatened to fail again, just as it had in Durban, but Hoggard capped an amazing performance with the ball by claiming the last wicket shortly before six o'clock. That night in the team hotel, we celebrated (rather too well!) one of the most exhilarating days of cricket I was ever involved in.

All we needed was a draw in Centurion to take the series. When the first day was rained off and we then dismissed South Africa for 247, defeat was hard to contemplate. We would have had to lose 20 wickets inside three days. But having waited too long to bat in Johannesburg, I found myself hurrying out to the middle when three wickets tumbled in the space of 19 balls.

I cannot help but reflect on how I would have played in my early days. At 29 for three, I would deliberately have gone after the bowling and counter-attacked with pulls against the short-pitched ball and a few flat-footed drives. I would have pushed their field back, bit by bit. They would have put a man out on the hook and soon gone down to two slips and two gulleys. But now, I had to fight so hard just to keep them out.

It was a very similar innings to the one at Durban – a tight corner, a lot of grit, and a bit of luck early on. Strauss and I stayed together for over two hours before Fred and I had another long stand of 141 in three hours. We weren't taking any risks, there was absolutely no need, and Fred's fifty was the slowest he had ever scored for England. It was quite funny batting together in a way that wasn't natural to either of us and we both had a laugh about why we were desperate to pick up the bonus money for winning the series. I had some legal bills to pay and Fred, who was getting married a few weeks after the tour, needed to pay Bill Wyman to sing at the wedding!

I dearly wanted a second century in the series but when I'd reached 86 and was approaching my seventh hour at the crease, Andre Nel produced an absolute jaffa, an inswinging yorker that clipped the bottom of the stumps. Because of the pitches I'd been brought up on, I'd never been a big mover of my front foot, but there was not a lot I could have done about it. Nel said it was the best ball he'd ever bowled in Test cricket.

We took a first-innings lead of 112 and although South Africa managed to bat themselves into a position to declare and have a go at bowling us out on the final afternoon, they only gave themselves 44 overs at us. Despite losing three early wickets for a second time, we managed to hold out for the draw. With defence the only name of the game, this time I managed to bat more than an hour for eight!

I was surprised South Africa didn't try harder to declare earlier. Jacques Kallis is a world-class player with a fantastic technique, but I had to question what he was doing on the last day, when he appeared more interested in batting for his hundred than making quick runs for his team. If he had been a player in his early twenties and just setting out, I could have perhaps understood it, but he was secure in his place. Even when he got to his hundred, he didn't swing from the hip, even though he looked capable of hitting boundaries wherever he wanted. I felt sorry for Graeme Smith, an honest, hard-working captain who was trying to take his team forward. He tried very hard to gee up his team in that game.

Overall, I was pretty satisfied to finish the series third in our batting averages behind Strauss and Trescothick. I was slightly concerned with how I'd played, but was confident that I could sort out things over the course of a few early-season championship matches with Surrey. I believed I still had plenty to offer England.

NINETEEN

Ashes . . . to Ashes

THINGS DIDN'T work out as planned in the summer of 2005. If I could have written the script, I'd have played my hundredth Test match against Bangladesh – which I did, having started the season on 98 caps – and taken a full part in the Ashes series, and retired from Test cricket with a quiet announcement after the finish at the Oval, ideally as an Ashes winner.

But the cherished hundredth cap apart, it didn't happen anything like that. I was rarely fully fit and, even before I'd set foot on the field for England, some informal conversations with members of the management made it plain that they were unsure if there was a role for me in the Ashes. These conversations actually influenced my decision to bring forward my retirement plans more than anything that passed between myself and David Graveney around the time the England team was chosen for the first Test against Australia. What the chairman of selectors and I said to each other then became the subject of some controversy but these earlier exchanges, until now unrecorded, were the indications that the end was in sight.

By the time the decision was made to drop me from the team, it was hardly a surprise. As Steve Waugh once said, there aren't many Cinderella stories in sport. Most players are dropped in the end; few get to go at a time of their choosing.

So, no Ashes, and no going quietly. I think most people in the game knew that I would not be playing for England beyond the summer. They knew I was working on an autobiography and, as Michael Vaughan quipped, had known for some time that I was quite old. But I'd not made a public announcement because I feared it would compromise my position. I found myself in the classic dilemma facing every top sportsman when he approaches the end. Do you give notice that you intend to quit, and probably face having your commitment questioned and calls for you to give way to a younger man, or do you keep your plans to yourself until you've played your last game? I preferred the second course, which would keep down the media attention, but my plans were overtaken by events.

Unsurprisingly there was a huge build up to the Ashes series, and the team selection. For some reason that I never understood, the media kept talking about the selection dilemma of whether to pick Thorpe or

Pietersen. Ian Bell had come into the side for the two games against Bangladesh earlier in the summer and played well, but I was still surprised that there was no debate over his place in the side. After all, the Aussies were a different prospect altogether. Surely my experience and a good record against them would be valuable? Still, when the team was announced with Bell and Pietersen in the side, the media seemed happy enough.

But things can change very fast in the media. When England's batting failed in the first Test against Australia, suddenly there was a great deal of debate over the way I was dropped and whether I should have played instead of Bell. What a wonderful thing hindsight is! There was also talk about whether I should have remained available for the rest of the series. Perhaps England might yet need Thorpe, it was argued. But it was clear to me that England had made up their minds to do without me, and to move in another direction. So I felt there was no point hanging around once I'd been dropped. If I'd played my last Test, I wanted to go in a dignified manner.

After my retirement from Test cricket was announced on the second morning of the first Test, and, perhaps more importantly, after England had lost the game on the fourth day, David Graveney, the chairman of selectors, denied he'd given me the impression that I wouldn't be required later in the series. After witnessing the defeat at Lord's, the media were out in force to find someone to blame. I watched as the selectors came under fire for their decision to drop me, and I've got to be honest – it wasn't unpleasant!

It's always nice when you feel wanted, even though this seemed very much a case of closing the stable door after the horse had bolted. Graveney knew I was planning to announce my retirement and it was at his request that I held off making an announcement until after the first Test had started so as not to distract England's preparations. He could have tried to stop me but didn't.

In my opinion there were a number of ways the selectors could have played it if they had indeed wanted me on stand-by for the remainder of the series. They could have included me in a squad of 13, or just told me outright that I wasn't needed for the first Test but might well be needed in the others. I wasn't even told I was first in line if anyone was injured, for goodness sake. And the fact was, I was so desperate to play that had I had any straw to clutch onto that there might have been a chance to play later on in the series, I may have taken it. As it happened, I think Graveney made it pretty plain at the press conference at Lord's the next morning that he thought I might consider retirement in the light of my omission: that I had a pretty big decision to make over the next few days. I thought so too, and after taking the time to think things over duly came to the obvious conclusion. It was time to go.

If I had any criticism at all about the way the whole thing was handled, it was that I was disappointed that the selectors didn't see fit to keep me informed during the summer about their thoughts and maybe keep me in the loop a bit more. Maybe if that had happened, I might have been able to plan my retirement with the selectors, as opposed to it ending up looking like a bit of a squabble.

I know how fast people can fall out of favour in sport, but I admit I was taken aback at how the management's thinking appeared to be changing even before the first Test of the summer against Bangladesh, when I spoke to Michael Vaughan and Duncan Fletcher and got the definite impression that even then they were considering moving on.

I honestly don't think England intended going back to me, however badly things went against Australia. The days of chopping and changing the team were long gone, and the longer the Ashes series went on the less point there would have been in going back to me. Far better to look to fresh blood. My experience of the England management was that once they'd made their minds up, that was it. It was important for them, and for me, to move on.

When I did retire, there were some people who questioned whether I still had the appetite for Test cricket and was fully committed to playing in the Ashes, but I wouldn't have had a series of big injections to try to settle down my back if I hadn't been serious about playing against Australia. My desire remained as great as it had ever been. I couldn't have been in a happier state, with Amanda due to have our first child in early August. It was just my body that was ailing.

When I spoke to Duncan after the team had been announced, I told him that I too would have had Kevin Pietersen in the team. Pietersen was a South African guy who had qualified for England only nine months earlier and who burst onto the scene with three spectacular centuries against South Africa in a one-day series for which he was chosen only at the last minute when Andrew Flintoff withdrew.

I don't say that in any critical sense. I have no complaint with his background. He was raised in South Africa, but one of his parents was English and he spent four years qualifying. Nor would I question him being picked for Test cricket chiefly on the back of one-day performances. This had sometimes happened in the past and proved a mistake. What people do in one-day matches doesn't necessarily mean that much when it comes to Test cricket. They can't always play the short ball or handle the pressure. But KP was clearly different.

I was on holiday in Thailand with Amanda during the one-dayers in South Africa, and only heard about what he'd done when I got back home, but the way everyone was talking about him made it clear that he'd done something pretty special. The way he'd played, and his obvious enthusiasm for the big-match atmosphere, marked him out as very special. Anyone with a hairstyle like his doesn't lack star quality or confidence. Dressing-rooms need guys who are prepared to take the limelight. As long as he produced the goods, no one would care a jot how he looked or behaved.

I knew immediately that it was going to be hard for England to leave him out against Australia. He was a power-player and was clearly not going to be fazed by the Aussies. I knew, too, that his arrival on the scene might have implications for me, the oldest man in the team and whose fitness was suspect. I had already been aware that there would be plenty of attention on how I performed for Surrey in the early weeks of the season. Now I knew the pressure would be greater still, the greatest it had been since I came back at the Oval in 2003. But I also knew the selectors had some room for manoeuvre because there were doubts over Mark Butcher's fitness and Robert Key, his replacement, hadn't yet cemented his place.

But the speed of KP's emergence was another reminder that you can never take things for granted. One day you're integral to the team's plans, the next day you're not. I'd spent a fair time over the previous 12 months thinking about how my England career might end. I realized that the end might be bad (with injury and/or loss of form) or wonderful (lots of runs and winning the Ashes). Whatever might happen, I was ready. Part of me even hankered for the end just to get rid of the stress of not-knowing. But when the end came, it hurt.

STILL, I COULD have started the season later than I did but, given what had happened in South Africa, I was keen to get my body moving again and get some runs under my belt. Also, I'd not spent much time with Surrey's coach, Steve Rixon, so I wanted to see what he was like and how he was going to run things. Even if I played in all seven Tests – the two against Bangladesh and the five Ashes – I was still going to spend a fair time with my county. Rixon, who had kept wicket for Australia and worked with New Zealand, had a different style from Keith Medlycott. He was more orthodox and less *laissez-faire*, but perhaps that was what we needed as we tried to build a new side.

Things started okay for me, in a low-key way. I got through pre-season nets pretty happily, scored fifty in our rain-affected opening championship match against Sussex with the help of only one painkiller, and made 33 in the Totesport League at Durham. So far, so good. But by the time of our second championship game at Cardiff, where I failed to make double-figures in either innings, things weren't right with my back. I'd put in a lot of physical training before the season but that wasn't the same as being out in the middle, and two weeks of cricket was enough to leave my lower back cripplingly tight. I sat out our C&G Trophy match in Leek and hoped it would settle down, but the spasms were worse than ever in the championship match against Notts.

I worked with Surrey's physio, Greg Mullins, on a daily basis to try and put things right. I tried acupuncture and wearing a corset but with little success. Another double failure, 9 and 0 – I didn't bat or field much during the Notts game – alerted the media to the fact that, with the announcement of the first Test squad of the summer (against Bangladesh) a week away, I was woefully short of runs in county cricket. But so were Andrew Strauss, Marcus Trescothick and Michael Vaughan.

I underwent a scan that showed nothing was seriously amiss, but as a precaution missed Surrey's next four-day game. So when Graveney chaired the first selection meeting with Fletcher, Rod Marsh and Geoff Miller on May 13, I was the proud owner of a batting record that read . . . runs 111, average 15.9. But, as I say, I was not the only one to start the season quietly. The big difference was that whereas the other guys were fit and strong and sure of their places, I wasn't.

I felt I was picking up the ball okay at the crease – I don't think rumours that my eyesight was going were true – but my body couldn't do everything I wanted. And in addition to my poor mobility, it was taking days to recover from any exertion, and that ate into the time I could spend in the nets. The back pain hadn't been so bad for years. It was a battle of endurance, and one that I was losing. I was popping painkillers like they were going out of fashion. For every day that I felt okay, there were two when I didn't.

In the week before the selection meeting, Graveney came to see me during the Notts match to see how I was. I told him about my back, but that I was hoping it might settle down with a week's rest. I knew that I'd altered as a batsman, that perhaps I couldn't flick the 90mph balls through midwicket as I used to, but I still believed that, if I could sort out my back, I could still bring something of value to the team in terms of experience and expertise, especially as Butcher's wrist injury had ruled him out. The other batsmen in the mix appeared to be Key, Pietersen and Ian Bell, who had been scoring heavily for Warwickshire. All short of Test caps, but strong on potential.

Graveney seemed to go away from our chat happy. His message to me was, in a nutshell, 'make sure you're fit for the Ashes'. And the rest did do me some good. So I was pretty confident of making the team. But I wasn't really prepared for what happened next.

On the evening after the selection meeting, he phoned to tell me that I was, sure enough, in the squad, before adding rather ominously, 'Obviously, it was very close between you and Kevin Pietersen . . .' Oh right, thanks Grav. Thanks. I was glad I was 35 years old and not 25 because it wasn't the sort of lukewarm endorsement I'd have wanted at that age. I got off the phone, turned to Amanda and said, 'Great. I've been picked. But there's a noose around my neck.'

It later turned out that the selectors had decided that one batting place had come down to a choice between myself and Pietersen, and another was between Bell and Key. Bell had won that particular contest, which surprised me because I rated Key and felt he had done enough to hold onto his place. I still don't know why the selectors came to this unusual, strategic decision. Why couldn't the selectors just pick the batsmen they considered the best? That was the normal way of doing things. In terms of style, the player most like me was Bell. But I knew that I might struggle if the whole debate became Thorpe *v* Pietersen because I could see he had impressive credentials.

Ironically, in the light of later events, Graveney's phone call got me thinking again about what I'd do after I'd stopped playing. I'd been putting out a few feelers. I'd spoken to a few TV companies the previous year about my chances of doing commentary work, and had made a few enquiries about building up my coaching qualifications. I didn't know if I'd make a good coach, or whether I even wanted to coach, but it had crossed my mind that I could perhaps get a coaching job somewhere overseas in the winter and see how I took to it. I'd spoken to Rixon about whether there might be openings in Australian grade cricket, but I'd done nothing more about it. But when I told Amanda what Grav had said, she encouraged me to get something arranged.

Amanda and I had also talked about the possibility of perhaps relocating to Australia or New Zealand. I would never have considered emigrating had I thought it would be possible to see Henry and Amelia on a regular basis, but the more infrequently I saw them, and the more hassle I had in my dealings with Nicky, the more attractive such an idea became. But it was only a vague plan. My first priority was to find a new job. So I phoned David Gilbert, Surrey's former coach, who was now chief executive at the New South Wales Cricket Association. I told him that my England career was coming to an end, and that I was interested in doing some coaching in Australia. Did he know of anything in Sydney?

He came back to me in a matter of days. He said he'd come up with an idea that the association was happy with that would involve me acting as some kind of an assistant coach/player with New South Wales. I'd coach at a local club but join the state team for their training sessions, and help in whatever capacity was deemed appropriate. The state side had lost a lot of experienced batsmen in recent seasons – the Waugh twins, Michael Slater who had retired and Michael Bevan who'd left for Tasmania – so Dave felt that my experience of international cricket around the world would be useful. He also said that New South Wales would register me as a player and use me in the unlikely event of a spate of injuries. It all happened very fast but it sounded ideal, and I had no hesitation in agreeing to start work in January 2006.

Then came the complication. The following week, Dave called me early one morning to say that New South Wales were required to provide Cricket Australia with a list of their players for the next season, and the list would be made public. Would that cause me a problem?

Naturally, I hadn't yet mentioned the job to anyone connected with the England team. It had only come up a few days earlier, and had no relevance to my immediate commitments with England. But it showed beyond doubt that I was not planning to make myself available for England beyond the Ashes.

I took Dave Gilbert's call in the team hotel near Lord's two days before the first Test against Bangladesh. From what he said, I realized that I had to tell the management immediately. I was aware that for news of what amounted to my impending retirement to come out during preparations for a Test match was not ideal, but there was nothing I could do about that. I got dressed and went downstairs. Fortunately, Duncan was having breakfast by himself. I joined him and told him everything.

Like Vaughan, Duncan had a good idea that I was not thinking of carrying on with England for much longer, and his general attitude towards senior players like myself who were thinking of retiring was to encourage us to go only when we were absolutely sure that we were ready. He also felt that anyone who had played for his country over a long period did not deserve to be dumped unceremoniously, but was entitled to a dignified departure.

He slightly surprised me, though, when he asked whether I was going to retire after the Bangladesh series, before the Ashes. 'No,' I said. 'My heart and my mind are set on playing against Australia. Whether my body gives me the opportunity, or you give it me, is another thing, but I want to play.'

We talked a bit about my fitness. He'd seen how I'd physically struggled in South Africa, and he said something about Gary Kirsten, the South Africa batsman whom he knew well, telling him how he'd still enjoyed his cricket at the end of his career, but that his body had begun to pack up. At one point Duncan said, 'I have to say that I can't guarantee you starting against Australia.'

He suggested that we speak to Andrew Walpole, the ECB's media liaison officer, about how best to handle the announcement. A press release was issued later in the day. I knew that there had been times in the past when I didn't handle things as well as I could have done, but in this instance I felt I did the best I could in the circumstances.

During practice at the ground that day I saw Graveney

and asked him if Walpole had told him my news, and he said that he had. He didn't seem too concerned, only that I should be fit enough to play. But some comments he later made to the press suggested he was unhappy about the timing of the announcement. The newspapers inferred that had I told the selectors of my plans earlier they might not have picked me (unfortunately, the Lord's Test was pretty one-sided and the media were on the look-out for juicier things than the match to write about). Later in the summer I saw Geoff Miller and he, too, said he had been disappointed at the timing of the New South Wales announcement. 'You must have been thinking about it for a long time,' he said. Well, I hadn't been. I couldn't have told them about the job before they picked the Test team against Bangladesh because I didn't know anything about it then.

Frankly, I was amazed at the management's attitude. If they held that incident against me – and I strongly suspect they did – then they had no right to. As they very well knew, the English game had a real problem with unemployment among retired players. There had been suicides, attempted suicides and depression. I'd have thought they might have been pleased that a player who was approaching the end of his playing days had got off his backside and found himself a job.

My sense of foreboding was not alleviated by a conversation with Vaughan the next day at the end of nets. We were talking about how my back was feeling – 'Not too bad' was the answer – when he just said, 'Look, mate, if your back is really playing up, then just tell us. There's no difference between 99 and 100 Tests and I'd like to get KP in to give him a game before the Ashes . . .'

'Yes, of course, Mick . . . No problem . . .'

I walked back to the dressing-room in a daze, thinking to myself, *Hang on . . . Did that really just happen?!* I'd always thought of Vaughan as a pretty shrewd character, but that remark suggested a certain naivety. *No difference between 99 and 100 caps?* I wondered if he would view it the same if he was ever in that position.

So going into that first Test of the summer, I knew how vulnerable my position in the team had become. I felt under a serious amount of pressure, a ridiculous situation really, given that the opposition was Bangladesh. Two days later – the day I was to bat – I saw Nasser in the morning and told him that I feared I was on the way out. He told me that he had felt the same towards the end of his career but that it was something you learned to live with. You knew the axe was hovering, and that if you failed there was no way back, but you got used to it.

Still, it was hardly a tough situation. I went out to join Ian Bell at 415 for 3, and by the time I'd reached the middle I'd pretty much cleared my mind of all the mess of the previous two days. I decided that if this was going to be my last innings for England, I was going to have a good look around and enjoy it, and not throw my wicket away.

If I was a bit crabby and cautious in the way I played then, that's probably because that's how I felt. It was a pretty good wicket and a fairly undemanding attack, and I contributed 42 to an unbroken partnership with Bell of 113 before the declaration came. I showed I'd not completely lost it in the field by taking a sharp reflex catch at short leg to dismiss Javed Omar, and we completed the easiest of innings victories early the next morning.

There was a bit of media speculation that the selectors might not pick me for the second Test at Durham because they now knew of my retirement plans, but I wasn't too worried. I'd parted company with both Duncan and Mick at Lord's with them saying: 'See you next week.' Still, you never knew, and it was a relief to hear from Grav a couple of days later that I had kept my place. However, I had a scare when I realized I'd left my mobile phone off for a few hours and when I switched it on and picked up a message from him asking me to call him. Maybe it was bad news? But it wasn't. It seemed he just wanted to tell me the good news in person. As it turned out it was to be the last good news he would give me.

In the end, what with all the speculation going on about my retirement, it was a huge release to get to 100 caps. When I dropped out in 2002, I had 77 Test appearances to my name and gave myself little chance of playing once more, let alone another 23 times. I was only the eighth England player to reach the milestone and felt incredibly proud. I was presented with a commemorative bat during the game, but didn't really study the list it bore of all my games until after I'd returned home. Looking at all those Tests I'd lived through reminded me what an incredible journey I had been on.

Taking the field on the first morning, with the team lined up on either side, was pretty special but unfortunately Amanda couldn't be there to share it with me as she had a law exam. My parents could not attend either as they had a funeral to go to. So when Steve Harmison asked me if I had any spare tickets for his family as the match was at his home ground, he must have been surprised when I said he could have all of mine on my 100th Test!

Again we won easily, and again I batted with Bell. We put on 187 together before the declaration, my share being 66 not out. It was a nice enough way to celebrate your hundredth Test, although it might have been more satisfying to make runs against stronger opposition.

I enjoyed batting with Bell, who became yet another England team-mate I'd accompanied to his maiden Test century. I tried to give him as much advice as I could. I told him to take all the runs he could because there would be times when they wouldn't come as easily. I'd not really seen much of him before these two games, but it was clear he possessed a good technique and had been groomed from an early age to play for England. I thought his biggest challenge would be handling the public criticism that comes when you play a bad shot in a big game. He'd received a lot of hype earlier in his career and it had affected him then, but I knew from personal experience that heaps of criticism were even harder to take than heaps of praise. We had a chat about it during the series, and I warned him not to be fooled by the nice things being written about him, and to avoid the newspapers when things went wrong.

I WENT BACK to playing for Surrey. There were six weeks until the Ashes. With two weeks given over to the Twenty20 Cup, that left me three championship matches to get my form.

Things didn't go well. Two of the three games followed straight on from the Durham Test, and I got to bat only once both times and did nothing. I scored four at Middlesex and 10 at Hampshire, which meant that in six championship innings I'd amassed 33 runs.

Warne bowled for Hampshire. It was the first time I'd faced him in three years. He was a very different bowler from the one I'd first come up against. It was a first-day wicket, but even so it was clear he was bowling far more straight stuff than he used to. When he was in his pomp, I had four basic shots against him: the cut, the dab off my hip for one, the slog-sweep and the fine-sweep. I reckoned that if he was bowling more straight stuff, the sweeps might have to stay in the locker. I'd have to come up with some fresh strategies. He also bowled some leg-breaks and even a couple of googlies, a ball some reckoned he had lost. I would have liked to face him for longer but got out at the other end to a good ball from Chris Tremlett. Even from quite a brief view, I could tell that Warne remained incredibly smart and skilful. But then he'd seen something of me, and I reckoned he could tell how weak my back was, and that it was preventing me moving properly around the crease.

By then I'd already decided on a last throw of the dice. With a break for the Twenty20 competition, I arranged to see a specialist for a series of massive pain-killing injections that would free up my lower back for several weeks – hopefully right through to the end of the Ashes in early September. I would need several days to recover but that was possible if I acted swiftly. I had a major epidural and four cortisone injections on 22 June. Three days earlier, in his first one-day international appearance against Australia, Pietersen had played an incredible innings of 91 off 65 balls to win the game for England in Bristol. The day after that, Rod Marsh stepped down as a selector, an event I might once have greeted with relief. Now I reckoned it would make little difference. All the selectors were probably starting to back Pietersen, and I couldn't blame them.

The one thing I did do when I realized I had a few

days off was to try and make arrangements to see the children. I texted Nicky to ask if I could see them for the day on the following Saturday. She said that I could see them from 5 until 9pm in the evening, and that I could take them to the cinema and for a pizza in Epsom. I called her to ask why I couldn't see them during the day; after all, wasn't that quite late for them to be out? Nicky made her feelings pretty plain: She said she didn't want them coming to my home and playing happy families, she didn't want them to see 'that woman' (Amanda), Kitty or the baby when it arrived and that I could see them only if I was on my own. I wasn't really surprised, just sad that we didn't appear to have moved any further forward after three and a half years.

Knowing that my international career was coming to an end also meant that I would no longer be able to pay Nicky the sort of maintenance that I had been. I dreaded starting yet more legal proceedings, and wrote to Nicky in the hope that we might be able to sort something out ourselves, thereby saving legal fees. But she wouldn't hear of it and so began another full-blown legal procedure. My solicitors told me that one of the factors that would influence my application was that Nicky had now been co-habiting with Kieron for over three years and he could be expected to contribute to the household. The last time the maintenance figure was decided, Kieron had conveniently moved out of Nicky's home a few months earlier. This time Nicky informed my solicitors that

Kieron had recently become unemployed. I couldn't believe it – did this man have no pride?

It was all very frustrating. I had started the proceedings as I would no longer be able to afford the high maintenance payments once I'd retired, but so far I hadn't saved a penny and the legal bills to date have exceeded £10,000.

MY FIRST MATCH back came two weeks later for Surrey second XI against Sussex at Cheam. It was another inglorious moment in an inglorious summer – I was out for nought – but my back was actually the best it had been for months. I went down to Bristol under a lot of pressure as it was my final championship match before the Ashes squad was announced. I scored 73, positively and without discomfort. It was my highest innings of the season. I spoke to both Duncan and Grav during the game and told them that I was feeling good. The anxiety was getting to me, though, and I asked them what they wanted to do. Both said they were still unsure. Grav told me: 'The one thing we don't want you to do is to retire.'

Pietersen hadn't done much in the one-dayers since Bristol but on the day before the selectors met he scored a hard-hit 74 against Australia at the Oval. I still don't know when the selectors finally made up their minds, but that performance may have clinched things for Pietersen. But as far as I saw it, there was still a good chance of me being named in the squad along with Pietersen.

I knew I'd be getting a call from Grav on the Wednesday evening, the night before the team was announced. I'd not had many anxious days waiting to hear whether I'd made the team in the previous 12 years but this was one. By the time Grav finally rang, at around 10pm, I was out in town having a meal with my old friend Ray Alikhan, who was over from Australia.

It was a pretty short call. 'Thorpey, it's Grav. I'm the bearer of bad news . . .'

'Oh . . .'

'I'm afraid we haven't selected you. We've gone with Pietersen instead.'

Then he added: 'The other week in Bristol, I did ask you not to retire. I realize I was wrong to do that now.' After thinking about it for a minute, I took that to mean that if I now wanted to retire then I could go ahead, as I wasn't going to be needed for the rest of the series either.

Even though all the media talk had been about Thorpe *v* Pietersen, I had hoped they would come round to the view that the debate ought to be about Thorpe v Bell, but apparently that never came into it. Of course, I had realized it had been a possibility that they wouldn't pick me, but it was still kind of shocking when it happened. The word was that they thought I hadn't had enough cricket and was too much of a risk, but

I felt I could have really done something had I been chosen.

When I had pulled out of the tour of Australia in 2002, one of the things troubling my already disturbed mind was whether I'd be able to cope if the Australian fielders referred to my screwed-up private life. I could not be sure they would say anything but I had to be able to cope with it if they did. I came to the conclusion that I wasn't mentally resilient enough to do that and it contributed to my withdrawal. I had no such qualms now. I'd put most of my troubles so far behind me that they could have said what they liked, I wouldn't have listened. What's more, I was looking forward to renewing my duels with Warne and McGrath. I'd scored runs before against them – admittedly most of them quite a few years earlier – but I saw no reason why I couldn't again, provided my back wasn't restricting my movement. Now I would never know what I might have done.

I talked things over with Amanda that night. I was very disappointed but she encouraged me to be philosophical, saying: 'Maybe this was just the way it was meant to be.' We realized that at least my omission would allow me to be around in the days after the birth, something that hadn't been possible when Henry and Amelia were born. And it was true, it didn't take me long to get my head round it and start getting excited about the new baby. The timing was pretty perfect really, and I was almost surprised to realize that only a day later I had completely accepted and come to terms with the selection decision.

I had a game for Surrey in the C&G Trophy the next day, which was probably the best thing for me, and I enjoyed making another half-century in a spectacularly high-scoring game with Hampshire which we lost. The team was announced on the Thursday. On the Sunday, I rang Richard Bevan at the Professional Cricketers' Association and discussed how the remainder of my England contract would be affected, in financial terms, were I to retire straight away. The answer was 'not greatly', as I would revert to being an employee of Surrey for the remainder of the season.

I spoke to Grav the next day and told him what I was planning. He raised no objection but asked me to wait until the Lord's Test had started to prevent the captain and coach being forced to answer questions in the build-up to the game. I also spoke to Duncan, whose attitude was basically: 'It's your call.'

In the end, the ECB released the news on the Friday morning at Lord's after England had been dismissed for 155, which meant that despite a fantastic bowling performance the day before, they had gone behind on first innings.

I was playing in a championship match for Surrey at the time and fielding on the boundary at Guildford when an old boy with a radio shouted: 'Hey, Graham! They're saying you've retired. Why's that? You'll be in by the third Test!'

One hundred and fifty-five all out. I've been there, I thought. Yes, I've been there.

Graham Thorpe's Career in Figures

A MILESTONES IN FIRST-CLASS CAREER

DEBUT: 11 June 1988 v Leicestershire at The Oval

CAP: 1991

FIRST CENTURY: 100* v Cambridge University at The Oval 1998
Thorpe moved from 50 to 100 in 31 balls in a match in which his future long-term Surrey colleague, Martin Bicknell, took 9 for 45, against a University team captained by his future long-term England colleague, Michael Atherton.

15,000th FIRST-CLASS RUN: v Western Australia (Perth) 1998/99

20,000th FIRST-CLASS RUN: v Vice-Chancellor's XI (Sir Frank Worrell Memorial Ground, Jamaica) 2003/04

FIRST WICKETS: D I Gower lbw b Thorpe 3; P Willey c Lynch b Thorpe 10

Wisden Cricketer of the Year 1998 – with Matthew Elliott, Stuart Law, Glenn McGrath and Matthew Maynard

He was Surrey's leading batsman on aggregate (1863) in 1992 and had the highest average (51.75) in the same year. He also had the highest average (69.60) in 1996 and again in 1997 (70.70), but international commitments have prevented his featuring strongly in Surrey lists.

B MILESTONES IN TEST CAREER

DEBUT: 1 July 1993 v Australia at Trent Bridge, with fellow debutants Mark Ilott, Mark Lathwell and Martin McCague

FIRST CENTURY: 114* in the second innings of his début match. He shared a partnership of 150 with captain Graham Gooch, making a major contribution to a drawn match which brought to an end a sequence of seven Test defeats. Thorpe was the 60th player and 14th Englishmen – and the first for 20 years – to make a century on début. He became the second Surrey player to do so – after Peter May at Headingley in 1951.

LAST CENTURY (his 16th): 118* v South Africa at Durban 2004/05

LAST APPEARANCE (his 100th): v Bangladesh at Riverside 2005

C SUMMARY OF ALL FIRST-CLASS MATCHES

by season

	M	Inns	NO	HS	TOTAL	100	Ave	Ct
1988	3	6	2	100*	158	1	39.50	3
1989	18	30	5	154	1132	2	45.28	12
1989–90 (Zimbabwe)	2	2	0	98	142	0	71.00	2
1990	18	28	6	86	608	0	27.63	9
1990–91 (Pakistan)	1	1	0	98	98	0	98.00	1
1990–91 (Sri Lanka)	3	4	0	68	188	0	47.00	4
1991	23	38	9	177	1203	4	41.48	8
1991–91 (West Indies)	4	7	0	57	226	0	32.28	2
1992	24	41	4	216	1895	3	51.21	19
1992–93 (Australia)	3	5	1	96	215	0	53.75	2
1993	17	31	2	171	1043	3	35.96	17
1993–94 (West Indies)	9	14	0	86	370	0	26.42	9
1994	16	25	4	190	1136	2	54.09	11
1994–95 (Australia)	10	20	3	123	756	1	44.47	9
1995	16	30	0	152	1223	2	40.76	13
1995–96 (S Africa)	9	14	4	131*	415	1	41.50	3
1996	16	29	4	185	1569	6	62.76	18
1996–97 (New Zealand)	5	6	0	119	324	2	54.00	7
1996–97 (Zimbabwe)	4	8	1	65	187	0	26.71	1
1997	14	23	4	222	1160	3	61.05	17
1997–98 (West Indies)	9	15	4	103	603	1	54.81	9
1998	9	13	1	114	314	1	26.16	10
1998–99 (Australia)	4	8	3	223*	438	1	87.60	4
1999	13	21	4	164	708	2	41.64	18
2000	11	16	0	115	376	1	23.50	9
2000–01 (Pakistan)	5	8	1	118	420	1	60.00	10
2000–01 (Sri Lanka)	5	9	2	113*	366	1	52.28	9
2001	5	7	0	148	430	2	61.42	8
2001–02 (India)	2	4	0	111	111	0	27.75	2
2001–02 (New Zealand)	4	8	2	200*	285	1	47.50	8
2002	8	14	0	143	526	2	37.57	6
2003	13	20	2	156	1019	2	56.61	9
2003–04 (Bangladesh)	2	4	1	64	136	0	45.33	0
2003–04 (Sri Lanka)	4	7	0	57	218	0	31.14	2
2003–04 (West Indies)	6	8	3	119*	417	1	83.40	3
2004	10	17	3	114	770	2	55.00	7
2004–05 (South Africa)	6	12	2	118*	298	1	29.80	5
2005	9	13	3	95	418	0	41.80	4
Totals	**340**	**566**	**80**	**223***	**21901**	**49**	**45.06**	**290**

by opponents

for England

	M	Inns	NO	Highest	TOTAL	100	AVE	Ct
Australia	16	31	4	138	1235	3	45.74	19
Bangladesh	4	6	3	66*	244	30	81.33	4
India	5	9	1	89	283	30	35.37	8
New Zealand	13	23	6	200*	905	34	53.23	16
Pakistan	8	14	1	138	671	32	51.61	13
South Africa	16	29	4	124	897	32	35.88	8
Sri Lanka	9	16	2	123	699	32	49.92	9
West Indies	27	47	6	119*	1740	33	42.43	27
Zimbabwe	2	4	1	50*	70	30	23.33	1
TOTAL	**100**	**179**	**28**	**200***	**6744**	**16**	**44.66**	**105**

for Surrey

	M	Inns	NO	Highest	TOTAL	100	AVE	Ct
Derbyshire	10	16	3	185	809	2	62.23	7
Durham	4	7	1	62	214	0	35.66	4
Essex	14	22	2	143	536	1	26.80	6
Glamorgan	9	17	4	222	995	3	76.53	5
Gloucestershire	8	15	4	81	483	0	43.90	6
Hampshire	13	23	1	164	924	3	42.00	1
Kent	14	22	2	154	900	2	45.00	14
Lancashire	12	19	0	66	565	0	29.73	6
Leicestershire	11	19	1	154	678	1	37.66	6
Middlesex	14	21	1	117	520	1	26.00	9
Northamptonshire	11	18	5	148	824	3	63.38	7
Nottinghamshire	12	18	1	100	689	1	40.52	12
Somerset	11	17	1	216	747	3	46.68	10
Sussex	14	21	5	177	1238	5	77.37	12
Warwickshire	9	17	0	114	533	1	31.35	11
Worcestershire	10	17	3	190	737	2	52.64	7
Yorkshire	8	10	3	79	368	0	46.00	4

Bowling

Tests

Overs	Mdns	Runs	Wkts	BB	Ave	SRate	Econ
23	7	37	0				1.60

First-Class

Overs	Mdns	Runs	Wkts	BB	Ave	SRate	Econ
397.5	72	1378	26	4–40	53.00	91.80	3.46

D FIRST-CLASS HUNDREDS

for England (16)

200* v New Zealand (Christchurch) 2001/02
138 v Australia (Edgbaston) 1997
138 v Pakistan (Old Trafford) 2001
124 v South Africa (The Oval) 2003
123 v Australia (Perth) 1994/5
122 v Sri Lanka (Edgbaston) 2002
119* v West Indies (Bridgetown) 2004
119 v New Zealand (Auckland) 1996/97
118* v South Africa (Durban) 2004/05
118 v Pakistan (Lahore) 2000/01
114* v Australia (Trent Bridge) 1993
114 v West Indies (Old Trafford) 2004
113 v Sri Lanka (Colombo) 2000/01
108 v New Zealand (Wellington) 1996/97
104* v New Zealand (Trent Bridge) 2004
103 v West Indies (Bridgetown) 1997/98

for Surrey (30)

222 v Glamorgan (The Oval) 1997
216 v Somerset (The Oval) 1992
190 v Worcestershire (The Oval) 1994
185 v Derbyshire (The Oval) 1996
177 v Sussex (The Oval) 1991

171 v Worcestershire (Worcester) 1993
164 v Hampshire (Guildford) 1999
156 v Sussex (The Oval) 2003
154 v Kent (The Oval) 1989
154 v Leicestershire (The Oval) 1996
152 v Kent (Canterbury) 1995
148 v Northants (Northampton) 2001
143 v Essex (Southend) 1996
143 v Hampshire (Southampton) 2002
138* v Northamptonshire (Northampton) 1999
130 v Sussex (Guildford) 1996
117 v Middlesex (Lord's) 1991
116* v Northamptonshire (Northampton) 1999
115 v Hampshire (Basingstoke) 1989
115 v Somerset (The Oval) 2000
114* v Cambridge University (Fenner's) 1992
114 v Derbyshire (The Oval) 1994
114 v Warwickshire (Edgbaston) 1998
110 v Sussex (Horsham) 1995
106* v Glamorgan (The Oval) 1991
106 v Sussex (Hove) 1997
104 v Glamorgan (The Oval) 1993
100* v Cambridge University (The Oval) 1988
100* v Somerset (Taunton) 1996
100 v Nottinghamshire (Trent Bridge) 1992

for other teams (3)

223* England XI v South Australia (Adelaide) 1998/99
141* The Rest v England A (Chelmsford) 1996
131* England XI v Free State (Bloemfontein) 1995/96

E LIMITED OVERS MATCHES

	Matches	Inns	NO	Highest	TOTAL	100s	Av'ge
for England	84	79	13	89	2433	–	36.86
for Surrey	244	277	36	145*	7733	9	40.48

for other teams

England A	10	9	3	78	296	0	49.33
England XI	19	17	6	95	409	0	37.18
All 'List A'	357	332	58	145*	10871	9	39.67
Twenty20	5	4	–	50	95	–	23.75

F LIMITED OVERS HUNDREDS

for Surrey (9)

145* v Lancashire (The Oval) NatWest Bank Trophy 1997
126* v Nottinghamshire (Guildford) Norwich Union League 2000
115* v Lancashire (Old Trafford) Refuge Assurance League 1991
114 v Gloucestershire (The Oval) Norwich Union League 2002
112 v Gloucestershire (The Oval) Axa, Equity & Law League 1995
103 v Lancashire (The Oval) Benson & Hedges Cup 1993
102* v Yorkshire (Scarborough) NatWest Bank Trophy 1997
102* v Somerset (Taunton) C & G Trophy 2003
100* v Yorkshire (The Oval) Axa Life League 1997

Thorpe never scored an international limited overs century. He made the Australian unlucky number of 87 on two occasions – v Zimbabwe at Brisbane in the Benson and Hedges World Series Cup in 1994/95 and v Holland at Peshawar in the Wills World Cup in 1995/96.

G TEST HUNDREDS

First 114* v Australia (Trent Bridge) 1993

Biggest 200* v New Zealand (Christchurch) 2001/02

Made in 231 balls, the seventh fastest in terms of balls faced, and subsequently eclipsed by Nathan Astle's double century in 153 balls, the fastest double century in Test history by some distance

Best 118 v Pakistan (Lahore) 2000/01

Against county colleague, Saqlain Mushtaq, who had figures of 74–20–164–8 in an innings of 480–8 dec. Thorpe's century is believed to be the only one in Test cricket to contain only one boundary.

Bravest 114 v West Indies (Old Trafford) 2004 with broken finger.

Missing A century v Australia at The Oval in 2005 on a farewell Test appearance – never made following his omission from the England team for the first Test and consequent retirement from international cricket. It would also conceivably have been his 50th first-class hundred.

Thorpe also contributed in a way to a missing first-class hundred by another player, being at the other end when his Surrey colleague, Alex Tudor, batting as nightwatchman, scored 99 not out in the seven wicket defeat of New Zealand at Edgbaston in 1999.

Most wanted 124 v South Africa (The Oval) 2003 on return to England squad after an absence of over a year. It was Alec Stewart's final Test and Thorpe made an important contribution to England's victory on which bookmakers were offering 40–1 at the beginning of the second day.

H RECORD PARTNERSHIPS

for England

v Australia

4th wicket: 288 with Nasser Hussain (Edgbaston) 1997, the eighth highest fourth wicket partnership in Tests.

v Bangladesh

4th wicket: 187* with Ian Bell (Riverside) 2005

v New Zealand

6th wicket: 281 with Andrew Flintoff (Christchurch) 2001/02, a record partnership for this wicket against all countries.

v Sri Lanka

3rd wicket: 167 with Nasser Hussain (Kandy) 2000/01
10th wicket: 91 with Matthew Hoggard (Edgbaston) 2001

v West Indies

5th wicket: 150 with Alec Stewart (Bridgetown) 1993/94
6th wicket: 205 with Mark Ramprakash (Bridgetown) 1997/98

for Surrey

v Glamorgan

4th wicket: 211 with David Ward (Neath) 1992

v Kent

2nd wicket: 260 with Darren Bicknell (Canterbury) 1995

v Somerset

2nd wicket: 190 with Mark Butcher (The Oval) 2000

v Sussex

3rd wicket: 243 with Alec Stewart (Horsham) 1995

v Worcestershire

6th wicket: 220 with Adam Hollioake (The Oval) 1994

for England XI

5th wicket: 377 with Mark Ramprakash (Adelaide) 1998/99, the ninth highest in first-class cricket and a record for any wicket by a touring team in Australia.

I BEST BOWLING

Although Thorpe was described by *Wisden* on his début as 'Surrey's 18-year-old all-rounder', it as a batsman that he will be remembered, his back problems preventing his being used a serious bowler in the latter part of his career. His best figures were 4 for 40 for Surrey against the Australians in 1993, the last occasion Surrey hosted a first-class fixture against a senior touring side. His wickets were those of Mark Waugh, Tim Zoehrer, Brendon Julian and Paul Reiffel. It was in the second innings of the same match that Tim Zoehrer equalled the English record for the number of wicket-keeping victims in an innings, Thorpe being one of them, c Zoehrer b Warne.

J COMPARISONS

Statistical comparisons, particularly trans-generational ones, can be misleading, as the circumstances in which runs are made differ from match to match and the value of a century on a flat pitch against modest bowling in a dead match will be different from one which contributes to a result against a quality attack in bowler friendly conditions and cannot be measured in statistical terms. However, although statistics never reveal everything, they rarely reveal nothing and against a sufficient number of contemporary or near-contemporary comparators, they may begin to acquire some meaning.

(1) with other Test Centurions

Thorpe is the most recent of eight English players to collect a century of Test caps. His batting average is superior – if only marginally – to that of any of them with the exception of Geoffrey Boycott's.

	Matches	Inns	NO	Highest	TOTAL	100s	Avg
G Boycott	108	193	23	246*	8114	22	47.72
G P Thorpe	**100**	**179**	**28**	**200***	**6744**	**16**	**44.66**
D I Gower	117	204	18	215	8231	18	44.25
M C Cowdrey	114	188	15	182	7624	22	44.06
G A Gooch	118	215	6	333	8900	20	42.58
A J Stewart	133	235	21	190	8463	15	39.54
M A Atherton	115	212	7	185*	7728	16	37.69
I T Botham	102	161	6	208	5200	14	33.54

(2) with other left-handers

Thorpe's Test performances compare not unfavourably with the world's highest scoring left-handers.

	Matches	Inns	NO	Highest	TOTAL	100s	Avg
A R Border	156	265	44	205	11174	27	50.56
B C Lara	112	197	6	400*	10094	26	52.34
D I Gower	117	204	18	215	8231	18	44.25
G S Sobers	93	160	21	365*	8032	26	57.70
G P Thorpe	**100**	**179**	**28**	**200***	**6744**	**16**	**44.66**

(3) with other England no 5s

His performances at no 5 are superior in aggregate and average, hundreds and fifties, to any other England batsman in that position.

	Runs	Average	100s	50s
G P Thorpe	**3265**	**54.41**	**10**	**17**
M C Cowdrey	2377	49.52	6	16
D I Gower	2131	49.55	7	8
A J Lamb	1803	40.06	5	8
K W R Fletcher	1774	46.68	5	9

K TEST PERFORMANCE AGAINST THE WORLD'S LEADING BOWLERS

	Times dismissed	Average
C A Walsh	10	41.40
C E L Ambrose	9	34.33
S K Warne	9	46.44
M Muralitharan	7	27.57
C L Cairns	5	29.20
G D McGrath	5	52.40
S M Pollock	4	12.5

L THORPE'S 78 ENGLAND TEAM-MATES IN HIS 100 TESTS

67 Michael Atherton, Alec Stewart
59 Nasser Hussain
42 Marcus Trescothick
41 Andrew Caddick
39 Mark Butcher
35 Michael Vaughan
34 Darren Gough
33 Ashley Giles
32 Graeme Hick
30 Dominic Cork
29 Andrew Flintoff, Matthew Hoggard
26 John Crawley, Angus Fraser, Mark Ramprakash

23 Jack Russell, Phil Tufnell
19 Robert Croft, Steve Harmison
17 Robin Smith
16 Craig White
14 Geraint Jones, Devon Malcolm
13 Simon Jones, Nick Knight, Alan Mullally, Andrew Strauss
12 Dean Headley, Chris Lewis
11 Chris Read
10 Graham Gooch
8 Mark Ealham, Peter Martin
7 Gareth Batty, Phil DeFreitas, Richard Illingworth, Steven Rhodes, Ian Salisbury
6 Robert Key
5 James Anderson, Mike Gatting, Mark Ilott
4 Neil Foster, Adam Hollioake, Mike Watkinson
3 Martin Bicknell, Jason Gallian, Ronnie Irani, Martin McCague, Mark Saggers, Peter Such, Alex Tudor, Ian Ward
2 Ian Bell, Rikki Clarke, Paul Collingwood, John Emburey, Aftab Habib, Alan Igglesden, Richard Johnson, James Kirtley, Mark Lathwell, Matthew Maynard, Min Patel
1 Joey Benjamin, Simon Brown, Richard Dawson, Ed Giddins, Ben Hollioake, Steve James, Darren Maddy, James Ormond, Ryan Sidebottom, Chris Silverwood, Ed Smith, Mike Smith, Alan Wells

M EXTRAS

Conversion rate

A criticism often made of Thorpe in the early days of his international career was that his half-centuries were not often enough converted into centuries. After his maiden Test century, only one of next twenty fifties became a century. In a feature in the June 2005 edition of *Wisden Cricket Monthly* Thorpe commented that in three-day cricket a quick 70 or 80 met the requirement, but in Test Matches, 150 or more was the requirement. However, the following figures point to an increasing maturity of approach and an improvement in the conversion rate.

Graham Thorpe's Career in Figures

	50–99	100+	Conv Rate
Tests 1–34	19	2	9.52%
Tests 35–100	20	14	41.17%

Overseas tours

Between 1989/90 and 1998/89, Thorpe was on tour every winter with either England or England A.

Captaincy

Thorpe captained England in three Limited Overs Internationals in Sri Lanka in 2000/01 when Hussain was injured. Matches were at Dambulla (the first on the ground), R Premadasa Stadium, Colombo and Sinhalese Sports Club, Colombo. All were lost, the last by ten wickets.

Fielding

Thorpe's 105 Test catches place him joint 18th in the all-country list with Mohammad Azharuddin and Ian Chappell and 5th in the England list after Ian Botham, Colin Cowdrey, Walter Hammond and Graham Gooch.

His six catches in an innings for Surrey v Kent at The Oval in 1998 stand second only to Mickey Stewart's seven against Northamptonshire in 1957.

Freak average

In the 1999 NatWest Trophy, he had a freak batting average of 234 (39* v Scotland, 91* v Worcestershire, 42* v Northamptonshire and 62 v Somerset)

Man-of-the-Match Awards

Thorpe has received 17 of these.

Statistics compiled by Keith and Jennifer Booth as at 8 August 2005. Sources: Wisden Cricketers' Almanack, Wisden Cricket Monthly June 2005, Cricinfo, Cricket Archive, Graham Thorpe Benefit Brochure 2000, Surrey County Cricket Club Records Book.

Index

Index

Index

Index

Index

Index

Index

Index